Milton Among the Romans

Medieval & Renaissance Literary Studies

General Editor:
Albert C. Labriola

Advisory Editor:
Foster Provost

Editorial Board:
Judith H. Anderson
Diana Treviño Benet
Donald Cheney
Ann Baynes Coiro
Mary T. Crane
Patrick Cullen
A. C. Hamilton
Margaret P. Hannay
A. Kent Hieatt
William B. Hunter
Michael Lieb
Thomas P. Roche Jr.
Mary Beth Rose
John M. Steadman
Humphrey Tonkin
Susanne Woods

MILTON
Among the Romans

The Pedagogy
and Influence
of Milton's
Latin Curriculum

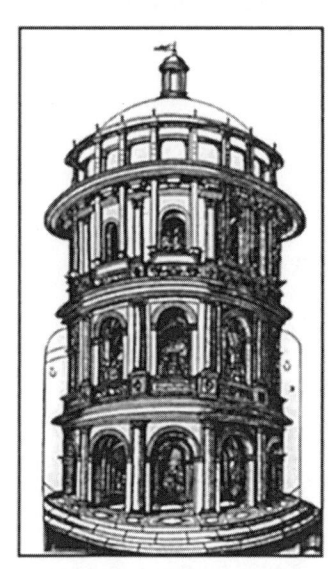

Richard J. DuRocher

DUQUESNE UNIVERSITY PRESS

Copyright © 2001 Duquesne University Press
All Rights Reserved

Library of Congress Cataloging-in-Publication Data

DuRocher, Richard J.
  Milton among the Romans: the pedagogy and influence of Milton's Latin curriculum/Richard J. DuRocher.
    p. cm. — (Medieval & Renaissance literary studies)
  Includes bibliographical references and index.
    ISBN 0-8207-0328-1 (hardcover)
    1. Milton, John, 1608–1674 — Knowledge — Rome. 2. Latin literature — Study and teaching — England — History — 17th century. 3. Milton, John, 1608–1674 — Contributions in education. 4. Milton, John, 1608–1674 — Knowledge — Literature. 5. Epic poetry, English — History and criticism. 6. Milton, John, 1608–1674. Paradise lost. 7. English poetry — Roman influences. I. Title. II. Medieval and Renaissance literary studies.
    PR3592.R65 D87 2001
    821'.4—dc21

                                                              2001004468

∞ Printed on acid-free paper.

For Scott Elledge, *in memoriam*,
and
Mary Ann Radzinowicz

Contents

	Illustrations	viii
	Acknowledgments	ix
	Abbreviations	xiii
	Introduction: Reading the Romans	1
One	Conning the Creature	35
Two	Careful Plowing	54
Three	Building Pandaemonium	74
Four	A Marriage Made in Heaven	94
Five	The Wounded Earth in *Paradise Lost*	130
	Conclusion: Regenerating Rome	152
	Appendix	171
	Notes	176
	Works Cited: Primary Sources	188
	Secondary Sources	193
	Index	205

Illustrations

Figure 1. Title page, *Rei rusticae auctores Latini veteres* 61
Figure 2. "Homo ad Quadratum." 85
Figure 3. "Homo ad Circulum." 85
Figure 4. Vitruvian figure. 87
Figure 5. Cathedral design. 88
Figure 6. Vitruvian figure. 90
Figure 7. Theatre design. 91
Figure 8. Aerial view of the Church of Santa Maria della Consolazione, Todi, Italy, completed 1508. 93

Acknowledgments

If you ever write a book, Horace advises in the *Ars Poetica* (386–90), let it fall upon the ears of a few wise judges, then put your parchment in a closet and keep it back until the ninth year. Largely because of my daughter's extended illness, I have followed Horace's advice in my own way. Over the nine years of the book's composition I have incurred many debts, and I gratefully acknowledge them here. Thanks to a grant from the National Endowment for the Humanities, I began work on this project, then entitled *"Paradise Lost* and the Sacred Earth," in the summer of 1992. A grant from St. Olaf College released me from teaching duties in spring 1995 and thus enabled me to extend my inquiry into Milton's Latin tutorial. Librarians at the Rølvaag Memorial Library at St. Olaf, the Wilson Library at the University of Minnesota, the Newberry Library in Chicago, and the Olin Library at Cornell University helped me on numerous occasions: Fred Hoxie, Mary Sue Lovett, and Mary Beth Rose, in particular, provided exceptional assistance. Dean Jim Pence and Associate Dean James May of St. Olaf quite simply made completion of the book possible by providing financial support, opportunity to travel, and release time for faculty development.

The first respondents to ideas presented in the book were my students at St. Olaf College. I especially wish to thank Michael Antenbring, Jennifer Benson, Ann Kathan, Jen

Okerlund, and Sarah Solum, who undertook advanced work on Milton, and the Milton and Theory group comprising Andrea Gronstal, Hadley Johnson, Katie Larson, Amy Nelson, and Todd Sorensen. My faculty colleagues in the English Department sustained me with their good humor and scholarly acumen. The Northfield Renaissance Colloquium and the Language and Literature Group, particularly Dick Bodman, Laurel Carrington, John Day, Karl Fink, Michael Foote, Doug Green, Jeanine Grenberg, Anne Groton, Lowell E. Johnson, Ronald J. Lee, Frank Morral, R. G. Peterson, and Cathy Yandell, thoughtfully responded to my presentations of Milton's gleanings from the Romans. With characteristic grace, Diane Kelsey McColley invited me to present a paper on the wounded Earth, the earliest version of chapter 5, for a special session on "Images of Nature in Early Modern Europe" at the 1995 MLA convention. Alan Rudrum organized a panel with a similar focus for the 1996 Renaissance Society meeting at the Huntington Library, at which I presented a paper that eventually grew into chapter 1. In 1997, at the Renaissance Society conference in Vancouver organized by Paul Stanwood, I gave an early version of the third section of chapter 4 on Manilius. Three parts of the book — the first subsection on Vitruvian architecture, the heart of the conclusion dealing with the so-called "rejection" of classicism in *Paradise Regained*, and the discussion of astrology in Milton's divorce tracts — were first presented as papers at the conferences on John Milton in 1995, 1997, and 1999. It is a pleasure to thank the three organizers, Charles W. Durham, Kevin J. Donovan, and Kristin A. Pruitt, who made the recurrent pilgrimage to Murfreesboro possible. In the final year of the book's composition, Tim Raylor and Mark Greengrass offered valuable suggestions concerning educational methods in Milton's day that informed the introduction. When the manuscript was accepted, Kristina Alton and Sue Oines helped convert it from MLA to Chicago style. Mark Murakami meticulously checked my quotations and translations, preventing me from many errors. All that remain are mine. Susan Wadsworth-Booth, editor, and Albert C. Labriola, editor of the Medieval and Renaissance Literary Studies series at Duquesne University Press, serenely guided the manuscript into print. Of those contributing to this project whose names I forgot or never knew, including the consultant reader for the press, I am nonetheless grateful. At the same time, I remain mindful of substantive suggestions and collegial criticism from the following: Diana Treviño Benet, Dennis Danielson, J. Martin Evans, Achsah Guibbory, William B. Hunter, W. R. Johnson, Carol V. Kaske, William J. Kennedy, John Leonard, Anthony Low, John Mulryan, Anna K. Nardo, Stella Revard, John T. Shawcross, and James H. Sims. A smaller, eccentric circle — among whom I happily name David Booker, Steven Buhler, W. Gardner Campbell, Robert Entzminger, Raphael Falco, Louis Schwartz, Elizabeth Skerpan-Wheeler, and Shari Zimmerman — shared my passion for Milton occasionally mingled with good food, strong coffee, and the music of Bob Dylan and Bill Monroe. In the smallest but most important circle of my family, I remain indebted to my wife and colleague, Karen Cherewatuk, and to my children, Helen Lorraine and Mary Clare, for their daily inspiration and enduring gifts of love.

Three essays representing earlier versions of arguments in the book have previously appeared in print. I thank the following for permission to reprint:

> "Careful Plowing: Culture and Agriculture in *Paradise Lost*," from *Milton Studies* XXXI, ed. Albert C. Labriola. c 1995. Reprinted by permission of the University of Pittsburgh Press.
>
> The Editor of *Studies in Philology*, for permission to republish "The Wounded Earth in *Paradise Lost*," *Studies in Philology* 93 (1996): 93–115.
>
> "Building Pandemonium: "Vitruvian Architecture in *Paradise Lost*," originally published in *"All in All": Unity, Diversity, and the Miltonic Perspective*, ed. Charles W. Durham and Kristin A. Pruitt. Selinsgrove: Susquehanna University Press, 1999.

In addition, I gratefully acknowledge the following for permission to reprint images from their collections: For figure 1, DePauw University Archives and Special Collections; figures 2, 3, 5, 6, and 7, the Newberry Library; figure 4, the Special Collections and Rare Books Department, University of Minnesota Libraries; and figure 8, the Photo Laboratory of Vincenzo Benigni, Todi, Perugia, Italy.

Finally, because I could not thank them enough, I dedicate this book to the two people who made me a Miltonist, Scott Elledge and Mary Ann Radzinowicz.

Abbreviations

CC *The Cambridge Companion to Milton*. Ed. Dennis Danielson. Cambridge: Cambridge University Press, 1989.

CE *The Works of John Milton*. Ed. Frank Allen Patterson et al. 18 vols. New York: Columbia University Press, 1931–40.

French J. Milton French. *The Life Records of John Milton*. 5 vols. New Brunswick, N.J.: Rutgers University Press, 1950; rpt. New York: Gordian Press, 1966.

Hughes Merritt Y. Hughes, ed. *John Milton: Complete Poems and Major Prose*. Indianapolis: Odyssey Press, 1957.

Masson David Masson. *The Life of John Milton*. 7 vols. London: Macmillan, 1859–94; rpt. New York: Peter Smith, 1946.

OED *The Oxford English Dictionary*. 20 vols. Prepared by J. A. Simpson and E. S. C. Weiner. Oxford: Clarendon Press, 1989.

Parker William Riley Parker. *Milton: A Biography*. 2 vols. Oxford: Clarendon Press, 1968; 2nd. ed., edited by Gordon Campbell, 1996.

YP *Complete Prose Works of John Milton.* Ed. Don M. Wolfe et al. 8 vols. New Haven, Conn.: Yale University Press, 1953–82.

INTRODUCTION

Reading the Romans

Between 1640 and 1646, John Milton systematically read and taught an extensive body of ancient Roman texts. The reading took place in the course of a private tutorial that included, among other students, his sister Anne Phillips's two sons, Christopher and Edward. In his brief work on the life of Milton, Edward Phillips recalled ten Latin authors he studied under his uncle's tutelage:

> And here by the way, I judge it not impertinent to mention the many authors both of the Latin and Greek, which through his excellent judgment and way of teaching, far above the pedantry of common public schools (where such authors are scarce ever heard of), were run over within no greater compass of time, than from ten to fifteen or sixteen years of age. Of the Latin, the four grand authors *De Re Rustica*, Cato, Varro, Columella and Palladius; Cornelius Celsus, an ancient physician of the Romans; a great part of Pliny's *Natural History*; Vitruvius his *Architecture*; Frontinus his *Stratagems*; with the two egregious poets, Lucretius and Manilius. (Hughes, 1029)[1]

Immediately, speculation quickens about the pedagogical objectives underlying this curriculum, even more about its effects on both students and teacher. What ends was this peculiar educational experiment meant to serve? What would a participant in Milton's tutorial come to know and be prepared to do? Perhaps more important, in what ways did the tutorial influence John Milton's thought and imagination? In particular, are there ways in which this classical curriculum makes a difference in understanding *Paradise Lost*? For, as Edward Phillips also recalled, it was during the same period as the tutorial that Milton composed the earliest lines of *Paradise Lost*, Satan's first soliloquy in book 4.

In order to understand Milton's Latin curriculum, I decided to experience it as fully as possible as his students did. Between 1993 and 1999, I read the Latin texts Phillips describes in the order given above. While attempting to recreate Milton's tutorial, however, I labored under certain restrictions. I began the tutorial as a 30-something English instructor with a passion for Latin literature, not a 10-year old English boy in 1640. More than that, I submitted to Milton's curriculum not as a young person in the process of being prepared for a career of public service (which Milton's tract *Of Education* describes as his program's main civic purpose), but as a career academician at a liberal arts college, and what is worse, a committed Miltonist. With the hindsight provided by Milton's oeuvre, I undertook the classical curriculum chiefly as a way to learn more about the poet. Throughout my inquiry, one question remained preeminent: How do Milton's writings, especially *Paradise Lost*, appear when seen in the light of his classical curriculum? This book, the record of my pedagogical experiment, provides my answer.

The chapters that follow trace a sequence of defining moments throughout Milton's career in which he extensively and intensively engages with his Roman precursors. Chapter 1 shows how Milton in his tract *Of Education* provides both a rationale for using the natural knowledge provided by the Romans and sets limits to that knowledge. Further, that chapter isolates as paradigmatic Milton's treatment of two creatures in *Paradise Lost*: the amarant and the serpent. Milton's approach to those creatures, I argue, amounts to an instrumental use of natural science. Chapter 2 examines the references to agriculture in *Paradise Lost*, beginning with the opening line of the epic and focusing primarily on the debated simile of the "careful Ploughman" in Book 4. Those references show Milton's grounding not only in contemporary issues such as enclosure and farm management but in the ancient theory and practice of agriculture expressed by Cato, Varro, Columella, and Palladius. Chapter 3 shows how Pandaemonium arises in *Paradise Lost* as a curiously successful architectural achievement, deriving largely from the demonic builders' use of Vitruvian principles. The success of Mulciber in building his masterwork raises questions that Milton, as a builder of verses, is forced to confront within the fabric of his poetic edifice. Chapter 4 traces Milton's surprising use of the *Astronomica*, the didactic epic on astrology by Marcus Manilius. Milton's use of Manilius appears in a series of authorial comments on human love and spiritual aspiration, beginning with *The Doctrine and Discipline of Divorce* and culminating in Adam and Eve's spiritual marriage in *Paradise Lost*. Chapter 5 takes us to the narrative climax of *Paradise Lost*, at which Milton tells of the Earth's wounding at the moment of the human Fall. That pivotal moment takes on even greater significance when placed within the sequence of allusions to Roman precursors — to the personified Earth of Pliny and Lucretius as well as Vergil. In the conclusion, I consider Milton's putative rejection of the classics generally and Roman learning and culture specifically in *Paradise Regained*.

Before considering this sequence of Milton's poetic achievements, however, I examine first of all the shape and significance of Milton's curriculum as an educational venture. While innovative, Milton's academy was not entirely without precedent, as it developed along lines suggested by several European reformers, notably J. A. Comenius, Samuel Hartlib, and, above all, John Dury. Nonetheless, his classical curriculum emerges as *sui generis* and distinctive in several regards. Milton's eclectic scheme, as we shall see, strikes a delicate balance — adopting on the one hand traditional training from the wisdom of the ancients and on the other the latest suggestions toward reforming the forward youth of the 1640s in yet unrealized ways.

Milton's Classroom, Educational Theory, and the Temple of Wisdom

As a pedagogical experiment, Milton's tutorial has several distinctive features. Most noticeable in its day would have been the technical as opposed to verbal emphasis of Milton's curriculum. In contrast with the standard grammar school curriculum built around the trivium of grammar, logic, and rhetoric, Milton's program emphasizes *res* instead of *verba*, things rather than words (Mulder, 19–24). Completing Milton's tutorial meant that he and his students became acquainted with how to plant, tend, and harvest crops; how to choose a building site and build a house or fortification; and how to dress a wound and navigate by the stars. For the seventeenth century, Milton's reading program devoted unprecedented attention to practical matters. Whatever changes radical reformers might have effected around them, Milton's students were prepared if necessary to rebuild their world from scratch.

The classical cast of the tutorial may lead one to underestimate its relevance to the world outside Milton's classroom. As early as the 1920s, however, James Holly Hanford argued that Milton's curriculum was designed to prepare young men to become leaders within the broad cultural context of Renaissance humanism. For example, Hanford accounted for the inclusion of military study and discipline in the curriculum, represented by Frontinus's *Strategemata*, as "an essential part of Milton's attempt to carry out consistently in a definite educational program the humanistic ideal, so nobly formulated by the scholars, philosophers, and poets of the Renaissance, of a trained leadership, in which practical skill is integrated with and based on liberal culture" (Hanford, 187). Within that ideal, Hanford observed, military training had always held a prominent place. Without denying the endurance of the humanist ideal, Martin Dzelzainis and Robert T. Fallon have documented the pressing need in the early 1640s among parliamentary sympathizers for a "trained leadership." Both scholars discuss the immediate relevance of Milton's educational philosophy, as articulated in *Of Education*, published in June 1644, to the problem of discipline that plagued the parliamentary forces during the early years of the English Civil War. Martin Dzelzainis argues that the tract's repeated insistence on inculcating fortitude, while traceable to Cicero's classic call for fortitude in *De officiis*, reflects Milton's awareness in 1644 that fortitude was precisely the virtue the parliamentary leaders lacked (Dzelzainis, 13–14). Robert Fallon observes that even the medical training in the curriculum, represented by Celsus's *De medicina* in the Latin tutorial, reflects warfaring England in the 1640s. Milton's young scholar is to study "Physick" so that he may not only heal himself and his friends but perhaps even "save an Army by this frugall and expenceless meanes only; and not let the healthy and stout bodies of young men rot away under him for want of this discipline" (YP 2:393). For Fallon, this formulation calls to mind "the sorry spectacle of Essex's army sitting outside London in the spring and summer of 1643, reduced by neglect, disease, and desertion to a pitifully ineffective remnant, defenseless against the attacks of Rupert" (R. Fallon, 66). At the same time, Milton's inclusion of the 1644 tract *Of Education* in the 1673 reissue of his 1645 *Poems* suggests that he saw his didactic experiment as still worthy of emulation, long after the particular needs of the parliamentary forces during the 1640s had passed.

However effective Milton's curriculum may have been in

preparing young men for military service, he insists in *Of Education* that his educational program is superior to those given over to a single purpose, such as military or mental readiness. While closest in design to the ancient Athenian and Spartan academies, his curriculum has a balance they lacked: "But herein it shall exceed them, and supply a defect as great as that which *Plato* noted in the common-wealth of *Sparta*; whereas that city train'd up their youth most for warre, and these in their Academies and *Lycaeum*, all for the gown, this institution of breeding which I here delineate, shall be equally good both for Peace and warre" (YP 2:408). Comprehensiveness is the hallmark of Milton's curriculum, as his definition of a complete education shows: "I call therefore a compleate and generous Education that which fits a man to perform justly, skilfully, and magnanimously all the offices both private and publike of peace and war" (YP 2:377–79).

As that definition indicates, Milton believed that education ought to equip citizens to perform their proper "offices" — in the Ciceronian sense of "duties." How education could best be organized so as to enable young persons to perform those duties, however, had become the subject of vigorous debate and experimentation during the early decades of the seventeenth century. The humanist ideal had been creatively complicated by the European movement of universal education. Martin Bucer has been credited with first promulgating the notion of universal education, which logically arose as a corollary of the Reformation emphasis on the individual believer's need to come to terms with Scripture (Webster, 207). The impetus for reviving this ideal during the 1630s and 1640s, however, came from the Moravian polymath, Jan Amos Comenius. At the invitation of Samuel Hartlib, Comenius visited London during 1641–42. There he met with Hartlib as well as with John Dury, known on the continent as a proponent of Judeo-Christian ecumenism (Milton, "Peacemaker" 95–101). Shortly before the Long Parliament reconvened in October

1641, Hartlib, Dury, and Comenius collaborated for an extensive period on a variety of projects, among them several plans for educational reform (Popkin, 119). In March 1642 the three men entered into a formal compact whereby they agreed to work together toward three goals: to promote peace among the religious denominations; to fashion the education of Christian youth according to the true aim of a higher Christianity; and to reform the study of true wisdom (Turnbull, 363, 459). Following their meeting, Hartlib himself translated one of Comenius's works and had it published in 1642 under the title *A Reformation of Schooles*. This work, and the far-reaching educational innovations of the Comenian troika generally, would have been of immediate interest to Milton as he was conducting his academy in London. Although Milton did write to Hartlib in *Of Education* (June 1644) expressing his disinclination "to search what many modern *Janua's* and *Didactic's* more then ever I shall read, have projected" (YP 2:264), his statement at the very least shows his familiarity with the major Comenian educational titles — the *Janua linguarum* and *Janua rerum* and the *Didactica Magna*.[2]

A summary of Comenius's educational philosophy, the work of a lifetime, would be fraught with peril. Nevertheless, any account of his views would surely feature the Comenian masterconcept of pansophie or pansophy. The end of education, Comenius stressed, is gaining wisdom — the comprehensive kind of wisdom he called "pansophie":

> It must therefore be agreed upon, that Wisdome is the thing we are to seeke. And because Wisdome is said to be the worker of al things, Wisdome 7.22, it is evident, that learning ought to be used, and improved as the meanes to bring us unto the universall knowledge of all things, (unto Pansophie, that is, a Wisdome every way compleat, both in the largenesse of its extent, and in its perfect agreement with it selfe) that we be not ignorant of any thing which is secret, or knowne, Wisd. 7.21. That so mans mind may become indeed, as it ought to be, the image of God, who knoweth all things. (Comenius, 4)

Comenius refers to two verses from the apocryphal book, the Wisdom of Solomon, which the Latin Vulgate Bible had entitled "*Sapientia*," that is, simply, "Wisdom":

> Et quaecumque sunt absconsa et improvisa didici:
> Omnium enim artifex docuit me sapientia.
> (Wisd. of Sol. 7.21–22)

> I learned both what is hidden and what is manifest,
> For wisdom, the fashioner of all things, taught me.
> (RSV)

As the *artifex omnium*, the maker of all things, Wisdom has a Godlike power in this account. A logical corollary would be that the student who has acquired pansophy has the potential to become a kind of magus. Comenius's ultimate educational objective of making the human mind the perfect reflection of the all-knowing God is a lofty goal indeed. Nonetheless, it strikes me as harmonious with Milton's soaring pronouncement on the end of learning in *Of Education*: "The end then of learning is to repair the ruins of our first parents by regaining to know God aright, and out of that knowledge to love him, to imitate him, to be like him, as we may the neerest by possessing our souls of true vertue, which being united to the heavenly grace of faith makes up the highest perfection" (YP 2:366–68). In associating learning with the superlative values of "true vertue" and "the highest perfection," Milton, like Comenius, upholds education's potential to unite the human mind with the mind of God. Milton's notion of education differs fundamentally from that of Comenius, however, in its less optimistic view of human nature. For Milton, education is for the fallen. We can at best use learning to "repair" those "ruins" in order to "know God aright," and even then we must rely upon that gift of the Spirit, "the heavenly grace of faith," to approach perfection in this fallen state. The potential transformation of the learner that Milton outlines remains circumscribed by that Protestant vision. Both Milton and

Comenius descend from such heights of educational aspiration in rapid succession, and both move on to confront the practical challenges and common faults in the seventeenth century schoolroom.

One specific connection between Comenian pansophy and Miltonic instruction deserves mention in this regard. In attempting to articulate his vision of a "Universal Temple of Wisdom," Comenius offers as an illustration a passage from Lucretius's *De rerum natura*. Hartlib translates the passage in *A Reformation of Schooles* as follows:

> That so there may be erected some universall Temple of Wisdome, truly glorious, and refulgent with the ornaments of Harmony, and the light of Truth; Such as wee might justly apply that of *Lucretius* unto it,
>
> *Sed nil dulcius est bene quam munita tenere*
> *Edita Doctrina sapientum Templa serena,*
> *Despicere unde queas alios, passimque videre*
> *Errare, atque viam palantis quaerere vitae.*
>
> Thus in English.
> No worldly pleasures may compare
>   With this: well fenced to possesse
> Faire Wisdomes Temples (beauties rare)
>   High rais'd on learnings solidnesse.
> Thence you may see, how others goe astray
> As men bewild'red, groping for the way.
>
> (Comenius, 23)

The Lucretian passage invoked is the celebrated introduction to book 2 of the *De rerum natura*, which Hartlib translates loosely. What he renders as "Faire Wisdomes Temples" derives from the Latin phrase "templa . . . serena," which literally means "peaceful dwelling places" (Bailey, 1798). In general, Comenius had less confidence than Milton in the educational value of instruction in ancient Greek and Latin. Their shared use of Lucretius, however, indicates common ground in their use of Latin literature as a resource for ideas and expression.

At the very least, Comenius provides Milton with a strong endorsement for using the Romans to articulate the search for wisdom.

Perhaps an even closer analogue to Milton's Latin curriculum than the Comenian goal of pansophy comes from John Dury's projected scheme for an ideal pre-university education. Some consider Dury's plan for a Noble school the most complete educational scheme produced during the Puritan Revolution (Webster, 214). Published in London in 1651, Dury's plan overlaps with Milton's in several particulars. To begin with, Dury shares Milton's conviction that education serves not only a civic but a spiritual purpose. Focusing on students from ages 13 or 14 to 19 or 20, Dury compiles a complete list of "all the Usefull Arts and Sciences, which may fit them for any employment in Church or Common-wealth" (57). This list, particularly in its first three points, is strikingly similar to the Latin curriculum Edward Phillips recalled:

> 1. The Latine Authors of Agriculture Cato, Varro, Columella, may be put into their hands by parcels, to be an enlargement unto that which they have alreadie been taught concerning Husbandry.
> 2. The Naturall History of Pliny and Others, by choice parcels are also to be perused by them; and brought home to what they have formerly seen; together with the Histories of Meteors, Minerals, etc.
> 3. In like manner some Models and books of Architecture, Enginry, Fortification, Fire-works, Weapons, Military Discipline, and Navigation are to be lookt upon.
> 4. The Greek Authors of Morall Philosophie, Epictetus, Cebes, Arianus, Plato, Xenophon, Plutarch; and some Latin Tracts in this kind should be read by them; and an account taken of their proficiencie thereby.
> 5. The Doctrine of Oeconomicks, of Civill Government, and Naturall Justice and Equitie in the Laws of Nations should be offered unto them; the grounds of that *Jurisprudentia* whereof the summe is to be given out of the Institutiones of Justinian and Regulae Juris.

6. The Theorie of all the Mathematicks, with the full Practise of that which was deficient in their former Institution; where the Opticks with the Instruments belonging thereunto, and the Art of Dialing is to be entertained; and in Arithmetick the way of keeping Accounts.

7. The Principles of Naturall Philosophie and the Main Grounds of Medicin, with the Instruments of Distilling and other Chimicall Operations, and the Art of Apothecaries, are to be offered unto them partly in books, partly in the Operations themselves by an ocular inspection thereof, and of their drugges.

8. The Art of Chirurgery described in books, with an ocular inspection of all their tooles, and Compositions of plaisters and ointments, and the use thereof.

9. The Rules of Logick, Rhetorick and Poesie; shewing them first how to Analyse Authors, and observe their Art of Reason and Utterance to persuade: and then how to order their owne thoughts and expresssion, to search out Truths and declare the same Historically, Philosophically, Oratorically, Poetically.

10. Directions for the studye of all Humane Histories and what to observe in them, for the attainement of Wisdome and Prudencie in the Government of a mans owne life; where with the Directions to observe the wayes of others; the Rules of Judgement, Discretion, Prudencie and Civill Conversation to order their owne wayes aright towards all, are to be given unto them which is to be concluded with a special recognition and insight into Salomons Proverbs, and Ecclesiastes. (Dury, 58–60)

In his first three points, Dury seems to be matching Milton's Latin curriculum step by step. In points four through nine, Dury takes a much more utilitarian, "hands on" approach to various studies than does Milton. Whereas Milton seems primarily concerned to instill an awareness or conceptual understanding of various arts and sciences in the liberal arts manner, Dury aims to promote vocational or technical training. In the final section, with an eye toward the student's self-government, Dury urges "the attainement of Wisdome," reserving for last a special recommendation of Proverbs and

Ecclesiastes. In short, Dury begins with Milton, moves to Hartlib, and ends with a bow to Comenius. Determining lines of influence or indebtedness among Dury, Comenius, and Milton is not the issue here. What is most important is the way the other educators serve to clarify Milton's distinctive views.

Clearly, as I shall argue more fully in chapter 1, Milton sees in education not only a civic function but a religious purpose, a lifelong — even species-long — endeavor (Fallon, 64) to "repair the ruins of our first parents by regaining to know God aright" (YP 2:366–67). Focusing on the role that classical studies could play in this spiritual agenda, Milton took another distinctive step. His curriculum tacitly insists that reading Latin science and poetry can serve the religious purpose of education. In this regard, he parted company from Comenius and others. Comenius wrote: "If we would have a reformation of Schooles... profane, and Heathen Authors must be either quite rejected, or used with more choice and caution" (YP 2:366, n. 12). In *The Reformed School* John Dury refined this rejection somewhat, laying down as his first rule of teaching: "The teaching of Arts and Sciences ought not to be suspended upon the teaching of unknown Tongues, but made familiar unto the childrens capacity in their Mother-Tongue first; and afterward enlarged by the Use of other Tongues" (51). For Milton, in contrast, "languages are to be mastered (which means to write and speak, as well as to read them), as instruments indeed, but for the acquisition not merely of factual information, but of the whole cultures incorporated in them" (YP 2:202). Reading the Romans in their original tongue remained instrumental, first and last, to Milton's purposes.

Milton's innovative program, in other words, used readings in the classics to help train students to develop practical skills, but those skills were not to be seen as ends in themselves. By the same token, while learning to read Latin gave Milton's students practical benefits in their society, he specifically warns against learning languages for their own sake or for oratorical display. "[L]earning meere words" (YP 2:376), as Milton accuses the universities of doing, runs contrary to the ends of learning he expresses in *Of Education*. Learning Latin in particular enabled the student to take part in the dominant discourse of Europe. John Hale points out that post-Enlightenment readers often fail to consider the *questione della lingua*, the choice Milton's contemporaries faced of writing in Latin or the vernacular (*Milton's Languages*, 2–3). For example, late in his career, even when completely blind, Milton chose Latin for political and pedagogic topics — in particular for the *Artis Logicae* and *Defensio Secunda* — no doubt imagining their reception by a literate, that is, Latinate, European readership.

The sequence of texts Phillips recalled also hints at Milton's distinctive aim of training students, certainly to appreciate, and possibly to aspire to, the goal of poetic creativity. Phillips's list begins with the Latin authors of rustic matters and practical science, but it ends with the two "egregious" poets, Lucretius and Manilius. Thus it literally parallels the ideal sequence of disciplines set forth in Milton's tract *Of Education*, which likewise culminates with study of the "organic art" of poetry. Poetry, Milton writes, is to be made "subsequent, or rather precedent" to logic and rhetoric (YP 2:403). With Balachandra Rajan, I take this paradoxical utterance to mean that while the composition of poetry is to occur after rhetoric, poetry remains precedent in its value and worth (Rajan, 8).[3] Certainly Milton's scheme is to delay the composition of poetry and oratory until his students, "fraught with an universal insight into things" (YP 2:406), have worthy matter for their verbal compositions to express. It was the Romans, even more than the Greeks, who had emphasized the utility of poetry in forming students' character and in preparing them for public service (Sikes, 28–32). In Horace's epistle to Augustus, for example, Horace tells how poets serve the state. The poet can mold the tongue, the heart, and the eye of the young, he writes, by setting before them memorable precepts and examples (Horace,

Epistles 2.1.126–31). Rather than a harmless diversion or a means of self-expression, writing and reading poetry was vital to the health of the Roman state. The same conviction underlies the work of our English poet-teacher.

Of course, by filling his tutorial with readings in accomplished writers and poets, Milton served his own development as a writer as well. Phillips concludes his remarks on Milton's tutorial by observing that his teacher "thus increased his own knowledge, having the reading of all these authors as it were by proxy" (Hughes, 1030). The subject matter included within the tutorial is broad, even encyclopedic. This breadth reflects the ambitious discipline of its teacher-poet, who in *An Apology*, written in the midst of the tutorial, insisted that "he who would not be frustrate of his hope to write well hereafter in laudable things ought him selfe to be a true Poem, that is, a composition, and patterne of the best and honourablest things; not presuming to sing high praises of heroick men, or famous Cities, unless he have in himself the experience [including literary experience] of all that which is praise-worthy" (YP 1:890). Given this Miltonic commitment to composing his life, one of the chief outcomes of Milton's tutorial during the 1640s must have been self-education. Moreover, as Stella Revard forcefully maintains, Milton's reissue in 1673 of his 1645 collection of *Poems*, with its signature pairing of Latin with English poems, shows that "what he had learned about the neoclassical poetry of the Renaissance and had adapted to [his] first book of poetry continued to inform structurally and thematically his later poetry" (Revard, 266). Milton's development as a poet, moreover, never outgrows the didactic role of the teacher-poet. Among many articulations of that role, the most inspiring is found in *The Reason of Church Government*. There Milton writes that literary forms "are of power beside the office of a pulpit, to imbreed and cherish in a great people the seeds of vertu and publick civility, to allay the perturbations of the mind, and set the affections in right tune, to celebrate in glorious and lofty Hymns the throne and equipage of Gods Almightinesse. . . . Teaching over the whole book of sanctity and vertu through all the instances of example" (YP 1:816). Indeed, John T. Shawcross maintains that the great goal of Milton's life, whether one considers his classroom teaching, his prose, or his poetry, is education (*John Milton*, 97–99).

Whether discussing fertilizer or fate, the Roman authors in Milton's curriculum share certain characteristic habits of thought. All carefully observe phenomena, rigorously systematize their investigations, and readily acknowledge a divinity in natural things beyond human comprehension. The Romans' love of wordplay and lapidary syntax in articulating these matters was frequently emulated by Milton. The Romans' confidence in addressing and solving technical problems, whether through Vitruvian engineering or Lucretian therapy, however, is redefined within Milton's epic narrative. There it becomes a fatal form of self-reliance, a reflection of Satanic hubris. To the wealth of technical knowledge that the Romans made available to Milton, the poet attaches two caveats: the sacred quality of nature, and the limited capacity of human beings to comprehend the natural world. Those principles underlie not only Milton's epic argument but also his use of Roman science and learning in *Paradise Lost*. Such learning is radically paradoxical: incapable of solving the dilemma of the Fall, it remains potentially beneficial by enabling human agents to cope with the forces of nature while provoking them to seek spiritual understanding and humility.

Early Objections, Theoretical Defenses, and the Sacred Earth

Two standing objections to Milton's tutorial — and hence to my extensive study of it — demand responses at this point. In his *Life of Milton*, Samuel Johnson famously objected that Milton's tutorial gave so much emphasis to the acquisition of scientific knowledge that it scanted students' moral education:

But the truth is that the knowledge of external nature, and the sciences which that knowledge requires or includes, are not the great or the frequent business of the human mind. Whether we provide for action or conversation, whether we wish to be useful or pleasing, the first requisite is the religious and moral knowledge of right and wrong ... Physiological learning is of such rare emergence that one man may know another half his life without being able to estimate his skill in hydrostatics or astronomy, but his moral and prudential character immediately appears. (393)

Johnson's objection to Milton's tutorial is that it is *too* scientific in the narrow, technical sense and thus irrelevant to the "great business" of everyday life: moral discrimination. Surprisingly, the Christian moralist Johnson fails to recognize that the technical or scientific details in the Latin texts emerge in a highly moral and spiritual climate. For example, the technical information about farming in Cato is inseparable from the author's emphasis on farming as a good way of life, a way to cultivate the soul. Pliny, too, is concerned not merely to compile data about various species but to articulate a Stoic philosophy about nature and the proper role of human beings toward it. If anything, the epic poets Lucretius and Manilius weaken their objectivity as scientists by pressing their moral and philosophical views. Johnson's claim that these works lack moral fiber, and that Milton by teaching them thereby impoverished his students' moral development, is uncharacteristically shortsighted.

Virtually the contrary objection to the tutorial was raised by Milton's great Victorian biographer, David Masson. While Johnson claims that Milton taught too much science, Masson feels that Milton did not include enough. In his *Life of John Milton and History of His Time* (1896), Masson argues that the weakness of the tutorial was its reliance on dead ancient languages. Milton's error, he writes, lay in mingling the acquisition of knowledge with Latin and Greek. Milton followed the practice of his day in using Latin and Greek books, Masson admits.

> Even then, however, he perhaps overrated the necessity of Latin and Greek for this particular business of education, and underrated what could be done in sheer English. And, now that Science has burst all bounds of Latin and Greek, and it would be ludicrous to go merely to the Greek and Latin authors named by Milton for our Geography, or Astronomy, or Natural History, or Physics, or Chemistry, or Anatomy and Physiology, it is clear that the claims of Latin and Greek in education must not rest on their instrumental value in giving access to the stores of science, but on quite another basis. In short, that in Milton's scheme which is now obsolete is its determinate intertwining of the whole business of the acquisition of knowledge with the process of reading in other languages than the vernacular. This taken out of the Scheme, all the rest lasts, and is as good now, and perhaps as needful, as it was in Milton's time. (3:252)

Masson likes best about the tutorial what neither its students nor its teacher ever advocated: its total dedication to scientific advancement. Thus for Masson, if only the Latin and Greek languages could be purged from the experiment, Milton's scientific program could remain up to date. More than its anachronism vitiates Masson's critique: Why would gentle families in the 1640s *want* their sons to be trained exclusively as scientists? Masson's contempt for language study, in a biography of a writer remarkable for his love of languages, momentarily clouds his narrative. Well aware of the dangers of force-feeding foreign languages to unwilling students, Milton writes in *Of Education* that "language is but the instrument convaying to us things usefull to be known" (YP 2:369). Perhaps the "but" oversimplifies. Conveying information may be the primary, but it is by no means the *only* value of language study. Anyone who has thoroughly studied a language knows that mastering a language means learning the ways of the culture that produced it. If one has truly come to know Mandarin, one has a key — perhaps the only possible key — to understanding Chinese culture. If one has truly come to know the Latin of Lucretius and Manilius, one gains insight not merely into the "scientific" content of their texts, but into their cultures, convictions, and worldviews.

The Roman authors in the tutorial were, as Phillips wrote, "scarce ever heard of" in seventeenth century public schools; some twentieth century readers, too, may find them unfamiliar. Thus, my appendix provides a brief introduction to the ten Latin authors included in Milton's tutorial and a brief summary of their included works. This summary is not neutral, of course; it is written with an eye toward the significance of the ten authors for Milton. Hence, in the appendix, I discuss the limited appearance in Milton's works of Frontinus and Celsus. However significant in themselves, these authors prove not to be major precursors for Milton's art. Thus, they did not merit treatment in additional chapters.

Upon recognizing that Milton is referring to a precursor's text, readers move through awareness of the shared content between the texts to questions of method and significance. In other words, we wonder *how* Milton read the Romans, and how to interpret the record of that reading in Milton's works. In considering how Milton read those Roman texts, I take as the most reliable guide Milton's discursive responses to them. The two concepts that best describe those responses are allusion and imitation. Long before Milton's works join the tradition, the process of allusion was an integral feature of Roman literature. Following Gian Biagio Conte's analysis of Latin poetry, I regard allusion as a figure crucial to the creation of poetic tradition. "In the art of allusion, as in every rhetorical figure," Conte writes, "the poetry lies in the simultaneous presence of two different realities that try to indicate a single reality" (38). To illustrate this phenomenon, Conte discusses the gap that the competent reader perceives between the immediate scene, or "letter," of the allusive passage and its "sense" in the reality of the earlier text. As a paradigm, Conte shows how Anchises's greeting of Aeneas with "Quas ego te terras et quanta per aequora vectum/accipio quantis iactatum, nate, periclis!" ("I receive you, my son, borne through what lands and over how many seas, tossed about by how many dangers!" *Aeneid*, 6.692–93) links Vergil's hero — through the intermediary echo of Catullus's elegiac address to his brother, borne through many peoples and many seas ("Multas per gentes et multa per aequora vectus") — to the heroic wanderings of Odysseus, famously tossed about across the Mediterranean. Milton's allusions to Roman tradition create similar confrontations in the echo chamber of poetic memory. A major example is Milton's allusion to Roman literary tradition in describing the Earth's wound at the climactic moment in *Paradise Lost*. Thus, as I shall show in detail in chapter 5, Milton expands the sense of the Genesis Fall account to include the accounts of a wounded Earth debunked as mythology by Lucretius, recast as natural history by Pliny, and resurrected as Roman religion by Vergil. An equally inventive Miltonic allusion that I shall explore in chapter 4, and one that has heretofore escaped critical discussion, is the double claim of novelty in Milton's opening proclamation to be pursuing "[t]hings unattempted yet in prose or rhyme" (1.16). In addition to alluding to Ariosto's *Orlando Furioso*, as is well known, Milton also thereby recalls the opening of Manilius's epic.

While deriving from the strategy of an author, allusion requires the reader's memory for its effect; as Conte puts it, allusion "*establishes* the competence of the Model Reader" (30). In contrast, the Renaissance practice of *imitatio*, while depending on both the general reader and the particular imitator as reader, focuses primarily on the author's intentional relationship with the precursor. Renaissance writers including Pico, Petrarch, and Erasmus described this intentional relationship as *aemulatio* or emulation, which they regarded as a subspecies of *imitatio* (Pigman, "Versions of Imitation," 1–32). In his magisterial account of Renaissance imitation, Thomas Greene takes Milton's *Paradise Lost* as a chief example of what he terms "heuristic" imitation. Heuristic imitations advertise their derivation from the subtexts they carry with them, but also distance themselves from those subtexts and force us to recognize the distance crossed. *Paradise Lost* in particular, Greene writes, "established firmly a strong if sometimes complex relationship with each work and each tradition that it draws upon, according to each its own cultural weight and situation. It underscores rather than obscures the historicity of its sources, and so it permits a flood of imaginative energy to flow through it unimpeded" (40). This notion fits Milton's practice in parts of the epic quite well. As I have argued elsewhere, however, much of Milton's imitative strategy accords better with Greene's category of "dialectical" imitation, which "required the writer both to assume the vulnerabilities of his own specific moment and to reach out for the specificity of his subtext" in its own, far distant place and time (48).[4] Taken together, these two images — Milton as confident cultural historian, marshalling and dispatching literary traditions for his purposes; and Milton as isolated champion of classical learning, desperately appealing to the ancients for authoritative precedents for his own endangered literary experiment — epitomize Milton's overall imitative strategy in *Paradise Lost*.

Conte warns against the tendency among philologists tracing *imitatio* of falling into a psychological reconstruction of motive, whether admiration or emulation (26–29). Harold Bloom's approach to Milton and his heirs in *The Anxiety of Influence*, for all its brilliance, represents this psychoanalytic tendency. I would balance this salutary warning against overpersonalizing imitation with a warning against reducing literary relationships to an impersonal system of intertextuality, a mere intersection of *langue* and *parole*. This is a danger to which Conte and his followers are prone, given their primary concern with literary systems and issues such as textual production and readability.[5] Literary tradition maps the intersection of a talented writer's work with the precedents that the individual chooses to confront. To take T. S. Eliot's formulation in "Tradition and the Individual Talent," what makes a writer traditional in the positive sense is a keen awareness of the presence of the past, "not of what is dead, but of what is already living" (*The Sacred Wood*, 59). Such an awareness derives from an underlying historical sense "that the whole of the literature of Europe from Homer and within it the whole of the literature of his own country has a simultaneous existence and composes a simultaneous order" (49). G. W. Pigman has argued that the major intellectual achievement of the Renaissance is the development of an historical sense recognizing the fundamental differences between the ancient and early modern worlds (281–82). While Conte is right that "any author's text is already composed of many texts and codes" (29), each fully realized traditional poem nonetheless remains a distinctive creation. Readers have no trouble, despite the intricate plurality of codes that coalesce within one text, recognizing the distinctive features of an author's style. They readily make the synecdochic substitution by which "Milton" or "Lucretius" comes to stand for that author's style or works.

From what records survive about humanist education, the practice of *imitatio* was an entrenched and everyday feature of the Renaissance classroom. Well documented is the practice of early humanists such as Petrarch, Erasmus, and More in basing first their Latin letters, then their literary works in Latin, on ancient Roman models. By Milton's time, the practice of *imitatio* had in English grammar schools crystalized into such practices as double translation, grammatical parsing, and attempts to capture in English poetic forms (say, rhymed decasyllabic couplets) the sense and flavor of Roman forms (such as dactyllic hexameter and Ovid's elegiac distich).

Despite Milton's variation from the choice of texts common in grammar schools of his day, the analytical method practiced in classes such as Charles Hoole's and those of his own grammar school at St. Paul's would certainly be a part of his own training and practice (Harding, 28–33; Clark, 104–06; DuRocher, 39–42).

When we turn our attention from classroom practice to the production of mature poetry, certain shifts in our understanding of *imitatio* need to occur. Renaissance theorists, including George Puttenham and Francis Meres, distinguished between the specifically imitative concentration on a model text and the more broadly paradigmatic uses of the ancients. Thus, as Jonathan Bate explains (84–85), Meres argues that whereas Shakespeare's *Venus and Adonis* imitates Ovid's narrative of that myth, the account of Pythagorean metempsychosis serves as a paradigm for Shakespeare's sonnets. Instead of Shakespeare regarding Ovid's text as a source to be mined or a model to be closely imitated, "the principle of metempsychosis which Book Fifteen [of the *Metamorphoses*] articulates is enacted in the metempsychosis of Book Fifteen into the sonnets" (85). The flexibility implied in such paradigmatic uses of the ancients, along with enabling one to envision fluid relationships between Renaissance makers and antiquity, does beg questions concerning the limits of the process. To what extent in a paradigmatic relationship is a later author truly focusing on the precursor text? To what extent are paradigms escapable? For example, if Lucretius established a paradigm of the philosophical nature poem, may not every comparable work, from Aemilia Lanyer's "To Cookham," Ben Jonson's "To Penshurst," to Andrew Marvell's "Upon Appleton House," be said to be following that paradigm, regardless of the later author's knowledge or use of Lucretius?

Such questions are sobering. They are provocative in the best sense, challenging us to distinguish what constitutes genuine imitation. Two points seem to me essential. First, as Meres indicates, for a genuine paradigmatic relationship to arise, there must be palpable connections of ideas and expressions in both works. In the example cited, both Ovid and Shakespeare display self-conscious awareness of the shared principle, the transmigration of souls, in their respective works. Moreover, the exploration in both pieces of what Richard Lanham has called "the rhetorical way of life," the commitment to flexibility and adaptability in self-representation, runs deep. Second and no less important, Renaissance theorists insisted that difference along with similarity is essential to meaningful *imitatio*. What makes Shakespeare's use of Ovid's paradigm of metempsychosis so fascinating, at least in part, is his transplanting of Pythagoras's lesson from its didactic epic context to the new soil of the sonnet sequence. The application of Pythagoras's lecture to issues of love, friendship, and change articulated by the speaker of Shakespeare's sonnets renovates and reinvigorates the paradigm. Among less inventive writers, in contrast, the absence of palpable difference between the new work and the old paradigm results in mere copying, or in Renaissance usage, "aping." In a letter to Boccaccio written in 1366, Petrarch laid down the principle that the "proper imitator should take care that what he writes resembles the original without reproducing it":

> Thus we writers must look to it that with a basis of similarity there should be many dissimilarities. And the similarity should be planted so deep that it can only be extricated by quiet meditation. The quality is to be felt rather than defined. Thus we may use another man's conceptions and the colour of his style, but not use his words. In the first case the resemblance is hidden deep; in the second it is glaring. The first procedure makes poets, the second makes apes. (198–89; cited in Bate, 87–88)

Certainly Milton's resemblances with the Romans are "hidden deep." They are there nonetheless, awaiting our quiet meditation. Along with the pattern of allusion that I have sketched, I regard Milton's use of the Latin texts as a case of paradigmatic imitation. The Roman authors serve for Milton not as masters or sources but as respected precedents, precedents requiring his inventive and not apish adaptation.

Embodied in several of the Latin texts and adapted repeatedly in Milton's works is the notion that the Earth is a sacred, living organism. Perhaps the fullest expression of that notion among the Romans is Pliny's paragraph at the beginning of book 2 of his *Natural History*. I cite the Latin text from the 1635 London edition together with Philemon Holland's influential translation:

> Mundum, & hoc quodcunque nomine alio caelum appelare libuit, cujus circumflexu teguntur cuncta, numen esse credi par est, aeternum, immensum, neque genitum, neque interiturum unquam. Hujus extera indagere, nec interest hominum, nec capit humanae conjectura mentis. Sacer est, aeternis [sic], immensus, totus in toto, immo vero ipse totum, infinitus, & finito similis, omnium rerum certus & similis incerto, extra, intra, cuncta complexus in se: idemque rerum naturae opus & rerum ipsa natura.

> The World, and this, which by another name men have thought good to call heaven (under the bending cope whereof, all things are enmantled and covered), believe we ought in all reason to be a God, eternall, unmeasureable, without beginning, and likewise endlesse. What is without the compasse hereof, neither is it fit for men to search, nor within mans wit to reach and conceive. Sacred it is, everlasting, infinit, all in all, or rather it selfe all and absolute: finite and limited, yet seeming infinite: in all motions orderly and certaine: comprehending and containing all whatsoever, both without and within: Nature's work, and yet very Nature it selfe, producing all things.

Holland's halting rhythms express beautifully the syntactic reversals embedded in Pliny's sentences ("certus & similis incerto," "idemque rerum naturae opus & rerum ipsa natura"). The reversals thematically characterize the Earth as both created and creating. Pliny's account is the clearest proclamation of what Rackham describes as the Pythagorean and Stoic creed of the "world soul" (170, note a). As such, the doctrine would not easily find acceptance among Christian thinkers. Milton would surely reject the notion of the Earth's preexistence, which contradicts Genesis. For Milton, too, whatever "deity" the Earth possesses would be that of a creature subject to God's absolute authority. Yet the notion that the universe is sacred, living, and itself coterminous with God finds dramatic expression in *Paradise Lost* in Milton's simile of the universe as a flowering plant. In what Hughes calls the epic's "most beautiful and crucial ontological passage," Raphael explains to Adam:

> O *Adam*, one Almighty is, from whom
> All things proceed, and up to him return,
> If not deprav'd from good, created all
> Such to perfection, one first matter all,
> Indu'd with various forms, various degrees
> Of substance, and in things that live, of life;
> But more refin'd, more spiritous, and pure,
> As nearer to him plac't or nearer tending
> Each in thir several active Spheres assign'd,
> Till body up to spirit work, in bounds
> Proportion'd to each kind. So from the root
> Springs lighter the green stalk, from thence the leaves
> More aery, last the bright consummate flow'r
> Spirits odorous breathes.
>
> (5.469–82)

The epic simile of the flowering plant clarifies the tendency of living things in Milton's universe to grow upward: "Till body up to spirit work." While this view of nature was usually regarded by Christian exegetes as pantheistic and heretical, it nonetheless accords well with Milton's insistence on creation *ex Deo* (from or out of God) as opposed to the orthodox view of creation *ex nihilo* (Hughes, 193). If such a sacred, living universe set Milton at odds with Puritan interpretations of Genesis, Milton was apparently willing — perhaps eager — to link the animist Roman view with his distinctive recreation of Genesis. The Roman accounts of a living Earth, moreover, provide further support for Milton's ontological and poetic commitment to animist materialism or vitalism, a commitment John Rogers has persuasively established with reference to Milton's contemporaries, principally Jean Baptiste van Helmont, William Harvey, and Francis Glisson (8–12).

Likewise, Milton in his poetic account of Creation does not hesitate to adapt Lucretius's vivid celebration of the Earth's active role as mother, despite its obvious incongruities with a literal reading of Genesis. Lucretius describes the generation of creatures from Earth's womb, and thus concludes that the Earth's name of "Mother" is justified:

> Tum tibi terra dedit primum mortalia saecla.
> multus enim calor atque umor superabat in arvis.
> hoc ubi quaeque loci regio opportuna dabatur,
> crescebant uteri terram radicibus apti....
>   Quare etiam atque etiam maternum nomen adepta
> terra tenet merito, quoniam genus ipsa creavit
> humanum atque animal prope certo tempore fudit
> omne quod in magnis bacchatur montibus passim,
> aeriasque simul volucris variantibus formis.
>   (Rouse, ed., *De rerum natura*, 5.805–25)

> Then first the Earth produced the generations of living creatures. For there was great abundance of heat and moisture in the fields; therefore wherever a suitable place was found, wombs would grow, clinging to the earth by roots.... Which is why again and again the Earth deserves the name of Mother which she had acquired, since she created the human race out of herself, and brought forth almost at a fixed time every animal that ranges wild everywhere over the great mountains, and at the same time the birds of the air in all their varied forms.

Milton imitates this magnificent passage twice, first in his introductory description of conception in the Earth's womb, then in the return to womb imagery in his expansion of the scriptural account of day six of Creation:

> The Earth was form'd, but in the Womb as yet
> Of Waters, Embryon immature involv'd,
> Appear'd not: over all the face of Earth
> Main Ocean flow'd, not idle, but with warm
> Prolific humor soft'ning all her Globe,
> Fermented the great Mother to conceive,
> Satiate with genial moisture.
>
> (7.276–82)

> The Earth obey'd, and straight
> Op'ning her fertile Womb teem'd at a Birth
> Innumerous living Creatures, perfet forms,
> Limb'd and full grown: out of the ground up rose
> As from his Lair the wild Beast where he wons
> In Forest wild, in Thicket, Brake, or Den;
> Among the Trees in Pairs they rose, they walk'd:
> The Cattle in the Fields and Meadow green:
> Those rare and solitary, these in flocks
> Pasturing at once, and in broad Herds upsprung.
>
> (7.453–62)

Conspicuously and daringly, Milton's poem recalls both his great precedents: the Bible and the Epicurean poet. When Robert Boyle adopted atomism in *The Usefulness of Experimental Philosophy* (1653), he mined Lucretian concepts in order to refute its atheistical conclusions. While atoms apparently form the basis of all matter, Boyle argued, it was God who made the atoms, set them in motion, and formed them into complex creatures (Westfall, *Science and Religion*, 111–12). Likewise, Milton's majestic account echoes Lucretius in a way that shows the partial truth of the atomist's understanding of Creation. As it attempts to outdo Lucretius by showing the Roman writer's agreement with Scripture, Milton's account presents a radically new, hybrid argument that preserves its constituent parts. Through this stunning Creation account, itself emulating two memorable Creation narratives, Milton's universe begins with a true poem.

Beyond particular contributions to moments in Milton's works, can we offer a comprehensive account of the role the Latin tutorial played in shaping his imagination? Because there are several parts to this question, I offer several explanations. In the first place, Milton draws upon the Romans in depicting the Earth as a sacred, living creature because their accounts corresponded with his artistic needs. When one realizes that in *Paradise Lost* the Earth is named 94 times as a proper noun, more often than are major characters including Adam and Eve, then one is prepared to see the Earth as a full-fledged character in the epic. As Roman writers from Lucretius through Vergil and Seneca to Pliny and Columella had articulated a substantial conversation about the Earth as a living being, and as Scripture had relatively little to say on the subject, Milton naturally recalled the Romans in developing his characterization of the Earth. Certainly some kind of dialogic or dialectical exchange occurs as Milton mingles his scriptural narrative with the Roman accounts. Most important, as I will show in my chapter on the wounded Earth, Milton's account aims to emulate — that is, to overgo, even as it echoes — the specific accounts of a sacred, wounded earth presented by Lucretius, Pliny, and Vergil.

The suggestion that the Romans had more to say about the Earth than did Scripture introduces a larger question that chapter 1 will explore in depth. Precisely what for Milton is the relationship between the authority of Scripture and the authority of scientific and literary texts in human life? Milton's commitment to Scripture runs deep and along the lines of the radical reformers. He expresses as absolute the authority of the Bible, yet with the understanding that its language is best interpreted according to the Spirit, for "the Spirit which is given to us is a more certain guide than Scripture" (CE 16:279). The workings of the Spirit are crucial in opening biblical hermeneutics to human history and traditions. Recent scholarship has emphasized those scriptural texts, notably the Psalm texts, authorizing Milton and other reformers to delve confidently into nature. Mary Ann Radzinowicz and Dayton Haskin have demonstrated the particular significance in this regard of biblical commentary on the opening of Psalm 19: "The heavens declare the glory of God; and the firmament sheweth his handywork" (Radzinowicz, *Milton's Epics*, 207–09; Haskin, 202–16). Most notably, upon his first awakening described in book 8 of *Paradise Lost*, Adam reads the Book of Nature as the handiwork of "some great Maker."

Independently of scriptural proof texts, however, Milton voices his conviction that science, in the sense of the Latin *scientia*, is a powerful and pleasurable source of knowledge. In *Ad Patrem*, the Latin elegy to his father, Milton personifies *scientia* as a heavenly spirit made flesh, who can unfold all the knowledge that a generous father has enabled him to gain. Here the ambiguity of the poem's title — to the Father? to my Father? — is a potent poetic means of yoking John Milton, Senior, with the heavenly Father:

> Denique quicquid habet caelum, subjectaque caelo
> Terra parens, terraeque et caelo interfluus aer,
> Quicquid et unda tegit, pontique agitabile marmor,
> Per te nosse licet, per te, si nosse libebit.
> Dimotaque venit spectanda scientia nube,
> Nudaque conspicuos inclinat ad oscula vultus,
> Ni fugisse velim, ni sit libasse molestum.
>
> (86–92)

> And finally, whatever heaven contains and earth, our parent under heaven, and the air that flows between earth and heaven, and whatever the waters and the trembling surface of the sea cover, your kindness gives me the means to know, if I care for the knowledge that your kindness offers. From the opening cloud science appears, and, naked, bends her face to my kisses, unless I wish to flee or unless I should find her enjoyment irksome.

This dream vision describes a blissful encounter between the poet and science that can last as long as he can enjoy it. The ambiguous address of the poem to "*Patrem,*" that is, both to Milton's universal and his biological father, reinvigorates an otherwise commonplace metaphor. Likewise, the play on the Earth as the other parent under heaven renews and particularizes the stock personification of the Earth as mother. Not only does Milton thus link the Earth and John Milton Senior as benevolent parents and providers. The implicit point is perhaps more important for present purposes: Milton depicts science as the vital, intimate link between knowledge of the world itself and knowledge of God.

The end of learning, Milton writes in his educational tract to Hartlib, is nothing less than knowledge of God. Given human beings' limited means of perception, sensory knowledge is the clearest way to seek that end: "But because our understanding cannot in this body found it selfe but on sensible things, nor arrive so cleerly to the knowledge of God and things invisible, as by orderly conning over the visible and inferior creature, the same method is necessarily to be follow'd in all discreet teaching" (YP 2:367–69). This crucial epistemological sentence is at once a reply to the new science of Bacon and a credo of Milton's guarded confidence in scientific inquiry. It reflects not only Milton's instrumental view of Creation but also his awareness of the limits of natural knowledge, its dependence for its veracity on Scripture.

The relationship in Milton's time between the Bible and nature as authorities is in my view closer than has often been alleged. Scholars including Richard Westfall have emphasized how natural science "displaced" religion in the seventeenth century. Here I join with other voices who suggest that Scripture and science, properly understood, remained intertwined in the period. Sir Thomas Browne memorably described their relationship as that of God's two books, "besides that written one of God, another of his servant Nature." With Harinder Singh Marjara, I find that contemporaries of Milton "viewed nature as a created and a creative process set in motion by the command of God" (*Contemplation of Created Things*, 16). The definition of "Nature" in the *De doctrina christiana* resonates with that view: "Nature cannot mean anything except the wonderful power and efficacy of the divine voice which went forth in the beginning, and which all things have obeyed ever since as a perpetual command" (YP 6:131). That Miltonic conviction supports Alastair Fowler's reassessment of the long-held notion that the Renaissance amounted to a secular movement or involved desacralization of nature. During the seventeenth century nature was certainly revalued and represented through a variety of potent media, as Fowler extensively shows. "The idea of the divine universe," however, "far from dwindling, became strengthened, and its structures were established on a securer basis" (31).

Given Milton's insistence on returning to a securer basis for knowledge of the world and God, however, it is not surprising that he would ultimately depart from the direction of contemporary experimental science. Bacon's self-proclaimed "Great Instauration" required the separation of "things divine" from "things human" so that the new "logic" of scientific method could proceed toward its announced end: to conquer or command nature in action.[6] Despite all the benefits of the inductive method, to Milton such an objective places human beings in a destructive stance to themselves, their world, and their God. In the figure of Galileo, the one contemporary of Milton's who appears in *Paradise Lost*, we are shown precisely what modern science can do. Through his telescope or "Optic Glass," the "*Tuscan* Artist" discerns new features on the lunar landscape (1.286–91). Such knowledge, such improved vision, is revealing. It is also inherently incomplete. A more inclusive mode of seeing, Milton's poetry suggests, exposes the moon's "spotty Globe" as the shield of Satan. A final perspective, gained by stepping back from the moon-satanic shield image into the encompassing narrative of Satan's testing of human and angelic agents through God's permissive will, completes Milton's epistemologically educative argument.

A final question arises: Why would Milton choose a group of specifically Roman scientists and writers both as the basis of his educational scheme and as precursors worthy of imitation in his major epic? Part of my answer is a cultural one. As a British writer and historian, Milton did as Geoffrey of Monmouth did in his *History of the Kings of Britain*: he looked to Roman agents for the origin of his own culture. In fact, Milton included in his *History of Britain* a translation of Geoffrey's dialogue between Brutus and Diana about a "Sea-girt" land where Brut's descendants shall "find a lasting seat" and "another Troy shall rise" (YP 5:14). As a Renaissance artist, Milton turned to the exemplars of the arts and sciences that he and his contemporaries valued most. In many cases, these were ancient Romans. This focus on the ancients need not exclude attention to the moderns. In arguing that Milton drew upon the atomic physics and Epicurean philosophy of Lucretius, for example, I do not for a moment mean to deny Milton's familiarity with contemporary European disciples of Lucretius such as Pierre Gassendi, as Stephen Fallon has so capably demonstrated (20–21). I do insist, however, on Milton's primary engagement with Lucretius and the other texts in their original Latin, and on the metaphoric and linguistic depth that experience confers. English translations of the Roman texts were generally not available (even if they were desirable) for Milton's students. Accordingly, subsequent chapters describe Renaissance editions of the Roman texts that Milton and his students most likely used. These often contain illuminating front matter and surprising commentaries. For example, Georgius Alexandrini's index to Columella's book, typically appended to Renaissance editions *De Re Rustica*, provides a linguistic key to "Amarant," the unfading flower that Milton transplants to heaven in book 3 of *Paradise Lost*.

One wonders in Milton's case, however, if there might not be more intimate reasons for his focus on Roman precedents. Milton was simply fascinated with so many aspects of ancient Roman culture and its reflections in modern Italian culture. His memorable trip to Italy only confirmed and deepened his personal fascination, palpable in his early works, with Roman writers such as Ovid and Vergil. Milton's three Latin sonnets to Leonora Baroni, whom he heard singing in Rome, record one aspect of that passionate involvement; his poems to Salzilli and other Roman exemplars of the Italian academies record another. Even on the eve of Charles's restoration in 1660, the republican form of government exemplified by the early Roman republic remained Milton's urgent recommendation for reforming his country's governance in *The Ready and Easy Way*. Throughout his life, Milton's fascination with Christ's life and teachings would have brought him into frequent imaginative contact with Rome.

Milton faced enormous difficulties in promoting the Roman republic as a political or cultural precedent in his works, particularly among his Restoration readers. Before brilliantly demonstrating Milton's reassertion in *Paradise Lost* of Roman republican values, especially through sympathetic allusions to the tragic loss of liberty depicted in Lucan's epic *Pharsalia*, David Norbrook finds it necessary to counter an unwritten Act of Oblivion that since the collapse of the protectorate had in effect legislated forgetting the republican element in English cultural history (1–2). Milton's success in revaluing Roman precedents demands an audience capable of distinguishing between the enduring aesthetic power of classical culture and its spiritual emptiness. Focusing on the specific Roman form of the triumph, Laura Lunger Knoppers demonstrates that Milton in *Paradise Lost* "not only undercuts but outgoes contemporary political uses of the Roman triumph in the parody [sic] splendors of Hell and the truly glorious triumph of Heaven; the epic reflects the appeal, as well as the dangers of the triumphal mode" (96). Milton's brief epic, too, registers the splendor and the danger of ancient Rome. Satan in *Paradise Regained* shows the Son a panorama of imperial Rome:

> [T]here the Capitol thou seest,
> Above the rest lifting his stately head
> On the *Tarpeian rock*, her citadel
> Impregnable, and there Mount *Palatine*
> Th'Imperial palace, compass huge, and high
> The structure, skill of noblest architects,
> With gilded battlements, conspicuous far,
> Turrets and Terraces, and glittering Spires.
>
> (4.47–54)

In the military fortifications one hears Machiavellian echoes of Christ's Rome in bondage to worldly power, to Satan himself. A tone of strong disapproval emanates from Milton's representation of modern, Catholic Rome in the form of St. Peter's Basilica as Pandaemonium:

> Pilasters round
> Were set, and Doric pillars overlaid
> With golden architrave; nor did there want
> Cornice or frieze, with bossy sculptures graven;
> The Roof was fretted Gold. Not *Babylon*,
> Nor great *Alcairo* such magnificence
> Equall'd in all their glories, to enshrine
> *Belus* or *Serapis* their Gods.
>
> (1.713–20)

A different God, Milton believed, once walked among those graven temples in Rome. As a Christian poet, Milton sought to emulate the triumphal forms of Roman art while leading his "fit audience" to reject Roman excesses. His poetry takes readers down paths that Roman predecessors had provided, but at the end of our journey lies not the eternal city but a "a paradise within thee, happier far" (12.587).

ONE

Conning the Creature

Limits of Natural Knowledge in *Paradise Lost*

In the prose tract *Of Education*, written in reply to the educational reformer Samuel Hartlib, John Milton maintains that human beings can achieve knowledge of God "by orderly conning over the visible and inferior creature" (YP 2:369). Milton's precise formulation of this phrase reveals several dimensions of his complex attitude toward the nonhuman creation, an attitude expressed in intricate and stunning detail in the epic poem *Paradise Lost*. I will begin by teasing out Milton's view of the creatures from that passage in *Of Education*, then see how that attitude accords with Milton's treatment in *Paradise Lost* of one botanical species (amaranth), one zoological species (serpent), and one key scene showing the original human reaction to the creatures. What fascinates me about Milton's treatment of the creatures, and what my subsequent discussion will document, is the distinctive way Milton's poetry synthesizes relevant scriptural passages, mythological accounts, and scientific traditions. From the start it may be useful to observe that Milton, along with many contemporaries including Sir Robert Boyle, Galileo Galilei, Henry More, and Johannes Kepler, regarded questions of natural philosophy as inseparable from questions of metaphysics or theology. As Milton put it in *De doctrina christiana*: "Nature cannot mean anything except the wonderful power and efficacy of the divine voice which went forth in the beginning, and which all things have obeyed ever since as a perpetual command" (YP 6:131).[1] Instantly Milton's ambitious approach raises serious questions of veracity and authority. For example, how can the science in Milton's poem be reliable if it is blended with myths and fables? Assuming that Scripture was the ultimate authority for Milton, how do forms of knowledge such as science and legend interact with scriptural authority? As I hope to show, Milton's claim that systematic investigation of Creation leads to reliable knowledge of God marks a pivotal moment in the history of religion and of thought. Reflecting that bold claim, Milton's inclusion of various sources of knowledge within his poetic narrative amounts to a strategy with unparalleled potential to teach and delight. His inclusive and allusive poetry constitutes a form of "discreet teaching," and what it promises to teach is nothing less than the ways of God.

Early in *Of Education*, Milton sets forth what he sees as the "end" of learning, then immediately proceeds to unveil his essential teaching method. The passage conveys a full sense of its author's reforming spirit and his attitude toward the natural world:

> The end then of learning is to repair the ruins of our first parents by regaining to know God aright, and out of that knowledge to love him, to imitate him, to be like him, as we may the neerest by possessing our souls of true vertue, which being united to the heavenly grace of faith makes up the highest perfection. But because our understanding cannot in this body

found it selfe but on sensible things, nor arrive so cleerly to the knowledge of God and things invisible, as by orderly conning over the visible and inferior creature, the same method is necessarily to be follow'd in all discreet teaching. (YP 2:366–69)

For Milton, education involves moral improvement ("possessing our souls of true vertue"), but above all it aims at giving students knowledge of God. To approach that high goal from our fallen state, however, demands methodical knowledge of Creation. Georgia B. Christopher and Dayton Haskin have demonstrated Milton's contribution to the mid-seventeenth century debate among Reformation commentators about the proper relationship between scriptural and scientific knowledge. To use Sir Thomas Browne's influential terms in *Religio medici*, Milton's prose tract elegantly folds knowledge of God's written book into that of "his servant Nature" (24). Embedded in Milton's aim is both the Old Testament Fall narrative ("the ruins of our first parents") and the essence of Pauline, reformed theology ("the heavenly grace of faith"). Accordingly, later in *Of Education* Milton insists that students receive training in the original languages of Scripture in order to bolster their understanding of God. Thus for Milton, knowledge of Scripture underlies and sets boundaries to whatever science can show fallen human beings about the world.[2]

Three Ways of Looking at a Creature

It is specifically within Milton's sentence about his teaching method that his polysemous view of the creatures emerges. Milton's notion of "orderly conning over the visible and inferior creature" comprises three connected yet distinct dimensions of that view, each with several implications for approaching the nonhuman world.

1. Theologically Instrumental Dimension. We regard the creatures and thereby come to have knowledge of God. While containing the potential for abusing animals as existing solely for human purposes, this dimension ultimately requires the existence and flourishing of nonhuman creatures, without which human beings would lack that "visible" proof of God's ways and "things invisible." Milton's distinction between visible and invisible things in this method echoes Romans 1.20: "Ever since the creation of the world his eternal power and divine nature, invisible though they are, have been understood and seen through the things he has made." Exactly what about the divine nature may be understood by seeing the created universe, of course, was debated. Given the widespread increase in scientific investigation, seventeenth century theologians were forced to concede the usefulness of such investigation, however they might qualify the reliability of natural knowledge. The learned divine, H. F., for example, wrote a letter published with Philemon Holland's magisterial translation of Pliny's *Natural History*, arguing, like Milton, that the goal of repairing the Fall justifies the study of natural history:

> I am not of their minds, who desire that all humane learning in Arts and Naturall Philosophie should be reserved under locke and key of strange language, without the which no other man should have accesse unto it: For as such knowledge is a branch of that excellencie wherein man was formed, so the repaire thereof (though it be not the chiefe) is yet a thing unworthily neglected, as well in regard of our own comfort therein gained, as for the glory of God thereby promoted. (1)

H. F. qualifies his endorsement of natural philosophy, however, by insisting on the limits of its knowledge and the errors to which it is prone. Using a Miltonic metaphor of various degrees of light, H. F. distinguishes divine from natural knowledge:

> And though Plinie and the rest were not able by Natures light to search so far as to find out the God of Nature, who sitteth in the glorie of light which none attaineth, but contrariwise in the vanities of their imagination bewrayed the ignorance of foolish hearts, some doting upon Nature her selfe, and others

upon speciall creatures as their God: yet fear we not that Christians, in so cleare light should be so farre bewitched by such blind teachers, as to fall before those heathen Idols. (2-3)

Relying on the Anglican emphasis on the insufficiency of human reasoning to effect salvation together with a Jobean insistence on God's inscrutability, H. F. rejects as potentially idolatrous Milton's link between natural and divine knowledge. Nature did indeed become in effect the experimenters' God. Nonetheless, Milton's theologically instrumental view complements the Genesis notion of our first parents as stewards of the Garden: If we could not finally keep the Garden, perhaps we can work to repair it. From that theological imperative emerges an ecological one. While one could account for species depletion as a result of the Fall or later human error, any human misprision or mistreatment of creatures would counteract Milton's notion of looking to Creation for glimpses of the divine. Perhaps most significant in the context of the nascent Royal Society, Milton's view implicitly attacks as pointless "pure" research, or acquisition of natural knowledge for its own sake. Early in his career, by the way, Francis Bacon repudiated the posture of "detached" or pure research. "All knowledge is to be limited by religion," he wrote in *Valerius Terminus*, "and to be referred to use and action" (3.218; cited in Webster, 22).

2. *Methodical Dimension.* In Milton's formulation not only the adverb of manner ("orderly") but the essential process ("conning over") and the inclusive scope of the inquiry ("the visible and inferior creature"; that is, the physical Creation) indicate a commitment to consistency, care, and comprehensiveness in coming to understand creatures. As an example, in learning about the ant (the "emmet" in seventeenth century usage) the learner would seem required to do some sort of comparative study of ants along with other insects and higher animals in order to understand the ant itself and how

it contributes to knowledge of God. The methodical approach to the creatures would tend to temper — but not necessarily break — the habit of seeking analogies or similitudes that Foucault found predominant in sixteenth century representations of nature (32–40). Milton's "method," however, is not equivalent to the Baconian experimental method. While I would agree with Haskin that interpreting the Book of Nature was in Milton's view extremely difficult (237), Milton does present his method with apparent confidence in its efficacy. Perhaps one reason is that it does not require the specialized training and knowledge increasingly demanded by natural philosophers in his day.

3. Anthropocentric yet Self-Reflexive Dimension. The "visible and inferior creature" in Milton's phrase certainly includes the human creature shaping the phrase, for we are both with respect to an invisible and supreme Creator. Self-scrutiny is thus neatly and seamlessly presented as implicit in the process of studying Creation. While we examine the creatures around us, we also must examine ourselves as creatures. The metaphor of "conning over" Creation both elevates the human perceiver and shows us as centrally located to obtain natural knowledge. "Conning over" works both in its primary, temporal denotation — *OED* II.3, "to get to know; to study or learn, especially by repetition" — and figuratively in its spatial sense — as conning towers provide vistas from their elevated topographical positions over surrounding territory. There may be an echo in "conning over" of the biblical injunction that Adam and Eve were given "dominion over" all the earth (Gen. 1.26); one unfallen sign of that command and knowledge is Adam's naming of the animals (Leonard, 1–12). Yet, as we have seen, the Fall is a major element of Milton's overall educational scheme. Milton's view of natural knowledge in *Of Education* is consistent with the search for knowledge in *Areopagitica*, in which the searchers for Truth are forced to search throughout the world for the scattered pieces of her mutilated body. Overall, then, the human inquirer is a central figure superior to other visible creatures but limited and chastened by our creaturely status and fallen nature.

Creatures of Epic

To what extent does this threefold view of creatures in *Of Education* correspond with Milton's representations of creatures in *Paradise Lost*? To begin at the beginning of human views of nature, Adam's autobiographical account to Raphael of "how human life began" emphasizes rational interrogation of the creatures as Adam attempts to comprehend himself and his Creator:

> Thou Sun, said I, fair Light,
> And thou enlight'n'd Earth, so fresh and gay,
> Ye Hills and Dales, ye Rivers, Woods, and Plains
> And ye that live and move, fair Creatures, tell,
> Tell, if ye saw, how came I thus, how here?
> Not of myself; by some great Maker then,
> In goodness and in power preeminent;
> Tell me, how may I know him, how adore,
> From whom I have that thus I move and live,
> And feel that I am happier than I know.
> (8.273–82)

In a classic analysis in *Natural Supernaturalism*, M. H. Abrams has traced the Augustinian background of the topos of the *liber naturae*. Abrams contrasts theological conclusions such as Adam's with secular, Romantic interpretations, such as Wordsworth's emphasis in *The Prelude* on the creative interchange between physical nature and the poet's mind (Abrams, 88–94). Haskin points out that Adam's question anticipates the opening verse of Psalm 19: "The heavens declare the glory of God, and the firmament sheweth his handiwork" (202–03). With its emphatic echoing of "tell," Milton's verse reflects

Adam's assumption that the visible world does indeed in some sense declare and show God's glory.[3] Both contexts, the Augustinian spiritual autobiography and the psalmic hymn to nature, converge in Adam's question. At the same time, Adam's eloquent question exemplifies the regard for nonhuman creatures predicated in *Of Education*, not only in its aim of obtaining knowledge of God but also through its methodical procedure of moving from scrutiny of visible creation to "things invisible." Charles Webster observes that Adam and Eve's exquisite orisons or morning hymns (4.436–39; 5.153–59) trace the same pattern, moving from wonder about natural works to praise of the Creator (Webster, 16). The original human view of the creatures, emphasizing through repetition their "fair" aspect and the corresponding but preeminent goodness and power of their Creator, can perhaps best be described as respectfully inquisitive.

Perhaps the proof of Milton's stance toward the nonhuman creation lies not in how Adam talks to creatures but how he and others in the poem actually treat them. In *A Gust for Paradise*, Diane McColley brilliantly demonstrates how the arts as practiced and reflected in Milton's epic "alert us to the delicate microcosms of other lives and to our responsibility for our effects on them" (12). Thus Milton's epic is intrinsically ecological, in McColley's etymology, "that is, concerned with the knowledge of the *oikos*, the house living creatures share" (4). My examination of Milton's treatment of the creatures supports and extends that finding of an ecological ethic. Milton's artful allusions to ancient scientific writers on the creatures provide previously overlooked evidence of the essential relatedness among living things.

The first botanical species mentioned in *Paradise Lost* is the amaranth. The flower first appears in book 3, during Milton's account of the jubilant conclusion of the dialogue in heaven; it reappears in book 11 in the "blissful Bow'rs/Of *Amarantin* Shade" in which the angels dwell (77–78). As an illustration of alleged transplanting, the case of amaranth would be interesting botanically. But Milton does more. By creating a legend to account for the species' uprooting, he interweaves theological and cosmological significance into the plant's unique botanical properties. The legend emerges in the description of the angels' adoration of Father and Son:

>   lowly reverent
> Towards either Throne they bow, and to the ground
> With solemn adoration down they cast
> Thir Crowns inwove with Amarant and Gold,
> Immortal Amarant, a Flow'r which once
> In Paradise, fast by the Tree of Life
> Began to bloom, but soon for man's offense
> To Heav'n remov'd where first it grew, there grows,
> And flow'rs aloft shading the Fount of Life,
> And where the river of Bliss through midst of Heav'n
> Rolls o'er *Elysian* Flow'rs her Amber stream;
> With these that never fade the Spirits elect
> Bind thir resplendent locks.
>   (349–61)

This appropriation of the flower exemplifies the theologically instrumental view of Creation. Milton's subnarrative of the amaranth tells a story of the plant's double uprooting, with human sin forcing the removal of amaranth to whence it came, heaven. Milton's reasons for the transplanting of amaranth apparently have to do with theological notions about the nature of sin and its consequences (pure matter cannot remain in the presence of corruption; either the pure matter will be corrupted or it must, as in this case, be removed). 1 Peter 1.4 describes "an inheritance that is imperishable, undefiled, and unfading" (κληρονομίαν . . . ἀμάραντον) awaiting the faithful in heaven, but as D. C. Allen points out, Peter neither describes the unfading reward as a flower nor accounts for its transplanting. Allen argues that it was Clement of Alexandria, the second century church presbyter steeped in Greek philosophy and literature, who elaborated on the verse from Peter to characterize the unfading inheritance as a crown, then as a plant that grows not on earth but only in heaven:

> Ὁ γὰρ καλὸς τοῦ ἀμαράντου στέφανος ἀπόκειται τῷ καλῶς πεπολιτευμένῳ. Τὸ ἄνθος τοῦτο γῆ Βαστάζειν οὐ κεχώρηκεν. Μόνον δὲ αὐτὸ καρποφορεῖν ἐπίσταται οὐρανός. (Clement, *Paedagogus*, cited in Allen, "Milton's Amarant," 257–58)

> For the fair crown of amaranth is laid up for those who have lived well. This flower the earth is not able to bear; heaven alone is competent to produce it. (Clement, *Ante-Nicene Fathers*, II.ix.256)

Thus, Allen concludes, it was Clement who suggested to Milton the notion of amaranth's being transplanted to heaven ("Milton's Amarant," 257).

Yet both Milton's legend and Clement's commentary depend upon the etymological and botanical description of amaranth in a shared Latin precursor, the compendium of agricultural works by Cato, Varro, and Columella known in the Renaissance as *De Re Rustica*. Georgius Alexandrini, or George of Alexandria, wrote an index typically appended to Renaissance editions of that compendium. In the Paris, 1543 edition, page Aii, Georgius's index entry for *Amaranthus* reads as follows:

> *Amaranthus*: flos ab immortalitate nomen trahens,
>   unde immortalesque amaranthi: nunquam enim
>   marescit, sitque ab α privative particula &
>   μαραίνω sicco.
>   Col.lib.9.c.4

> *Amaranth*: A flower taking its name from immortality,
>   whence the saying, "the amaranthine gods": for it
>   never withers, and it may be [derived] from Greek alpha, α
>   the privative particle, and μαραίνω, to fade away.
>   Columella. book 9, heading 4 (lines 24–27)

Several features of Milton's poetic expression reflect that index entry. His phrase, "immortal amarant," literally translates

Georgius's Latin phrase, "immortales amaranthi." Milton's adoption of this phrase converts the amaranth to immortal, godlike status while literally carrying over the pagan deities ("immortales") into the Christian heaven. At the end of Milton's account he describes the amaranth and other Elysian flowers as "these that never fade," again closely following Georgius's etymological entry. Rather than being exploded as false, the lore about amaranth's immortality is integrated into a new Christian mythos. Milton's treatment of amaranth, then, amounts to a combination of instrumentality with etymology and etiology. It is a "just so" story of how human sin caused the removal of that etymologically never-fading flower.

The most extensively discussed creature in *Paradise Lost*, and therefore the ultimate test of Milton's attitude toward the nonhuman creatures, is the serpent. A surprising initial observation is how slight has been the scholarship on serpents in *Paradise Lost* compared with the voluminous work on the cognate topics of Milton's cosmology and the character of Satan.[4] When we place in context some overlooked details about serpents traceable to readings in the Latin tutorial during the 1640s, some crucial aspects of Milton's work become clear. Before examining those details, however, we need to bear in mind two compositional principles guiding Milton's representation of the serpent (as distinct from Satan) in his epic narrative.

First and foremost, in describing the serpent Milton follows the biblical accounts of the beast. Thus Milton's narrative superimposes the temptation by a mysterious, talking serpent according to Genesis 3, with the New Testament notion that Satan was in the serpent. In other words, in representing the serpent in his Fall story, Milton takes the Puritan approach of striving to accommodate above all the literal sense of Scripture, indeed of all canonical scripture of both testaments. To put it simply: however he might embellish or expand upon Scripture, Milton strove to avoid contradicting its plain meaning.

This self-imposed constraint of biblical literalism would seem too obvious to mention were it not for two attendant corollaries. First, against allegorical interpreters who posited that the "serpent" figured an internal temptation or an apparition or show (Thomas Cajetan argued for the allegorical reading; St. Cyril for the apparition; cited in Fowler, 462), Milton insists that there was an actual, ordinary serpent ("mere serpent in appearance," 9.413) that Satan inhabited for the purpose of the temptation. Thus Milton devotes considerable attention to describing the mechanism of Satan's possession of that serpent's body. The major upshot of maintaining that an ordinary serpent was used to effect the temptation, however, is that a creature acting according to nature, and not a supernatural phantasm, was involved in the temptation. A second corollary is that Milton reiterates (and apparently endorses) God's curse on the serpent, essentially versifying Genesis 3.14:

> Because thou hast done this, thou art accursed
> Above all cattle, each beast of the field;
> Upon thy belly grovelling thou shalt go,
> And dust shalt eat all the days of thy life.
>
> (10.175–78)

While perfectly in accord with a faithful representation of the scriptural record, Milton's repeating of God's curse on the serpent raises questions about God's seeming injustice to the innocent serpent. Why should the serpent be cursed when it was Satan who overpowered the helpless beast? Milton may have found convincing the line of argument taken by the Puritan exegete Mercurus, who writes: "God curseth the serpent because he was Sathans organe and instrument: and this standeth with Gods justice to punish the instrument with the principall. Lev. 20.15 ["If a man lie with a beast, he shall surely be put to death: and ye shall slay the beast."] . . . And though the serpent had no understanding, yet God curseth him for mans instruction, that he might see how much this their action in seducing him, was displeasing to God" (Willet, *Hexapla:*

Sixfold Commentary upon Genesis, cited in Fowler, 515). Harsh as it may sound, this argument and the verses it elaborates accord with several similarly hard passages in the Greek scriptures: Jesus' cursing of the fig tree (Mt. 21.18–22) and Christ's teachings about the instruments of sin ("If thy hand offend thee, cut it off. If thy eye offend thee, pluck it out"). To return to my overview of Milton's stance toward nature, his instrumental view is ultimately undergirded by a theology deeply committed to the reformed emphasis on the absolute and offensive character of sin. However much God loves the world, severe penalties await those creatures who, willingly or indirectly, do Satan's work. Perhaps this is a confirmation of the instrumental view, for God's anger motivating the curse is directed at a creature becoming an instrument of evil, parallel but contrary to Providence. Still, the instrumental view seems to have cast the creatures more as passive reactors than as agents with active roles to play in God's plan. We seem to be a long way here from Thoreau's dictum relating spirituality and nature: "In wildness is the salvation of the world."

The second principle about Milton's treatment of the serpent, and by extension of other creatures in *Paradise Lost*, is strongly indicated by Milton's mode of presentation in the epic. Together with the scriptural accounts of serpents, Milton mingles in his narrative a variety of material from secular authorities, from natural philosophers to mythological poets. The compositional principle to be inferred is that this material is relevant and integral to how Milton wants us to experience the creature. When, for instance, Satan first appears in the serpent before Eve, he is described as superior in beauty — which aids Satan's temptation — to a host of other legendary serpents:

> pleasing was his shape,
> And lovely, never since of Serpent kind
> Lovelier, not those that in *Illyria* chang'd
> *Hermione* and *Cadmus*, or the God

> In *Epidaurus;* nor to which transform'd
> *Ammonian Jove,* or *Capitoline* was seen,
> Hee with *Olympias,* this with her who bore
> *Scipio* the highth of *Rome.*
>
> (9.503–10)

That serpent in the garden, we are told, was "lovelier" than all those other positively lovely serpents of Greek and Roman legend. Milton's insistence on the superior beauty of that serpent serves the epic purpose of aggrandizing his subject, depicting it as larger than legend. For that strategy to succeed, the legendary material must not be merely exploded as false. It is never cast as merely erroneous by the workings of either heuristic imitation (as Thomas Greene would have it) or the corrective narrator, though certainly the narrator does comment frequently on the truth value of certain legends, as in the case of Mulciber, as in "Thus they relate,/Erring" (1.746–47). Nor is the extrascriptural material entirely restricted to similes (such as the bee simile in Book One)[5] or other putatively detachable parts of the poem, though Milton's similes have been justified to conscientious Christian audiences in that way, initially by Patrick Hume, in his *Annotations on Mr. Milton's "Paradise Lost."* Both of these ways of accounting for the extrascriptural, legendary lore assume that it is essentially false and meant somehow to be isolated and purged. Better than that presumption, surely, would be a criticism that confronts Andrew Marvell's fear upon beginning to read the poem that Milton would convert scripture to mere legend: "that he would ruine (for I saw him strong)/The sacred Truths to Fable and old Song" (7–8). Having confronted that danger, Marvell goes on to resolve the issue to his satisfaction: "Thou hast not miss'd one thought that could be fit/And all that was improper dost omit" (27–28). Marvell's solution of this dilemma recognizes that the mythic fables and natural science in *Paradise Lost* are indeed "fit" and proper to Milton's argument. Georgia Christopher writes: "Because Milton chose biblical 'fables' and classical forms, his major works inevitably evoke readings as pluralistic as the religious and intellectual traditions of his audience" (ix). The continuous hermeneutic struggle between sacred truth and ancient fable is integral to our experience of *Paradise Lost*.

A key site of that struggle is Satan's temptation of Eve. Milton's integral use of extrascriptural lore about serpents arises there in conjunction with Satan's story to Eve of how he, apparently a serpent, came to speak:

> I was at first as other Beasts that graze
> The trodden Herb, of abject thoughts and low,
> As was my food, nor aught but food discern'd
> Or Sex, and apprehended nothing high:
> Till on a day roving the field, I chanc'd
> A goodly Tree far distant to behold
> Loaden with fruit of fairest colors mixt,
> Ruddy and Gold: I nearer drew to gaze;
> When from the boughs a savory odor blown,
> Grateful to appetite, more pleas'd my sense
> Than smell of sweetest Fennel, or the Teats
> Of Ewe or Goat dropping with Milk at Ev'n,
> Unsuckt of Lamb or Kid, that tend thir play.
>
> (9.571–83)

While based on a false premise (Satan is not a serpent, and did not eat the fruit of the tree), Satan's claim that a creature can alter its thoughts by its diet accords with the poem's tragic story of Adam and Eve "eating death" and the more hopeful epistemological notion that "knowledge is as food." Moreover, Satan claims to have proof for that idea in his own experience. He asserts, in modern parlance, that he conducted an experiment, one by analogy able to improve Eve's lot: If I, a mute beast, ate the fruit, and became a speaking, rational being; you, a rational being, may become God by eating it.

Underlying that false representation is some apparently true information about serpents that Milton incorporates in Satan's speech. Milton knew that fennel was a serpent's favorite food from Pliny's *Natural History*, where the connection is amply established. Not only does Pliny describe the giant fennel as a snake's favorite food: "Reliqua sunt ferulacei generis, ceu feniculum anguibus, ut diximus, gratissimum" [There remain the garden plants of the fennel-giant class, which, as we have said, are most pleasing to snakes] (19.56.173); in addition, he accounts for snakes' affinity for fennel because of the plant's efficacy in both sloughing off their skin and sharpening their sight:

> anguis, hiberno situ membrant corpori obducta feniculi suco inpedimentum illus exuit nitidusque vernat; exuit autem a capite primum, nec celerius quam uno die et nocte, replicans ut extra fiat membranae quod fuerit intus. idem hiberna latebra visu obscurato marathro herbae se adfricans oculos inunguit ac refovet. (8.41.99)
>
> When a snake's body gets covered with a skin owing to its hibernation it sloughs off this hindrance to its movement by means of fennel-sap and comes out all glossy for spring; but it begins the process at its head, and takes at least a day to do it, folding the skin backward so that what was the inner side of it becomes the outside. Moreover as its sight is obscured by its hibernation it anoints and revives its eyes by rubbing itself against a fennel plant.

Pliny describes the many uses of fennel for snakes. Accordingly, Milton represents the appeal of fennel generally, not just as food: before the forbidden fruit, nothing "more pleased my *sense*" than fennel, Satan says. That general, synesthetic appeal supports Satan's appropriation of serpentine biology to human psychology: you, Eve, will surely want such a fruit that satisfies all of your senses. In this case at least, Pliny's "fable or old song" contributes to the psychological probability of Satan's temptation of Eve in serpent form. Of even greater importance for my argument, Pliny describes the snake's regard for fennel as instrumental. That is, a snake uses fennel sap for its own purposes. The awareness that every creature insists on its own viewpoint is one way out of the loop of anthropocentrism. While this pervasive purposiveness might lead some to consider Pliny's view of nature as Hobbesian, others might credit the Roman with a view of the creatures as comprising an intricately interactive ecosystem. Milton, apparently, found the latter view both accurate and appealing.

Contemporaries of Milton, including Edward Topsell and Thomas Mouffet, wrote about the creatures in ways close to the poet's. Works such as Topsell's *The History of Four-Footed Beasts and Serpents* and Mouffet's *The Theatre of Insects* display a Plinian (they cite Pliny above all other authorities) preexperimental view of the creatures, one imbued moreover with the sense that they ultimately reflect God's glory. In those texts, careful observations about animal physiology and behavior crowd up against fantastic stories and images of mythological beasts, of Lamia and Mantichora. The scientist in us wants to separate out the mythological from the factual, but doing so is not always easy and is perhaps finally not the best way to appreciate these speculative if erroneous accounts. Mouffet's theological ruminations on the glow worm send us back to the darkness visible of Milton's poetry:

> How wonderful the works of God are in our eyes, none can be ignorant, who shall diligently consider this little creature and weigh its nature, and its light resembling that divine light. For who is he that beholds the vanishing light of this, that doth not fix the eyes of his minde upon Christ, the lasting, true, and the chiefest light of the world; and doth not call to remembrance that holy Spirit which doth illuminate our spirits in the most obscure darkness of our understandings? (981)

Seen in the history of attitudes toward nature in the West, Milton's view expressed in *Of Education* and *Paradise Lost* makes a significant if Janus-faced contribution. This contribution emerges clearly when we set Milton between Bacon, on the one hand, and Diderot and d'Alembert on the other, as Robert Darnton has done. Darnton contrasts Bacon's epistemological scheme with that of the Encyclopedists through a familiar Edenic metaphor: "Bacon envisaged two trees of knowledge, one for revealed and one for natural theology, while the Encyclopedists grouped together revealed and natural theology on a single tree and subordinated both to reason" (201). Although Bacon acknowledged the force of inductive reasoning about God based on perception of natural phenomena, he considered the practice dangerous: "But on the other side, out of the contemplation of nature, or ground of human knowledges, to induce any verity or persuasion concerning the points of faith, is in my judgement not safe: *Da fidei quae fidei sunt*" [Give to faith what belongs to faith] (*Advancement of Learning*, 86). What Bacon saw as unsafe was ultimately subordinating theology to reason. Contrary to Milton in *Of Education*, Bacon had insisted that inductive reasoning from observed phenomena — arguments for theism from design — could never lead to knowledge of the true God: "So we ought not to attempt to draw down or to submit the mysteries of God to our reason" (86). Had Bacon lived to read it, he would have regarded Milton's notion of conning over Creation and thereby arriving at knowledge of God as a case of "conning" in the modern sense, that is, as a cheat. Those mixtures of religion and science that Bacon could imagine he regarded as injurious to both true religion and scientific advancement, citing in support the "extreme prejudice which both religion and philosophy hath received by being commixed together; as that which undoubtedly will make an heretical religion and an imaginary and fabulous philosophy" (87). Yet if Milton's view is reactionary from within Bacon's scientific outlook, it is visionary in anticipating Diderot and d'Alembert's Enlightenment position that theology and science cannot be separated. The Encyclopedists maintained that, in Robert Darnton's words, "to separate theology from philosophy [as Bacon had done] would be to cut the offshoot from the trunk to which it is united by its very nature" (300). For Milton as well, if for different reasons, knowledge of nature is connected with knowledge of God.

Fundamentally and consistently, Milton refused to separate knowledge of the created world from knowledge of God. Milton takes the wonders of Creation as seen through Adam's unfallen eyes as a confirmation of the scriptural revelation. More than that, those wonders begin to show the wisdom, might, and benevolence of the Creator even before He discursively manifests those divine attributes to Adam through dialogue. For the fallen, the long process of "regaining to know God aright" (YP 2:367) begins, logically and naturally, as we begin to explore the world around us. While the created world neither fully reveals nor contains Milton's God, respectful and rational investigation of the creatures remains the sacred ground upon which the divine presence manifests itself. With this epistemological foundation in place, Milton turns, as do we, to the fundamental science of agriculture, which serves as the basis or literal ground for his epic argument in *Paradise Lost*.

Two

Careful Plowing

Culture and Agriculture in *Paradise Lost*

"Fruit" and "Seed," in that order, frame the opening sentence of *Paradise Lost*. Surprisingly, Milton scholarship has not registered the significance of that emphatic arrangement. The poem begins as follows:

> Of Man's First Disobedience, and the Fruit
> Of that Forbidden Tree, whose mortal taste
> Brought Death into the World, and all our woe,
> With loss of *Eden*, till one greater Man
> Restore us, and regain the blissful Seat,
> Sing Heav'nly Muse, that on the secret top
> Of *Oreb*, or of *Sinai*, didst inspire
> That Shepherd, who first taught the chosen Seed,
> In the Beginning how the Heav'ns and Earth
> Rose out of *Chaos*.
>
> (1.1–10)

By placing "Fruit" and "Seed" at the line endings that open and close this grand opening utterance, Milton underscores the importance of those natural images to his epic argument. Both words are used initially in a figural sense. The "chosen Seed" describes the descendants of Abraham, God's chosen people. As the Israelites were taught by Moses, the "Seed" becomes by analogy Milton's audience, a people not so much chosen as freely choosing to learn of divine Creation. "Fruit" figures the consequences of the Fall, including human mortality, expulsion from Eden, and "all our woe." Adam reinforces that figural sense by using "consequence" as a gloss on "fruit" in book 8. Adam's speech there, recalling the divine command, takes us to the poem's moral center:

> This Paradise I give thee, count it thine
> To Till and keep, and of the Fruit to eat:
> Of every Tree that in the Garden grows
> Eat freely with glad heart; fear here no dearth:
> But of the Tree whose operation brings
> Knowledge of good and ill, which I have set
> The Pledge of thy Obedience and thy Faith,
> Amid the Garden by the Tree of Life,
> Remember what I warn thee, shun to taste,
> And shun the bitter consequence.
>   (319–28)

By the conclusion of Milton's epic, the figurative meanings of "Fruit" and "Seed" undergo a dazzling reversal summarized by the doctrine of the fortunate fall. Thus, the "Fruit" of the forbidden tree comes to include the incarnate Redeemer, who is specifically identified as both of "Abraham and his seed" and of "the woman's [Eve's] seed."[1] Perhaps this encouraging reversal of the fruit's negative consequences parallels the opening poem's inversion of the apparent biblical order of Creation and Fall, which Regina Schwartz has noted (2–3). Certainly Milton's reversal of the natural generative sequence in his word order, beginning with fruit and ending with seed, points to a continuing process of re-creation. Milton's poetic reversal anticipates George Eliot's metaphoric and philosophic assertion, in the pivotal chapter heading of *Romola*, that "Fruit *is* Seed."[2]

Because the figural senses of "Fruit" and "Seed" in *Paradise Lost* demand recognition, a reader may overlook the words' literal meanings. Yet fruit and seed in the literal sense carry great significance throughout the epic. For Milton as for Adam, the fruit of the forbidden tree actually hung in the garden of Eden.[3] The seeds of both plants and human beings appear literally many times in the poem. Variants and offshoots of fruit and seed — in leaves, stocks, and flowers — fill the physical landscape of the poem. To put it with childlike simplicity, *Paradise Lost* is a story about picking a fruit. By heralding the imminent significance of fruit and seed in the poem, the opening invocation reveals Milton's attention to the natural process of growth. More important, it implies that the natural process of growth underlies the argument of *Paradise Lost*.

Milton learned about nature as we all do, by experience and observation. Even when he lived in the heart of London, young John Milton grew up surrounded by flourishing natural growth. Despite the increasing urbanization of London during the earlier seventeenth century, England remained a predominantly agricultural society. While at Cambridge, Milton expressed his fascination with agricultural scenes in his Latin and English poetry, as *L'Allegro* most prominently shows:

> While the Plowman near at hand,
> Whistles o'er the Furrow'd Land,
> And the Milkmaid singeth blithe,
> And the Mower whets his scythe,
> And every Shepherd tells his tale
> Under the Hawthorn in the dale.
>
> (63–68)

Milton needed no more inspiration for these verses than what he saw and heard around him. Those tetrameter couplets happily wed images of rustic working life with the poem's spirit of mirth: no small achievement. Still, the plowman who carelessly whistles while he works here represents only a fraction of farming life; the "careful Plowman" whom Milton will include in an epic simile in *Paradise Lost*, the central focus of this essay, involves a more mature, rounded appraisal of agricultural life.

Milton in particular learned a great deal about natural growth through his reading and teaching. For Milton, the Bible held unique and absolute authority among all texts (YP 6:583–85). The primary biblical text concerning natural growth, which Adam's speech, quoted earlier, incorporates, is Genesis 2.15: "And the Lord God took the man, and put him into the garden of Eden to dress it and keep it" (Authorized Version). In Adam's speech, Milton has replaced the verb "dress" from the Authorized Version with "till." Tilling appears in the Authorized Version only after the Fall, at Genesis 3.23, as part of humanity's punishment for sin.[4] Milton's point is unmistakable. By making tilling the garden part of God's original command, the poet asserts that agricultural labor is part of the unfallen way of life.

Milton's treatment of labor in *Paradise Lost* forms part of a far-reaching poetic strategy, scholars have observed. In *The Georgic Revolution*, Anthony Low's sustained meditation on Milton focuses on the remarkably positive treatment of labor in *Paradise Lost*. Milton's Eden revels in what Thomas Rosenmeyer has aptly termed the "Hesiodic" ethic, demanding that a good life furnish evidence of effort and suffering, which is fundamentally opposed to the pastoral pursuit of *otium* (Low, 296–352).[5] Given the ethical dimension of labor, notably its association with the inward heroism celebrated in the proem to book 9 — "the greater fortitude of patience/And heroic martyrdom unsung" — one can easily see why Milton would endorse the georgic view of labor. In the poet's view, labor cultivates communities as well as individual souls, as Barbara K. Lewalski, Diane McColley, and Mary Ann Radzinowicz have eloquently argued.[6]

Although scarcely considered, Milton's sustained emphasis in *Paradise Lost* on agriculture itself — on tilling and seeding as well as on agricultural theory and practice generally — is also remarkable. The inclusion of agriculture is remarkable if only because Milton could have entirely avoided it. There are three "steps" in human civilization, the Roman linguist and farmer, Marcus Terentius Varro (116–27 B.C.), points out: first, the state of nature, "when men lived on those products which the virgin earth [*inviolata terra*] brought forth"; second, the pastoral stage; and third, the present agricultural age.[7] Milton's story, of course, takes place almost entirely within the original state of nature; the Edenic state is doubly removed from the harsh realities of agriculture. Yet Milton insists on using agricultural allusions throughout *Paradise Lost*. A cursory survey recalls the major agricultural images scattered throughout the poem: the "belated Peasant" in the darkness visible of book 1 who refigures Aeneas among the shades; the transplanted "immortal Amaranth" said to be growing in heaven in book 3; the "careful Plowman" simile concluding book 4; early in book 9, Satan's entry into Eden as a city dweller in farming country; Eve's touching yet ironic depiction at the Fall as the "Harvest Queen"; the simile of the mist rising at the "laborer's heel" marking Adam and Eve's departure from Eden at the poem's end. Before the Fall, Adam and Eve are repeatedly shown working their "field," whereas a garden plot would be more strictly accurate. One may even see God as a farmer, particularly in Creation and in response to the war in heaven (Low, 316–17).

Agriculture is the most fundamental of human sciences. In Milton's view, it is also fundamental to understanding the "organic" art of poetry. This is not to say that poetry requires agricultural metaphors. Rather, the point is that, as Milton explains in *An Apology Against a Pamphlet*, the epic poet must have the *experience* of agriculture — as well as of all essential arts and sciences — before attempting to sing of the subject. One need not harvest a cornfield to acquire agricultural experience any more than one need travel to hell to confront Satan. Led on by what he believed to be God's Spirit, Milton gathered experience about agriculture by reading and teaching. He taught the "four grand authors *De Re Rustica*, Cato, Varro, Columella, and Palladius" at the very beginning of his tutorial program, Edward Phillips recalled. With Milton and his students, we need first to retrace those beginning steps if we hope, by the end, to perceive the open goal announced in *Of Education*: "what glorious and magnificent use might be made of poetry, both in divine and humane things" (YP 2:405–06).

My discussion of *Paradise Lost* focuses on perhaps the most controversial of Milton's agricultural images, the figure of the "careful Plowman," which has been read allegorically — mistakenly, I believe — as either Satan or God. I choose the plowman image partly because its dependence on Roman literature is so clear, and partly because its workings, once understood, reveal Milton's characteristically luxuriant method of allusion in full flower. Further, I will show how the plowman image becomes the means by which the poet joins the seventeenth century controversy over enclosure. This chapter aims to retrace Milton's method of "seeding," that is, of cultivating readers by presenting images of moral choice that can lead to growth. If beginning with an image of harvesting and ending with seeding seems backward, it nonetheless conforms to Milton's organic artistry.

Cultivating Readers

As Edward Phillips's reference to the "four grand authors *De Re Rustica*" indicates, Milton taught his students the agricultural works of Marcus Porcius Cato, Marcus Terentius Varro, Lucius Columella, and Palladius. Phillips's Latin phrase implies that Milton used one or more of the Renaissance editions containing all four writers. Two notable examples are *Libri de re rustica*, which contains a fully annotated index by George Alexandrinos as well as commentary by diverse hands on Columella's versified book 10; and *Rei rusticae auctores Latini veteres, M. Cato, M. Varro, L. Columella, Palladius*, edited with an analytical index by Hieronymus Commelinus. Both texts were frequently reprinted throughout the mid-seventeenth century.[8] Moreover, Joan Thirsk has demonstrated that farming enjoyed a newfound favor among English gentlemen of the late sixteenth and early seventeenth centuries, thanks largely to the newfound influence of classical agricultural manuals ("Fresh Start," 15–34). Thus Milton could have readily acquired both texts, either in England or during his continental travels of 1638–39, before his teaching career. A brief survey of those agricultural texts enables us to grasp their relevance to *Paradise Lost*, their power to cultivate readers no less than crops.

Commelinus's edition of the Roman authors *De Re Rustica* has one immediately intriguing feature. On its title page appears a woodcut illustration that visually reinforces a cluster of points that Milton's poem makes verbally (see fig. 1). The central female figure of the woodcut, recalling similar figures of the Earth, Gaia, or Ceres, is the ruling genius, the proper tutelary deity, of agriculture. The pair of Greek legends encircling the various fruits of agriculture specifically identifies the figure as ΜΑΤΩΡΠΑΝΑ ΑΛΗΤΗΕΙΑ or TRUTH ALL-RULING. The animate sun in her right hand represents the common Renaissance fusion of Apollo, the pagan sun god, and Christ, the Son of God. In her left hand the woman holds both a book and a stalk, a composite emblem for the farming manuals contained in the text. Learning and fecundity, wisdom and plenty, are collectively promised by these ancient authors, the artist

REI RVSTICAE
AVCTORES LATINI
VETERES,

M. CATO M. VARRO
L. COLVMELLA PALLADIVS:

Priores tres, e vetuftiff. editionibus; quartus, e veteribus
membranis aliquammultis in locis
emendatiores:

*Cum tribus Indicibus, Capitum, Auctorum, & Rerum
ac Verborum memorabilium.*

Criticorum & Expofitorum in eosdem atque Geoponicos
Græcos Notationes feorfum dabuntur.

Ex Hier. Commelini typographio,
ANNO MDXCV.

Figure 1. *Title page*, Rei rusticae auctores Latini veteres.
Photo courtesy of DePauw University Archives and Special Collections.

suggests. The promise also carries a warning: As agriculture literally combines soil (*ager*) and tilling (*cultus*), no culture that violates the creative Earth will thrive.

The ethical dimension of agriculture implied by the title page perfectly matches the spirit of Commelinus's text. Turning to the first printed section, the reader encounters Cato's endorsement of farming as a vocation. Other vocations may be more lucrative, Cato admits, but none is more honorable:

> Est interdum praestare mercaturis rem quarerere, nisi tam periculosum sit, et item fenerari, si tam honestum sit. Maiores nostri sic habuerunt et ita in lebigus posiverunt, furem dupli condemnari, feneratorum quadrupli. Quanto peiorem civem existimarint feneratorem quam furem, hinc licet existimare. Et virum bonum quom laudabant, ita laudabant, bonum agricolam bonumque colonum. Amplissime laudari existimabatur qui ita laudabatur. (Commelinus ed., Cato, *De agricultura*, 1.1)
>
> It is true that to obtain money by trade is often more profitable, were it not so hazardous; and the same goes for money-lending, if it were as honorable. Our ancestors held this view and embodied it in their laws, which required that the thief be fined double and the usurer fourfold. One may infer from this how much less desirable a citizen they considered the usurer than the thief. And when they would praise a worthy man their praise took this form: "good tiller," "good farmer"; one so praised was thought to have received the greatest commendation.
>
> (my translation)

This classical view of farming as a praiseworthy way of life, as indeed the best way of life, Thirsk argues, brought hundreds of English gentlemen onto the land as direct overseers in the sixteenth and early seventeenth centuries ("Fresh Start," 15–20, 23–26). Unlike the absentee landlords typical before 1500, good farmers from Tudor days onward dwelt on their land and took a direct hand in its management. No hollow ideal, Cato's view literally caused a revolution in English agricultural practice 16 centuries later.

The Roman agricultural anthology repeatedly reinforces the

notion of farming as a morally honorable pursuit. For example, Columella begins his work by recalling the tale of Cincinnatus, who, summoned from the plough to the dictatorship in order to liberate a beleaguered consul, after victory readily relinquished power and returned to his small ancestral farm. At times, the lessons in the proper farming spirit are rendered in language with the timeless, philosophical tone of Ecclesiastes. Consider the following passage, which concludes Columella's first book. All of the rules and suggestions for farming ultimately reduce to one principle, Columella suggests: doing what is necessary at the proper time.

> Unum enim ac solum dominatur in rusticatione, quicquid exigit ratio culturae, semel facere, quippe cum emendatur vel imprudentia vel neglegentia, iam res ipsa decoxit nec in tantum postmodo exuberat, ut et se amissam restituat et quaestum temporum praeteritorum resarciat. (1.8.14)

> For there is one and only one ruling principle in agriculture: namely, to do once and for all whatever the method of cultivation requires; since when ignorance or carelessness is rectified, the matter at issue has already suffered impairment and never recovers afterward so much as to regain what it has lost, and to make up the profit of missed opportunities.

To everything there is a season; or more emphatically, every season demands that farmers do certain things. Palladius makes this same point by arranging his manual in calendrical fashion, with the various tasks appearing in their proper months. Linked with the cyclic pattern of a complete year, quotidian tasks and particular bits of advice accrue the timeless quality of the seasons.

At other places in the anthology, the language embodying the agricultural ideal has the salty, homespun quality of *Poor Richard's Almanac*.[9] For example, after discussing in detail the layout and management of a farm, Cato quips: *frons occipitio prior est* (IV, 7). One labors to convey in English the wit of this pithy Latin maxim. Literally, Cato writes, the forehead is better than the back of the head. More loosely, we might say, it's better to look ahead than back. We might come closest to Cato's meaning with an English aphorism: "Foresight is better than hindsight." Cato's remark also contains an extra layer of meaning lost in translation. The Latin word *frons* has the sense not only of the English word front but also of frond, that is, the first uncurling of a leaf. In an agricultural manual, that sense certainly is appropriate. A frond from the farmer's seed appears first (*prior*) in the growing cycle. This sense of *frons* may even carry the sense of an Aristotelian final cause. For a farmer, a growing frond or plant takes priority over everything else. It is the underlying reason for all of the farmer's ingenuity, labor, and anxiety.

Reading the Plowman

The "careful Plowman" appears toward the end of book 4 of *Paradise Lost*. The image marks the confrontation between Gabriel and his band of faithful angels, the guardians of Eden, on the one hand, and Satan alone, on the other, whom they have discovered "[s]quat like a Toad, close at the ear of *Eve*" (800). Gabriel's interrogation of Satan has broken down into threats to drag him to the "infernal pit" and seal him there, which provokes Satan to his own insulting, violent counter-threats. At that moment — that is, on the border between speech and violent action — the plowman image appears:

> While thus he [Satan] spake, th'Angelic Squadron bright
> Turn'd fiery red, sharp'ning in mooned horns
> Thir Phalanx, and began to hem him round
> With ported spears, as thick as when a field
> Of *Ceres* ripe for harvest waving bends
> Her bearded Grove of ears, which way the wind
> Sways them; the careful Plowman doubting stands
> Lest on the threshing floor his hopeful sheaves
> Prove chaff.
>
> (977–85)

As Joseph Summers has said of the epic's opening proem, everything in this magnificent poetic passage happens at once (12). While Satan speaks, the angelic band changes color, posture, and military formation. The simile of the field of grain specifically adumbrates the density ("as thick as") with which the faithful angels' spears surround Satan. Readers may find that emphasis on density hard to bear in mind, as Milton's verse rapidly unfolds a variety of animated images: the geometric shifting of the angels — from phalanx to crescent to circle; the dangerously swaying grain, in the guise of the goddess Ceres; the worried farmer, nonetheless standing in the scene, transported there by Milton's rapidly associative imagination.

In the midst of threatened violence, then, the figure of the "careful Plowman" appears. He effects a kind of countermovement to the participants' explosive rage in much the same way as Christ, the "one greater Man" of Milton's opening invocation, opposes the downward slide inherent in "Man's First Disobedience." Although "doubting," the Plowman "stands": a verb associated throughout the Miltonic canon with wise, moral action. "They also serve who only stand and wait," the conclusion of *Sonnet 19* goes; at the crisis in *Paradise Regained*, the Son will, miraculously, stand. Within the more immediate context of *Paradise Lost*, Adam and Eve have been introduced as "Two of far nobler shape [than the prone beasts] erect and tall,/Godlike erect" (288–89). In that context, we are prepared to see the Plowman as a morally upright figure, in short, as a good man. The Plowman does not, however, arrest the threat of angelic violence, which suggests that he lacks the Son's divine, restorative power. The opposing angels remain locked in their adversarial postures until the heavenly scales appear above them, and Satan flees, ending book 4.

Most of the controversy over the passage has focused on two questions: the Plowman's identity and the cause of his anxiety.[10] Most critics have attempted to see the Plowman as either Satan or God. For example, Alastair Fowler, in his edition of *Paradise Lost*, argues against the satanic reading of the passage advanced by William Empson. Satan is already described in a simile nearby, Fowler points out. He advocates the position that the Plowman represents not Satan but God. Fowler's reasoning is revealing: "The ploughman must in some sense be 'like' God" (251). Certainly Fowler's dismissal of the misleading identification of the Plowman as Satan is useful. Unfortunately, his black-or-white way of reading oversimplifies Milton's poetry. John Rumrich, eager to catch Gabriel in error, may himself err. He claims that Gabriel misreads the heavenly sign of the scales displayed by God, who, Rumrich assumes, "is compared to a 'careful plowman doubting' what action to take" (1041). Yet why should God, whose foreknowledge and providence are manifest in showing the scales, be in doubt about what to do thereafter? If the Plowman is neither God nor Satan, then who is he? What is a plowman doing at this point in the poem? These questions can be effectively addressed only if we meet the Plowman in the context from which Milton drew him. As my discussion indicates, that context is agricultural.

The exact phrase "careful Plowman" has a clear precedent in book 5 of Lucius Columella's *De Re Rustica*. Columella uses the phrase *sedulus arator*, or careful plowman, while explaining the precautions to be taken when cultivating vines:

> Nam in bracchiatis plerumque fit, ut aut cruere aut cornibus buom vitium defringantur, saepe etiam stiva, dum sedulus arator vomere perstringere ordinem, et quam proxinam partem vitium excolere studet. (5.5.12)

> For in vines which grow out into arms it generally happens that the small branches are broken off by the legs or horns of the oxen, and often too by the handle of the plough while the careful ploughman is striving to graze the edge of the row with the ploughshare and to cultivate the ground as near as possible to the vines.

Given the strong possibility of injuring the plants, the Latin *sedulus* conveys the same combination of anxiety and diligence embodied in the English word "careful." The first definition for "careful" in the *OED* — "Full of grief; mournful, sorrowful" — is appropriate to the losses contemplated by Columella's and Milton's plowmen. The fifth of the *OED*'s headings — "Applying care to avoid; on one's guard against, cautious, wary" (said to be obsolete after 1728) — perhaps best describes Milton's figure. Specifically, the Plowman in *Paradise Lost* is applying care to avoid the loss of his harvest.

In a passage that further clarifies the identity of Milton's figure, Columella describes the harvesting of grain in Book 2 of his *De Re Rustica*. Columella warns against a variety of dangers attending a harvest, and he gives a unique tip on precisely when to gather the crop:

> Sed cum matura fuerit seges, ante quam torreatur vaporibus aestivi sideris, qui sunt vastissimi per exortum Caniculae, celeriter demetatur; nam dispendiosa est cunctatio, primum quod avibus praedam ceterisque animalibus praebet, deinde quod grana et ipsae spicae culmis arentibus et aristis celeriter decidunt. Si vero procellae ventorum aut turbines incesserunt, maior pars ad terram defluit; propter quae recrastinari non debet, sed aequaliter flaventibus iam satis, ante quam ex toto grana indurescant, cum rubicundum colorem traxerunt, messis facienda est, ut potius in area et in acervo quam in agro grandescant frumenta. Constat enim, si tempestive decisa sint, postea capere incrementum. (2.20.1–2)

> But when the grain is ripe it should be quickly harvested before it can be parched by the heat of the summer sun, which is most severe at the rising of the Dog-star; for delay is costly — in the first place because it affords plunder for birds and other creatures, and, secondly, because the kernels and even the heads themselves quickly fall as the stalks and beards wither. And if wind-storms or cyclones strike it, the greater part of it is lost on the ground; for which reason there should be no delay, but

> when the crop is even golden yellow, before the grains have entirely hardened and after they have taken on a reddish color, the harvest should be gathered, so that the grain may grow larger on the floor and in the stack rather than in the field. For it is an established fact that, if cut at the proper time, it makes some growth afterwards.

Modern farmers carefully monitor percentages of moisture in determining when to harvest crops. Lacking such technology, early farmers could nonetheless rely on Columella's idea about color, harvesting the golden yellow grain at the first sign of reddening. In that context, Milton's depiction of the "Angelic Squadron" turning "fiery red" becomes significant rather than decorative. Presumably the red color of the angels extends to their spears, which become the spears of grain waving in the wind. The waving grain has reached the precise moment when it should be harvested. A corroborating sign from Milton's passage that the time is right is the description of the grain as "hopeful sheaves." The crop has ripened, but only the threshing floor will tell whether the ears will prove grain or chaff.

Anxiety runs through this sequence, to be sure. But it is no more God's anxiety than it is Satan's. The doubts of the careful Plowman are entirely human. The anxiety is precisely that of a careful farmer, properly concerned, understandably if overly fretful. For farmers are constantly reading the skies for signs of weather that threatens to devastate their crops. Such doubts and fears, quite familiar in the agricultural economy of Milton's day, place in human perspective the cosmic events of the passage. The confrontation between Gabriel and Satan thus acquires the high anxiety of harvest time. Despite the fear and concern everyone involved in the harvest experiences, the resolution of the crisis is generally positive and abundant. A rich harvest is also predicted in the eschatological sense to which Milton's epic gestures. The resolution of the harvest, as well as the plot of *Paradise Lost*, will eventually prove comedic, in Northrop Frye's sense of humanity assumed into divinity (43).

As a brief check on this interpretation, one might recall the role rustic figures play in Homeric similes. Richmond Lattimore maintains that Homeric similes carry readers from the scene in the poem to the outside, everyday world. Thus they provide a momentary "escape from the heroic" (Homer, 42). As an example, Lattimore cites *Iliad* 4.452–56. In this passage, a simile of clashing mountain streams illustrates the clash of heroic armies. The simile contains a precursor of Milton's Plowman: "As when rivers in winter spate running down from the mountains throw together at the meeting of streams the weight of their water out of the great springs behind in the hollow stream-bed, and far away in the mountains the shepherd hears their thunder; such, from the coming together of men, was the shock and the shouting." "Such similes," Lattimore concludes, "are landscapes, direct from the experience of life, and this one is humanized by the tiny figure of the shepherd set against enormous nature" (42). In Milton's poetry, the tiny figure of the Plowman does precisely that: he humanizes the remote, heroic world of clashing angelic forces. As with Homer, simile for Milton is neither decoration nor allegory. It is, in Lattimore's phrase, "dynamic invention" (45), which opens the epic argument into the strangely familiar world that the poet and reader share. As such, it renovates the epic argument by fusing it with the poet's own culture. Careful plowmen need to watch the swirling angels above, but, no less certainly, the angels need the Plowman if their spiritual struggle is to touch Milton's "fit audience."

Maintaining the Plow

While enjoying an epic precursor in Homer and reflecting the Roman agricultural writers whom Milton taught in school, the image of the "careful Plowman," then, refers to an agrarian world immediately recognizable to Milton's seventeenth century audience. If we place the Plowman precisely in that cultural milieu, we might gain even sharper resolution on

Milton's poem. What cultural associations would the "careful Plowman" carry for Milton's contemporaries?

For those resisting agrarian change in England, the Plowman would conjure up an image of established order. Thus Robert Cecil draws on the Plowman in a speech to the House of Commons in 1601, in supporting a bill intended to halt depopulation by the practice of enclosure. He proclaims, "I do not dwell in the Country, I am not acquainted with the Plough: But I think that whosoever doth not maintain the Plough, destroys this Kingdom."[11] Cecil's oratory prepares a charge of treason against anyone who would in any way fail to "maintain the Plough." Agrarian reformers would disagree that enclosure necessarily weakened or reduced agricultural production. Nonetheless, Cecil's rhetorical use of "the Plough" drives at something more intangible yet enduring: a vision of a thriving monarchical England upheld by its loyal farmer-citizens. Such a vision is the positive implicit in Cecil's threat: Those who maintain the plough strengthen the kingdom.

Thus one need not be surprised to find that, throughout the 1630s, King Charles and Archbishop Laud vigorously prosecuted landowners who violated antienclosure commissions, thus driving agricultural laborers off the land. One may speculate, as does W. E. Tate, whether Charles operated more out of concern for the poor uprooted rustics or out of desire to extort fines from offenders for his lavish expenses (126). Certainly the landowners were able to pay the fines, though a sign of their chafing appears in the charge against Laud in 1644 that "he did a little too much countenance the commission for depopulations."[12] As Charles's political situation became more precarious during the 1640s, the monarchy increasingly needed the support of traditional, loyal citizens. Charles took pains to appeal to yeoman and small farmers up to the end — even after his death, as his commissioning of the *Eikon Basilike* indicates.

Yet images of the plough and metaphors of plowing were used during the 1640s and 1650s to support a completely different political agenda, that of the radical left. The image of the plow appears in the Diggers' song, the refrain of which urges singers and listeners to recall that they are "Diggers all":

> With spades and hoes and ploughs, stand up now!
>   With spades and hoes and plowes stand up now!
> Your freedom to uphold, seeing Cavaliers are bold
>   To kill you if they could, and rights from you withold,
> Stand up now, Diggers all![13]

The plows incorporated in the Diggers' song have a literal quality, while the more abstract rights the Diggers claim derive from their farming implements.

Early readers of *Paradise Lost* would recall that the Diggers had physically enacted the program of their anthem beginning in 1649. According to the Council of State records for April 16 of that year, William Everard, a cashiered army officer who styled himself a prophet, had begun to dig up the common land on St. George's Hill in Weybridge, Surrey, and to sow it with carrots, parsnips, and beans. Everard was joined by roughly 100 to 200 followers; the names of 73 colonists are preserved (Hill, *World*, 91). Before being summoned, Everard and Gerrard Winstanley, the Diggers' leaders, appeared in person before the Council and unfolded a detailed Christian-communal-agrarian program. As Winstanley explained in the pamphlet, *The True Levellers' Standard Advanced*, the "first reason" for the digging is "that we may work in righteousness and lay the foundation of making the earth a common treasury for all, both rich and poor, that everyone that is born in the land may be fed by the earth his mother that brought him forth, according to the reason that rules in the creation" (84). The council tolerated the Surrey Diggers until the autumn of 1649, when they were forcibly dispossessed. Nonetheless, during the 1650s, groups of Diggers operated in similar fashion in

Middlesex, Bedfordshire, Berkshire, Buckinghamshire, Herefordshire, Huntingdonshire, Northamptonshire, Staffordshire, and Northumberland (Tate, 148–49).

The Diggers may have been motivated partly by a sheer instinct for survival. "The abysmal harvest of 1648 had led to widespread hunger and unemployment, especially among disbanded soldiers," Christopher Hill points out; moreover, the winter of 1648–49 was particularly harsh (*World*, 87; "Religion," 203). Visible from London, St. George's Hill apparently served as a beacon for the poor seeking sustenance. In terms of Milton's image of careful plowing, the Diggers may have contributed both a sense of urgency and potential failure to the scene. The Diggers succeeded in first plowing, then seeding, but they failed both literally and metaphorically to bring in a harvest.

In a work that resonates with the "careful Plowman" and the Digger song, Milton's *Sonnet 16* features the image of plowing as a measure of Oliver Cromwell's success as of May 1652. In the sonnet's opening quatrain, careful plowing is equated with wise, brave generalship:

> Cromwell, our chief of men, who through a cloud
> Not of war only, but detractions rude,
> Guided by faith and matchless Fortitude,
> To Peace and truth thy glorious way hast plough'd.
>
> (1–4)

Cromwell has plowed his glorious way to peace and truth, not only through military battles but through the uncertain political process (the "cloud"), by which he has endured harsh criticism ("detractions rude") for his actions. Cromwell's dual achievement, the sonnet insists, has been glorious. At its turn, however, the sonnet insists that Cromwell has more to do, "yet much remains/To conquer still; peace hath her victories/No less renown'd than war" (9–11). What remains for Cromwell and English citizens to achieve is an inner victory, a revolution that would "save free Conscience" from external, secular authorities — including Cromwell himself. The burden of the sonnet is to suggest that such a victory is at least as difficult and as glorious as Cromwell's military ones. Retrospectively, in light of the Plowman image from *Paradise Lost*, Cromwell needs to apply in this new field Gabriel's wisdom: "what folly then/To boast what Arms can do, since thine no more/Than Heav'n permits, nor mine" (4.1007–09). In working toward that inner revolution, violence will do no good. There is, however, a way. It is the Plowman's way. The wisdom, faith, and "matchless Fortitude" of a careful Plowman, standing through all the danger farmers know, represent all the resources that human beings can summon to bring in the harvest.

From the fundamental art of cultivation expounded by the agricultural texts, Milton's Latin curriculum moved to the practical science of building featured in Vitruvius's work on architecture. In Milton's view, the best followers of Vitruvius were Renaissance masters such as Leonardo da Vinci and demonic builders such as the architect of Pandaemonium. The next chapter seeks to account for their surprising Kinship.

THREE

Building Pandaemonium

Vitruvian Architecture in *Paradise Lost*

> And what will they at best say of us and of the whole English name, but scoffingly as of that foolish builder, mention'd by our Saviour, who began to build a tower, and was not able to finish it. Where is this goodly tower of a Common-wealth which the *English* boasted they would build to overshaddow kings and be another *Rome* in the west? The foundation indeed they laid gallantly; but fell into a wors confusion, not of tongues, but of factions, then those at the tower of *Babel*; and have left no memorial of thir work behinde them remaining, but in the common laughter of *Europ*.
> *The Readie and Easie Way* (YP 7:422–23)

I begin with this excerpt from *The Readie & Easie Way* because it draws together a cluster of Miltonic preoccupations that are fundamental to my discussion of architecture in *Paradise Lost*. In the prose passage, alluding to Luke's gospel and the Book of Genesis, Milton adduces images of towers from both the New and Old Testaments — in that characteristic, recursive order[1] — to chide his audience for their failure to advance "the Good Old Cause." While the passage seems primarily calculated to scold Milton's audience for their recent backsliding, the image of the "goodly tower," figuring a thoroughly reformed and reconstructed state, holds out the possibility of a positive future for England. In that sense the tower image has palpable rhetorical force, through its appeal to the English reformers to make good on their earlier boasting. Making good on a boast, one recalls from *Beowulf*, has long been a matter of honor for English speakers. Moreover, the image of the Commonwealth as a structure built to "overshaddow kings" is politically astute. On the occasion of the monarchy's impending restoration, Milton deftly sketches a tattling Europe in which a more or less thoroughly reformed England will find itself either a leader or a laughingstock. Placing the immediate situation in a longer temporal framework, Milton reminds the builders of the Commonwealth that they had for England a yet unrealized ambition: to be "another *Rome* in the west."[2] In *Of Reformation* (1641) almost twenty years earlier, Milton had advocated classical republican precedents for the political structure of the Commonwealth, including chiefly a theory of the "mixed state" that Polybius saw exemplified by the Roman republic.[3] While Milton's notion of the ideal political establishment in England evolved through the 1640s and 1650s, he continued to advocate the Roman republic, though tempered with Machiavellian realpolitik, as late as the second edition of *The Readie and Easie Way*, Nigel Smith contends (193–95). For Milton as for many supporters of "the Good Old Cause," ancient Rome embodied the premiere model of a flourishing culture and government that England should emulate.

These same Miltonic preoccupations — typological treatment of Scripture, architectural imagery, political briefing, classical Roman models — appear in a new configuration when

Milton describes the building of Pandaemonium in book 1 of *Paradise Lost*. The architectural part of that new configuration derives from the presence of another Roman author, Vitruvius Pollio, who in the first century before Christ was chiefly responsible for Augustus Caesar's public building campaign.[4] Vitruvius, in the ten books of his *De architectura* (ca. 28 B.C.), expounds the essential principles that Milton invokes in the scene. This is not to say that Milton was ignorant of other architectural models or that his Pandaemonium reflects nothing from architectural theory and practice among his near contemporaries such as Palladius, Leon Battista Alberti, Sebastiano Serlio, Giorgio Vasari, and Inigo Jones. A fuller, contextualized account of Milton's collective architectural inheritance than is possible here would surely enrich and complicate our understanding of Milton's notions of the art of building.[5] In any responsible account of Milton and architecture, however, I submit that Vitruvius would remain the central and primary figure. First of all, Vitruvius is the one architect whom Milton recommends by name. In addition to Milton's singling out Vitruvius in *Of Education*, Edward Phillips recalls in his brief biography of the poet that Milton included "Vitruvius his *Architecture*" in the curriculum of his private tutorial during the 1640s (Hughes, 634, 1029). While typically absent from academic curricula, the text of Vitruvius was often put to practical use by Renaissance builders. For example, one copy of Vitruvius published by Guinta in Florence, 1513, in a small octavo size, contains dozens of annotations of a practical, rather than scholarly nature.[6] All of the Renaissance architects mentioned above regard him as their chief authority and precursor. Breathtaking technical developments in single-point perspective and domed roofing, to name only two, are directly traceable to sentences in the text of Vitruvius. In short, Vitruvius was "highly valued by architects all over western Europe in the seventeenth century" (Hughes, 634 n. 34). I intend to focus on one well-known Renaissance architect whose exposition of Vitruvius adds a fresh perspective on the Roman architect's theory. To understand the building of Pandaemonium requires a reading of its double possibility akin to the hermeneutic Milton focused on the tower imagery in *The Readie and Easie Way*. To put it simply, Pandaemonium is designed to stand as an image of both good and bad building. Such a building is at once worse than the Tower of Babel and better than the unfinished "goodly tower of a Commonwealth." When we read Pandaemonium in this way, we stand to recover a sense of Milton's daring narrative strategy, inviting readers to marvel at demonic echoes of the architectural achievements of the high Renaissance.

We may begin with the more obvious sense in which Pandaemonium is a negative image. Traditionally, one way of reading Pandaemonium as an image *in malo* has been to regard the palace essentially as a locus of anti-Catholic satire. In 1931, Rebecca W. Smith drew a sharp distinction between the "generalized summary of Roman architecture" presented in Satan's panorama in book 4 of *Paradise Regained* and the "individual scene, with vivid, precise details and a definite location" of Pandaemonium in *Paradise Lost* (187). For the latter, Smith argues, Milton supplemented his reading with personal recollections of St. Peter's in Rome. For example, Milton's epic bee simile earlier in book 1 does more than imitate its Homeric and Vergilian precursors. At the Barberini palace Milton would surely have seen the bronze sculptures of bees emblematic of Pope Urban VIII. The subtly unresolved question in Milton's simile of who controls the bees would have recalled Protestant and Catholic arguments over the pope's putative supremacy, arguments Milton had disputed with Salmasius in *A Defense of the English People*. Likewise, through specific references to ecclesiastical terms such as "conclave" (1.795), by which Catholics designated an assembly to elect a pope, Milton in Smith's words "ascribes to the conferences of Satan and his peers the secrecy and dark designs that Protestants of his day denounced in the Church of Rome" (193–94). Taking Smith's analysis of the Roman church as the single, definitive source for Pandaemonium, William Riley Parker best summarizes the satiric reading of the scene. Parker links the account of Pandaemonium directly to Milton's visit to Rome in 1638: "Standing at last in St. Peter's, Milton must have felt it to be an architectural blasphemy, a perversion of true worship, a cathedral more fit for devils" (1:172–73).

The trouble with the satiric reading is not that it is false. Throughout his career Milton had rallied Protestant readers to his cause by mocking Catholic institutions. He does so most famously perhaps in his humorous indictment in *Areopagitica* of five imprimaturs conferring "in the Piatza of one Title page, complimenting and ducking each to other with their shav'n reverences" (YP 2:504). Certainly Pandaemonium is a place, in Parker's phrase, "fit for devils." To the extent that the quintessential Catholic structure would signal to Milton's readers a perversion of true religion, Pandaemonium delivers a satiric barb at the papacy. But would not Milton's "fit audience" take for granted the corruption of the Roman church? Why would Milton lavish such painstaking attention on an image he wished *only* to explode? Simply regarding Pandaemonium as the creation of demonic papists seems to distance and dismiss the scene too comfortably, in a way inconsistent with the troubling appeal of Satan himself in book 1.

Before asserting a positive view of Pandaemonium, one ought perhaps to anticipate the objection that the iconoclast Milton would oppose such a positive view of any church edifice. The evidence of the Lady Chapel at Ely Cathedral, where Cromwell's soldiers literally defaced or where possible beheaded the stone statues of Roman Catholic saintly icons, points to a literal iconoclasm of church architecture that Milton at least endured — if not applauded — without recorded objection. Milton's assaults on nonscriptural forms of worship and government do seem at times consistent with Puritan attacks on false icons. Thanks to Sanford Budick, Paul Stevens, David Loewenstein, Lana Cable, Michael Lieb, and others, however, Milton scholarship has come a long way from equating Milton's icastic imagination with simple-minded destructiveness or visual incapacity.[7] As an overview of this issue, W. J. T. Mitchell's summary best represents my position: "Milton's poetry is the scene of a struggle between iconoclastic distrust of the outward image and iconophilic fascination with its power" (36). In the opening invocation to *Paradise Lost* Milton asserts that the Spirit prefers "[b]efore all Temples th'upright heart and pure" (1.18); on a superficial reading, this line might be taken as a rejection of all houses of worship. Rather than denying that church buildings have any value, however, Milton's phrasing makes temples the positive standard that the worshipful human heart yet overgoes. To be sure, there are buildings as decadent as the cultures they represent: the Philistian temple in *Samson Agonistes* is the obvious example. Yet not even Samson's ultimate dismantling of the Temple of Dagon dismisses all building as vain or negative. After the tragedy, Manoa will bring Samson "[h]ome to his Father's house: there will I build him/A monument" which will commemorate Samson and rally "all the valiant youth," inflaming them to "matchless valor, and adventures high" (1739–40). It is precisely architecture's power to *impress* the observer, I shall argue, upon which Milton draws in *Paradise Lost*. And whereas the Son in *Paradise Regained* rejects Satan's impressive offer of the panorama of imperial Rome, that epic culminates on the pinnacle of the temple, with the Son embodying a typological kind of architectural flourish, before the victor returns to his mother's *house*. Parallel to the "goodly" but incomplete tower in *The Readie and Easie Way* that could "overshaddow kings," the palace of Pandaemonium reflects sound aesthetic and architectural principles. That these positive features are weighted down, even perverted by teleological misappropriation in no way cancels the architectural virtues of the edifice. Instead, such failings and exaggerations in demonic architecture may lead readers to reflect on the opportunities for appropriate building squandered by human architects. The Commonwealth, alas, was sorely in need of master builders.

The sequence by which Milton introduces Pandaemonium to readers of *Paradise Lost* hints at the double strategy of celebrating and undermining the structure. This doubleness is reflected in the two grammatical senses of "building": the gerund (as in "Building takes time") referring to an unfolding process; the substantive (as in "What a fine building!") to a finished product. The satiric coloring of Pandaemonium is applied to the finished structure only *after* we have seen the building process completed. For example, Milton's depiction of the assembly as a "secret conclave" (795), in the last sentence describing the scene, associates the devils' meeting with Catholic practice after we have seen the building rise. Likewise, the bee simile linking the palace with the Barberini papacy appears only *after* the devils have assembled or "swarm'd" into the completed edifice. Preceding that simile is the narrator's celebrated correction of human error in ascribing the name "Mulciber" to the palace's demonic architect. Indeed the collective effect of these authorial comments is to undermine whatever admiration readers may have felt about the glorious scene of Pandaemonium. Such a corrective strategy logically implies, of course, that an initially positive response to the place was expected and appropriate.

As a hinge between those later comments and the description of the actual scene of building Pandaemonium, Milton describes the impressive effect the palace has on those who enter:

>   The hasty multitude
> Admiring enter'd, and the work some praise
> And some the Architect: his hand was known

In Heav'n by many a Tow'red structure high,
Where Scepter'd Angels held thir residence.

(1.730–34)

The devils universally admire, but their differing responses divide them into two groups: some admiring the craftsmanship ("the work some praise") and others the architect. The doubleness in the devils' response may reflect the English Renaissance debate over the relative merits of architects and artisans. John Dee, in his 1570 preface to Euclid's *Elements*, had insisted on the gulf between the architect's intellectual achievement and the craftsman's handiwork. Paraphrasing Vitruvius, Dee claims that the architect is no mere "Artificer" but the "Hed, the Provost, the Director, and Judge of all Artificiall workes, and all Artificers" (d.iiij–v.). Likewise, Sir Henry Wotton writes in his *Elements of Architecture* that the architect's chief "glory" consists "in the Designment and Idea of the whole Worke, and his truest ambition should be to make the Forme, which is the nobler Part (as it were) triumph over the Matter" (11–12). Specifically, Wotton cites on this point Book 6, heading 2 of *De architectura*, which claims that an architect's greatest care must be to find the exact mathematical proportion that determines a building's design. Two factors point to Wotton as the conduit for Milton's awareness of this issue: Milton's cordial relationship with the English ambassador to Venice, attested by Wotton's glowing letter of introduction for the younger man; and their mutual reliance on Vitruvius, whom Wotton several times calls "our principal Master." In any case, Milton's verse paragraph makes one undeniable point: the architect behind Pandaemonium is the same architect renowned for designing many magnificent dwellings in heaven. Those structures are described in unequivocally positive fashion. The only note of discord in Milton's scene is the elegiac tone deriving from the past tense: "where Scepter'd Angels *held* thir residence" (my italics).

Assuming that the architect's skill remained constant from his tenure in heaven to his relocation to hell, a reader gathers from this transitional passage evidence attesting to the demonic architect's continuing mastery of the art.

A master architect's plan is likewise discernible in the initial description of Pandaemonium's rise. The principles of Vitruvius, adumbrated by several Renaissance architects, pervade Milton's description. To begin with, in describing the combining of various materials into a single "mould" for the building, he draws a precise musical analogy: "As in an Organ from one blast of wind/To many a row of Pipes the sound-board breathes" (708–09). In the surviving manuscript of book 1 edited by Helen Darbishire, a scribe alleged to be Edward Phillips has written "a row of" over the lined-out "an hundred" and added an "s" to "Pipe" (Darbishire, 68). The change focuses Milton's simile on an organ, making it at once more orderly and more visually concrete. The specific vehicle of Milton's comparison, the organ's sounding board that conveys architectonic unity and harmony, derives from Vitruvius. In discussing the design of theaters in book 5 of *De architectura*, Vitruvius tells how ancient architects considered acoustics:

> et quaesierunt per canonicam mathematicorum et musican rationem, ut, quaecumque vox esset in scaena, clarior et suavior ad spectatorum perveniret aures. uti enim organa in aeneis lamminis aut corneis echeis ad cordarum sonitum claritatem perficiuntur, sic theatrorum per harmonicen ad augendam vocem ratiocinationes ab antiquis sunt constitutae. (5.3.8)

> By the rules of mathematics and the method of music, they sought to make whatever voice from the stage clearer and sweeter to the listeners' ears. For as organs in bronze plates or horn sounding boards are tuned to the clarity of the sounds of stringed instruments, so through the harmonic arrangement of theatres the principles of acoustics were established by the ancients.

In keeping with his requirement that the perfect architect know all arts and sciences,[8] Vitruvius articulates an architectural principle that depends upon music and mathematics. He takes the harmonic tuning of the sounding board as the standard for acoustic design; Milton's devils rely on this notion in laying the foundation of Pandaemonium.

When we hear next in Milton's narrative how Pandaemonium arose on its site, Vitruvian doctrine and demonic practice unfold inseparably. Describing the distinctive features of the building from bottom to top, Milton's single, sinuous sentence mimics the vertical rise of Pandaemonium:

> Anon out of the earth a Fabric huge
> Rose like an Exhalation, with the sound
> Of Dulcet Symphonies and voices sweet,
> Built like a Temple, where *Pilasters* round
> Were set, and Doric pillars overlaid
> With Golden Architrave; nor did there want
> Cornice or Frieze, with bossy Sculptures grav'n;
> The Roof was fretted Gold.
>
> (710–17)

The generic term Milton uses to describe Pandaemonium is "Fabric." Vitruvius had used the Latin word *fabrica* to refer both to particular buildings and to the art of architecture. Accordingly, *"fabrica," "*fabric," or *"fabrique"* became the Renaissance terms of art for an architecturally composed building. Wotton routinely refers to buildings as "fabrics," pausing once to translate the term: "*Vna Fabrica ben raccolta*: as *Italians* use to speake of well united Workes" (68). Using the phrase "fabricke of man," Sir Thomas Browne in *Religio medici* extends the architectural term to human anatomy, and thence to an argument for the inorganic nature of the soul.[10] The various architectural features of the fabric that Milton describes can all be traced to Vitruvius, but they can just as easily be illustrated by dozens of Renaissance structures. Above all, Pandaemonium stands as a "a Fabric huge": it presents to the eye a grand spectacle of imperial power and magnificence.

Milton takes particular care to point out that Pandaemonium is "[b]uilt like a Temple." Rebecca Smith emphasizes the negative implication of that description. Pandaemonium is *not* a temple but a palace in temple style, she remarks, which reflects the devilish building's perversion (192–94). I suggest that the perversion Smith stresses coincides with an undeniably impressive aspect of Pandaemonium. To say that Pandaemonium is "built like a Temple," or built in the style of an ancient temple, is to say that it resembles in its basic design the grandest and most celebrated Renaissance churches. William A. McClung has recently added the Temple of Jerusalem, a scholarly reconstruction of which was published at Rome in 1604, to the list of possible precedents for Pandemonium. McClung notes the tradition that the Vitruvian canon informing that temple had been delivered by God to the Hebrews.[10] I caution, however, against the definite identification of any single edifice with Milton's poetic image of Pandaemonium. The ambiguity of Milton's poetic utterance "built like a temple," doubly indefinite through its use of simile and indefinite article, certainly creates space for a range of possible models. Rather than being modeled exclusively on St. Peter's in Rome, Pandaemonium more generally reflects the magnificent church buildings built along Roman lines that Milton knew.

Here again the revival of Vitruvius in the Renaissance provides illumination for Milton's verse account. Cesariano's commentary in his 1521 edition of Vitruvius had issued a sharp challenge to aspiring architects. Domestic architecture is easy in comparison with designing a sacred building, Cesariano writes, "with its fitting parts proportioned and diligently harmonized."[11] The comment may reflect credit on the builder of Pandaemonium, who previously had designed dwellings for the angels. In the opening chapter of the third book of *De architectura*, Vitruvius had introduced his famous observations on the proportions of the human figure which are to be reflected in the overall proportions of temples. Vitruvius explains how the human figure with extended hands and feet fits perfectly into the two putatively perfect geometrical figures:

Figure 2. *"Homo ad Quadratum." M. Vitruvius per Vocundum* (Venice, 1511). Photo courtesy of The Newberry Library, Chicago.

Figure 3. *"Homo ad Circulum." M. Vitruvius per Vocundum* (Venice, 1511). Photo courtesy of The Newberry Library, Chicago.

the square and the circle. Fra Giacondo, in his Venice, 1511 edition, provided woodcut illustrations of Vitruvius's "homo ad quadratum" and "homo ad circulum" (figs. 2 and 3). For Renaissance thinkers, Vitruvius's enclosure of the human figure within these perfect geometrical forms led to profound speculations, both architectural and theological. "This simple picture," Rudolf Wittkower remarks, "seemed to reveal a deep and fundamental truth about man and the world, and its importance for Renaissance architects can hardly be overestimated. The image haunted their imagination" (22).

Indeed, Renaissance commentators on Vitruvius elaborated, in a variety of ways, upon this picture of the human form circumscribed and ensquared. Cesariano's edition takes a graphic, mathematical turn by generating a circle within a grid of smaller squares inside a single square encompassing the human form (fig. 4). This geometric grid evokes a mechanistic view of the inscribed human being. A sequence of Cesariano's prominent illustrations, one each from books 1, 3, and 5 of Vitruvius's text (figs. 5, 6, and 7), constitutes a triptych visually linking cathedral architecture, the human body, and theatrical design. What draws these three images together is the combination of circles and squares, deriving from the measure of the proportions of the central human figure. Part of the wit of the triptych appears in the flanking illustrations, which display on the one hand the potential for creating the grandest space for worship of the divine, and on the other an impressive space for worldly display, with demonic figures perched in its highest spaces. Within Milton's poem, God's act of circumscribing the universe with "golden compasses" (7.225–27), thereby casting God as divine architect, is the central reflection of such geometrical anthropomorphism. In William Blake's vision a century later, Milton's account of the compass-wielding Creator has hardened into a mechanistic architect, one indistinguishable from the self-involved Newton

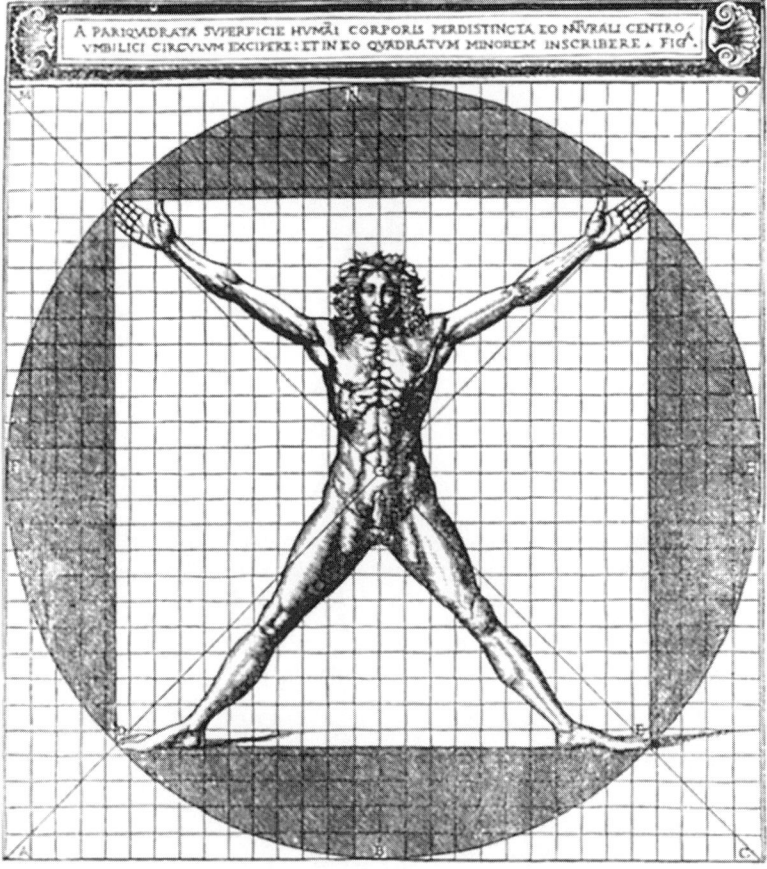

Figure 4. *Vitruvian figure.* Cesariano's *Lucio Vitruvio Pollione de Architectura* (Como, 1521). Courtesy of Special Collections and Rare Books Dept., University of Minnesota Libraries.

who, through the false liberation promised by the calculus, reduced human potential to a mere ratio.

Yet the ambiguous vision of Milton's poem resists the hard-edged mechanism of Cesariano's and Blake's illustrations. When Satan escapes the realms of Chaos and Night and once

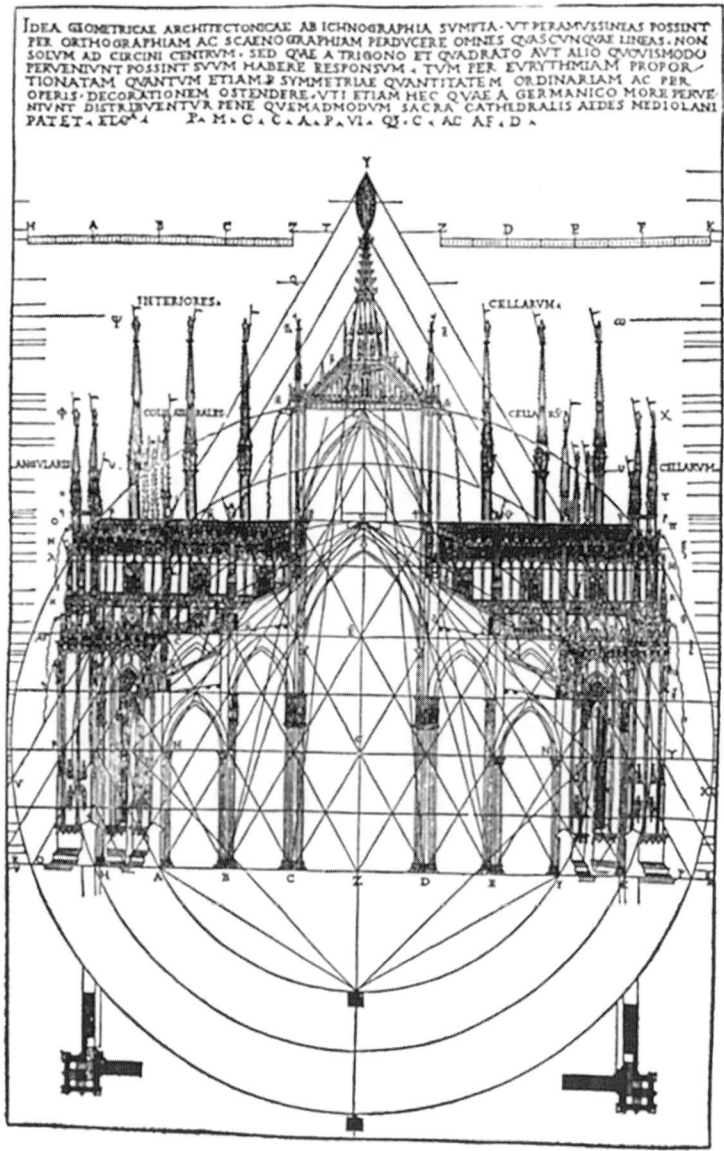

Figure 5. *Cathedral design*. Vitruvius, *De architectura*, book 1 (Florence, 1522). Photo courtesy of The Newberry Library, Chicago.

again glimpses heaven, his vision employs the geometric forms of circle and square, but the devil cannot resolve what he sees into one definite pattern. Satan beholds

> Far off th'Empyreal Heav'n, extended wide
> In circuit, undetermin'd square or round,
> With Opal Tow'rs and Battlements adorn'd
> Of living Sapphire, once his native Seat.
> (2.1047–50)

After the Fall, Sin mockingly asserts the superiority of Satan's "orbicular world" (10.381) to God's "quadrature," assuming that the sphere is a more perfect form than the cube. Sin's attempt to set these two forms at odds, however, ironically draws together what she would oppose, and moreover overlooks the mysterious fusion of spirit and matter in the human form typically symbolized by the squaring of the circle.[12] Indeed, from the sentence first naming Pandaemonium, Milton has playfully associated both circle and square with the fallen angels. There the demonic heralds proclaim:

> A solemn council forthwith to be held
> At *Pandaemonium*, the high capital
> Of Satan and his peers: their summons called
> From every *band* and *squared* regiment
> By place or choice the worthiest.
> (1.755–59; my italics, line 758)

The pun on "band" enables the word, with its double sense of a circle and a military unit, to balance "squared regiment." The "capital" in Milton's sentence has an obvious Roman precedent as well, alluding to the Roman capitol, where assemblies of leaders debated peace or war. As the dominating structure of Pandaemonium itself, the capitol has patent architectural significance.

Perhaps the illustration of Vitruvius most influential upon Milton's scene is also the most familiar. Behind Leonardo da Vinci's immediately recognizable drawing of a circumscribed

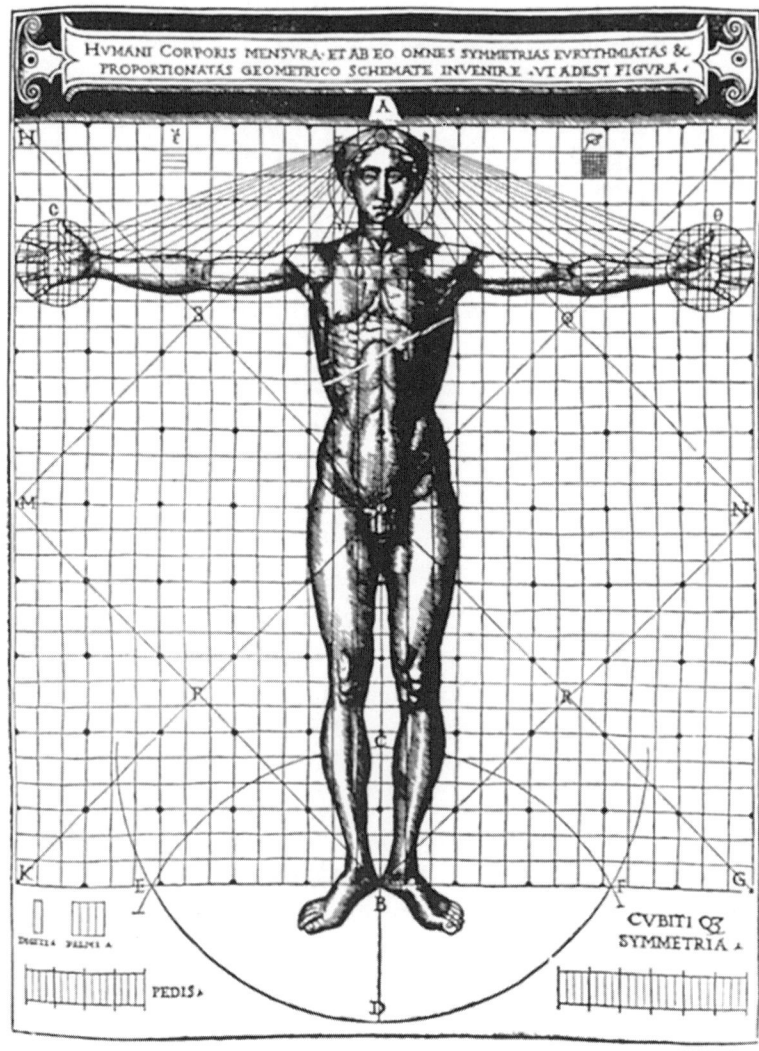

Figure 6. *Vitruvian figure.* Vitruvius, *De architectura*, book 1 (Florence, 1522). Photo courtesy of The Newberry Library, Chicago.

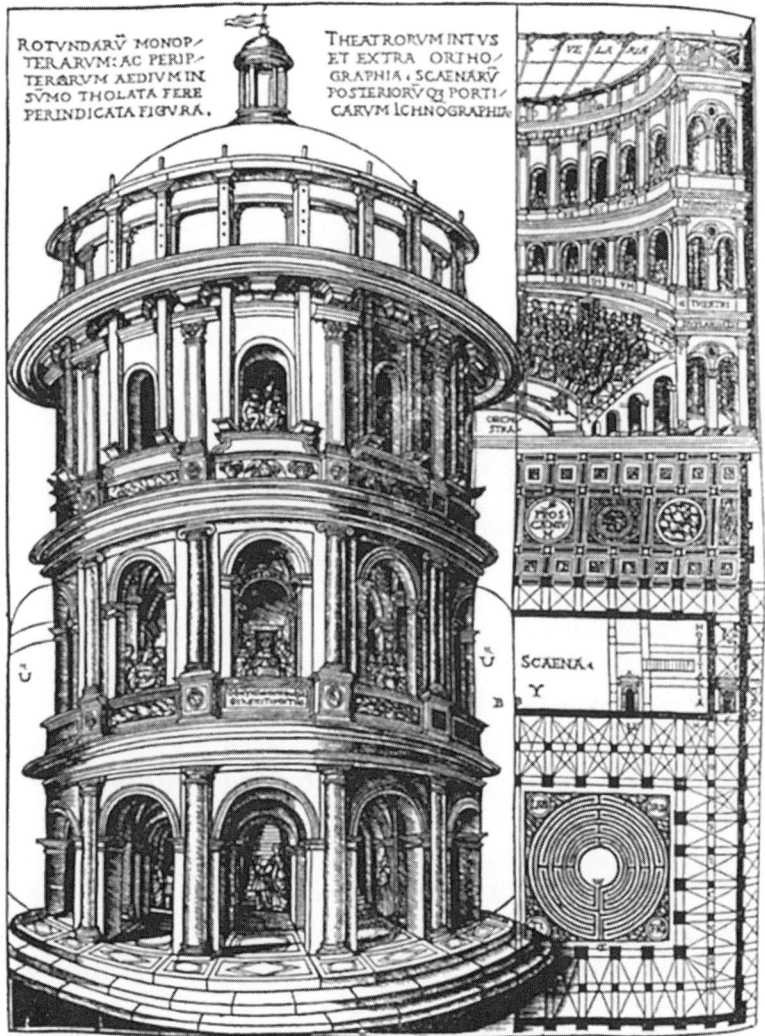

Figure 7. *Theatre design.* Vitruvius, *De architectura*, book 5 (Florence, 1522). Photo courtesy of The Newberry Library, Chicago.

human figure at Venice stands this same passage from book 3 of Vitruvius's *De architectura*. That drawing's combination of circular and square geometrical forms superimposed on the human body reappears in Leonardo's sketches of various church designs. These sketches remind us that, in its most basic definition, architecture is the creation of interior spaces for human occupants. Among many composed structures, those sketches are magnificently realized in the church of Santa Maria della Consolazione at Todi, which embodies Vitruvius's combination of circle, square, and human form along the lines of Leonardo's sketches (fig. 8). Responding to this fusion of Renaissance artistry and ancient theory, Rudolf Wittkower concludes: "How could the relation of Man to God be better expressed, we feel now justified in asking, than by building the house of God in accordance with the fundamental geometry of square and circle?" (25).

The Vitruvian background to Pandaemonium that I have sketched in this chapter should raise similar questions. Granted that the palace of Pandaemonium amounts to a perverted temple, a place of self-worship, is it possible that it also reflects a spiritual urge for harmonic relation with God? Whatever else they have lost, the fallen in *Paradise Lost* nonetheless seek encounters with goodness and divinity. Milton refers to the devils assembled in Pandaemonium as "[a] thousand Demi-Gods on golden seats" (796). Cesariano argues in his commentary on Vitruvius that master architects who can create the effects they desire appear like demigods, "come semi-dei" (1, fol. #2, 5). Blasphemy and aspiration to divinity are near akin. While Puritan reformers rightly mocked the greed and corruption of the imperial Roman church, seen in the lavish expenditure on St. Peter's no less than the "fretted Gold" crowning Pandaemonium, can the architectural achievements of Leonardo, Brunelleschi, Alberti, and Palladio be likewise mocked as merely wasteful? At the very least, should not a

Figure 8. *Aerial view of the Church of Santa Maria della Consolazione, Todi, Italy, completed 1508.* Courtesy of the photo laboratory of Vincenzo Benigni, Todi.

full response to Pandaemonium also credit the impressive act of creation that its architect has left as a memorial? The Miltonic narrator, by the way, includes a teacherly bit of commentary on Pandaemonium aimed at ambitious architects. In accord with my argument for both positive and negative aspects of Pandaemonium, the advice he gives to architects and poets is at once uplifting and humbling. By looking upon Pandaemonium, human builders may "learn how thir greatest Monuments of Fame,/And Strength and Art are easily outdone/By Spirits reprobate" (695–97).

FOUR

A Marriage Made in Heaven

Natural Astrology in Manilius and Milton

Questioning the Stars

When Eve speaks to Adam toward the end of book 4 of *Paradise Lost*, she raises a question about the stars: "But wherefore all night long shine these, for whom/This glorious sight, when sleep hath shut all eyes?" (657–58). Her question is compound, asking not only why the stars shine when she and Adam are asleep, but who benefits from this sight lost to them. Eve's question implies that God has created the heavens disproportionately, inefficiently, prodigally — an objection Adam elaborates upon while discussing astronomy with Raphael in book 8. Coming after the exquisite celebration of the sweetness Eve enjoys with Adam in all created things ("Sweet is the breath of morn"), Eve's query changes the mood in Eden from panegyric to analytic. Moreover, it raises the vertiginous possibility of Adam and Eve being unseated from their preeminent place in an orderly universe. Lurking just ahead, it seems, is Pascal's terrible *pensée*: "the eternal silence of these infinite spaces fills me with dread" (95).

In his immediate reply, however, Adam both credits Eve's intellectual curiosity and offers an explanation for the stars' continuous shining based on their ubiquitous illumination, opposition to darkness, and astral influence:

> Daughter of God and Man, accomplisht *Eve*,
> Those have their course to finish, round the Earth,
> By morrow Ev'ning, and from land to land
> In order, though to Nations yet unborn,
> Minist'ring light prepar'd, they set and rise;
> Lest total darkness should by Night regain
> Her old possession, and extinguish life
> In Nature and all things, which these soft fires
> Not only enlighten, but with kindly heat
> Of various influence foment and warm,
> Temper or nourish, or in part shed down
> Thir stellar virtue on all kinds that grow
> On Earth, made hereby apter to receive
> Perfection from the Sun's more potent Ray.
> These then, though unbeheld in deep of night,
> Shine not in vain.
>
> (660–75)

This is an elegant and beautifully rendered reply. Its account of the stars' "ministry" corresponds roughly with that given by Milton's God during the Creation account (7.340–52). "Common to both passages," Alastair Fowler observes in his edition of *Paradise Lost*, "are the duties of illumination and restraint of Night" (Fowler, 233).

Yet there is also a major difference between the accounts given by Adam and God. The passage in Book Seven exclusively amplifies its single, biblical source (Gen. 1.16–18); it is a case of versified theology. In contrast, Adam's reply is complex, moving from a rationale based in scientific astronomy through a mythology of stellar warfare to an appeal to the concept of influence described by astrology. The shifts between these diverse disciplines may either console or disturb certain readers. To state the case positively, through Adam's words we experience a unified mode of thought that reconciles and harmonizes diverse ways of knowing (science, mythology, astrology) that post-Enlightenment science regards as irreconcilable. In Milton's day such a syncretic epistemology was part of the intellectual and cultural legacy of the Renaissance. In particular, while the fundamental distinction between astronomy and astrology had been clearly and repeatedly made during the early decades of the sixteenth century, educated Europeans had no trouble, apparently, giving credence to both. D. C. Allen divides Renaissance writers into three broad groups: those who believed in judicial astrology, that given knowledge of the stars one could predict specific events; an opposing group denying that the stars have any particularized and predictable influence; and a middle group who, while admitting that current astrological practice was often erroneous, believed that the science might eventually be perfected. The revealing corollary is that *all* of Milton's contemporaries believed in some form of stellar influence. "There were no opponents of natural astrology," Allen claims, "no deniers of the general influence of the heavens" (*Star-Crossed Renaissance*, 147–48). Natural astrology had been authoritatively defined by John Dee in his preface to Euclid's *Elements* as an "Art Mathematicall, which demonstrateth reasonably the operations and effects of the naturall beams of light and secret influence of the Stars and Planets in every element and elementall body at all times in any Horizon assigned" (sig. G3). While Dee's essential characterization of astrology as an art and his allusion to its occult aspect ("*secret* influence") do deny it the status of an experimental science, his recognition of the ubiquity of influence and of natural astrology's reasonableness matches Adam's confident reply.

Despite the widespread Renaissance belief in natural astrology, Milton's attitude toward it remains a matter of debate. Christopher Hill has argued that radical Puritans used ambiguous terms from the language of astrology to encode "illicit meanings" (*English Bible*, 109). He cites as an example Milton's notorious simile of Satan as an eclipsed sun in *Paradise Lost* 1.596–99, which caught the licenser's attention. Ann Geneva insists that astrology spoke not in ambiguous terms but "genuine multiple denotations" that its practitioners such as William Lilly were able to divine (257–58). Whether Milton adapted the astrologer's verbal artistry to the multiple senses of his poetry Geneva does not speculate. The present essay suggests that while withholding credence from astrological prediction, Milton readily adapted its rich language to his complex verbal art.

Nonetheless, Adam's reply to Eve in book 4 leaves many unanswered questions. Some of those questions are philosophical or theological. Who controls the "various" and allegedly ubiquitous ("on all kinds") influence of the stars on earthbound creatures — God or Nature? Precisely how is that control exercised? How does the rather Manichean struggle between the heavenly stars and the forces of "old Night" interact with the poem's theology? Does stellar influence in any way compromise human freedom, which Milton's God has insisted upon in the dialogue in heaven? The greatest may best be described as structural. Why should Eve's love song segue into a colloquy about the stars? What does astrological inquiry have to do with Adam and Eve's relationship and with the argument of Milton's epic generally? If the connection between the ideal human relationship and astrology were isolated, one might regard the shift during Eve's speech as accidental. But this scene in *Paradise Lost* is actually one of several moments during Milton's career in which he interweaves the subject matter of the stars and human love. The first appears in *The Doctrine and Discipline of Divorce*, written during the mid-1640s, when Milton was simultaneously tutoring students in his private academy and beginning to compose *Paradise Lost*. After the present conversation in book 4, Adam's colloquy with Raphael in book 8 turns ultimately from the subject of astronomy to love. Thus the scene in book 8 completes this pattern of association chiastically by reversing the thematic order of the scene in book 4: Love–Stars: Stars–Love. Before examining these Miltonic discussions further, I propose to approach this thematic conjunction by tracing Milton's known reading about the stars in the *Astronomica* of Marcus Manilius. There we will find a poetic model that links curiosity about the stars with divine inspiration and epic aspiration, stellar influence with the power of spiritual love.

Leading the Magi

We know that Milton read and taught Manilius from Edward Phillips, the poet's nephew and pupil during the 1640s who left a brief biography of Milton. Phillips lists the many Latin works that he read under Milton's tutelage, concluding with the two "egregious" poets, Lucretius and Manilius (Hughes, 1029).[1] As one may infer from Milton's *Of Education*, in which the same sequence of texts obtains, the order in which Phillips lists the texts approximates the order in which they were read, beginning with the simpler and more technical works and ending with epic poetry. Thus, the "egregious" or outstanding poets Lucretius and Manilius conclude an ambitious reading program. While the *De rerum natura* was widely recognized as a seminal text in the seventeenth century, one used, for example, by writers as divergent as Thomas Hobbes and Andrew Marvell (Nigel Smith, 160–61, 327), Milton's choice of the *Astronomica* of Marcus Manilius is rather surprising, particularly as the tutorial's culmination. Nonetheless, Manilius's *Astronomica* uniquely serves Milton's interests, both as a teacher and a poet. Manilius himself is a self-consciously didactic poet.

Although almost nothing is known about Marcus Manilius personally, his poem gives several indications of its author's didactic aims. To begin with, the title of the poem, *Astronomica* or "Astronomics," begs for comparison with Vergil's didactic poem, the "Georgics" (Goold, xi–xii). A reasonable inference would be that the author is confident of his ability to cover the subject of astronomy with competence matching Vergil's handling of farming. The impression of magisterial self-confidence increases as one begins reading the *Astronomica*. In the opening proem, the speaker announces his aim: to be the first to sing of the stars in verse; and thus to bring into the sacred realm of Mount Helicon "strange lore untold by any before me":

> deducere mundo
> aggredior primusque novis Helicona movere
> cantibus et viridi nutantis vertice silvas
> hospita sacra ferens nulli memorata priorum
>
> (1.3–6)

> I endeavor to draw down from Heaven [the stars] and, first, to stir with new songs Mt. Helicon and the woods wavering on its green summit, a sacred guest relating things mentioned by none of my predecessors.

Thus, long before *Paradise Lost* but in strikingly similar language and tone, Manilius boldly asserts the intent of his "adventurous song" to "soar/Above the Aonian mount, while it pursues/Things unattempted yet in prose or rhyme" (1.13–16). Despite its signal appearance at the beginning of his epic, Milton's patent allusion to Manilius in these lines has hitherto escaped critical notice. Moreover, the allusion is as significant as it is striking, for Milton attempts to overgo Manilius by soaring over Mount Helicon while laying claim to expertise in the strange lore of astrology.

The teaching method of the *Astronomica* provides another reason for Milton to have studied Manilius's epic. After an early direct address to "Caesar" (1.7–10), Manilius turns to a second addressee, an astrological acolyte or student. Manilius's method involves directly intervening in the student's learning process through frequent uses of direct address and other techniques. Matt Neuberg has described as one of the hallmarks of Manilius's style the poet's habit of using the second person singular, typically in the remarkable negative form, in order to exhort the reader to believe or grasp what he is being told (261–62). "Don't be surprised," Manilius tells the reader time and again, by concepts new to you. In the very first instance of this form of address, for example, Manilius writes:

> Nec vero admiranda tibi natura videri
> pendentis terrae debet.
>
> (1.194–95)
>
> But the principle of the Earth's suspension
> should cause you no surprise.

This teacherly injunction strikes the same tone as the Miltonic narrator's comment to his readers against wondering at the presence of gold in hell: "Let none admire that riches grow in Hell;/That soil may best deserve the precious bane" (1.690–91). The pejorative observation that the narrator of *Paradise Lost* sounds too much like a pedagogue or schoolmaster is amply recorded in Milton criticism from Alexander Pope to Stanley Fish. The Manilian precedent may enable scholars to recover the positive side of that observation — that Milton's paideutic epic, like Manilius's, promises to transform the casual reader into a master of his art. Manilius's approach reminds us that the attempt to give readers mastery of complex matters requires a corresponding discipline.

The Roman narrator's quest for solitude and pursuit of a

selective audience provide further precedents for Milton as epic narrator. Solitude for Manilius is a requirement, or a self-imposed isolation from society, in order to pursue his art. Given his fascination with the stars, Manilius rejects the pursuit of worldly pleasure or political power. Manilius conflates the two notions of his own solitude and his elite audience, in a passage contrasting the appropriate isolation of the stargazer with the seductive diversions of the mass of humanity:

> nec in turba nec turbae carmina condam,
> sed solus, vacuo veluti vectatus in orbe
> liber agam currus non occursantibus ullis
> nec per iter socios commune regentibus actus,
> sed caelo noscenda canam, mirantibus astris
> et gaudente sui mundo per carmina vatis,
> vel quibus illa sacros non invidere meatus
> notitiamque sui, minima est quae turba per orbem.
> (2.138–44)

> Not in the crowd nor for the crowd do I compose my song, but alone, as though borne round an empty circuit I were freely driving my car with none to cross my path or steer a course beside me over a common road, I shall sing it for the stars to hear, while the stars marvel and the firmament rejoices in the song of its bard, and those whom the stars have not begrudged knowledge of themselves and their sacred motions — the smallest society on earth.

In strikingly similar terms, Milton articulates the cosmic scope of his epic hopes in the autobiographical digression in *The Reason of Church Government* (1642): "Time servs not now, and perhaps I might seem too profuse to give any certain account of what the mind at home in the *spacious circuits of her musing* hath liberty to propose to her self, though of highest hope, and hardest attempting, whether that Epick form" (YP 2:812–13; my italics). In this pivotal passage, written during the same decade as the Latin tutorial, Milton projects his epic ambition. The solitude enabling this projection is that of the young teacher at home, in the privacy of his father's house.

In sharp contrast to that domestic setting, the cosmic image of the "spacious circuit of her musing" suggests that Milton's epic ambition in his mid-30s is already moving away from local, British themes to lofty, heavenly concerns.

By the 1660s, however, Milton's career has taken unexpected turns. Solitude for the defeated revolutionary has come unwillingly through blindness and the failure of his political hopes. Solitude has become the bitter ground of experience from which to venture his mature epic ambition. The contrast between the bard's solitude and the noisy crowd of "*Bacchus* and his Revellers" in the proem to book 7 of *Paradise Lost* makes sense in political terms as a contrast between the faithful reformer and the triumphant celebrants of the Restoration, as Laura Knoppers has argued (87–91). If Milton's epic is to succeed under these conditions, it must truly be not his own doing but a gift from Urania, a gift from heaven. Seen in light of Manilius's repudiation of the crowd for spiritual purification, Milton's solitary stance as he appeals to Urania makes sense as the Christian poet's acceptance of humility:

> Standing on Earth, not rapt above the Pole,
> More safe I Sing with mortal voice, unchang'd
> To hoarse or mute, though fall'n on evil days,
> On evil days though fall'n, and evil tongues;
> In darkness, and with dangers compast round,
> And solitude; yet not alone, while thou
> Visit'st my slumbers Nightly, or when Morn
> Purples the East: still govern thou my Song,
> *Urania*, and fit audience find, though few.
>
> (7.23–31)

By specifying his footing on the Earth, Milton expresses not merely his location but his humility. He had "presum'd," during the dialogue in heaven in book 3, to have been a guest in the "Heav'n of Heav'ns" (12–14). Now he is expressly earthbound, "not rapt above the Pole," in a phrase which contrasts his humble attitude with the lofty, magisterial stance of the learned astronomer. Manilius, in contrast, confidently regards the heavens as the soul's true home, pausing only briefly to warn against the sacrilege of enslaving an unwilling heaven to one's earthly purposes (2.129–30). Solitude for Milton comes as the result of losses he must endure in his earthbound, fallen state. Yet there is a way out of this prison of isolation. The compensation for solitude is the company of the muse. In a sense, Milton is not alone, for the muse visits the blind poet in his slumber, and creates through his song a new society in his "fit audience . . . though few."

Like Milton, Manilius is highly conscious of his place in the epic tradition. In a passage anticipating the proem to book 9 of *Paradise Lost*, in which Milton distinguishes his epic argument from those of his precursors, Manilius devotes the bulk of his proem to book 3 of *Astronomica* to a rehearsal of earlier epic themes and a declaration of his unique contribution. Manilius takes a tone eerily reminiscent of Milton's unequivocal rejection of the matter of martial epic. Quoting Manilius's proem at length is necessary to convey the breadth both of his reading and epic ambition:

> non ego in excidium caeli nascentia bella,
> fulminis et flammis partus in matre sepultos,
> non coniurator reges Troiaque cadente
> Hectora venalem cineri Priamumque ferentem,
> Colchida nec referam vendentem regna parentis
> et lacerum fratrem stupro, segetesque virorum
> taurorumque trucis flammas vigilemque draconem
> et reduces annos auroque incendia facta
> et male conceptos partus peiusque necatos;
> non annosa canam Messenese bella nocentis,
> septenosve duces ereptaque fulmine flammis
> moenia Thebarum et victam quia vicerat urbem,
> germanosve patris referam matrisque nepotes,
> natorumve epulas conversaque sidera retro
> ereptumque diem, nec Persica bella profundo
> indicta et magna pontum sub classe latentem

immissumque fretum terris, iter aequoris undis;
non regis magni spatio maiore canenda
quam sunt acta loquar. Romanae gentis origo
quotque duces urbis tot bella atque otia, et omnis
in populi unius leges ut cesserit orbis,
differtur.

(3.5–26)

I shall not tell of war conceived for heaven's destruction and offspring buried by the flames of the thunderbolt in its mother's womb; or of the oath-bound kings and how, in Troy's last hour, Hector's body was ransomed for his obsequies and fetched by Priam; or of the woman of Colchis sacrificing to her guilty love father's realm and brother's mangled corpse, the crop of warriors, the bulls that breathed fierce flames, the unsleeping dragon, the restoration of the years of youth, the fires kindled by a gift of gold, and the children born in wickedness and yet more wickedly slain. I shall not sing of the agelong warfare for which Messene was to blame; or of the chieftains seven, the walls of Thebes saved by a thunderbolt from the threatened flames, and the city conquered because of its conquest; I shall not tell of them who were brother to their father, grandchildren to their mother, or of sons served up at table, whereat the stars recoiled and took away the light of day. Nor shall I tell of the Persian declaration of war upon the main, when a vast fleet hid the ocean, and a channel was let into the land, and a road laid on the waters of the sea. Of the feats of the monarch styled the Great, taking longer to record than to achieve, I shall not speak. The founding of the Roman nation, the periods of war and peace as numerous as the city's consuls, and the whole world's submission to a single people's rule, this I put off. (Loeb, 163–65)

Here Manilius shows his familiarity with a wealth of epic precursors: Hesiod's *Theogony*, the *Argonautica* of Apollonius Rhodius, the *Messeniaca* of Rhianus, the story of the Seven against Thebes, the tragic cycles of Oedipus and Thyestes, the *Persica* of Choerilus of Samos, Vergil's *Aeneid*, and the *Annales* of Ennius. Yet a curious thing happens in Manilius's summary. His compressed, lapidary syntax diminishes the other epic arguments even as it rehearses them. At several points Manilius mocks the prolixity of other epics: for example, he claims that the deeds of Alexander the Great took longer to describe than to achieve. Manilius also takes issue with the sensationalist aspect of much traditional epic and tragic material. Tales of various battles, however crucial to the Roman state, he passes over, seeming to regard them, as Milton said of "inditing" epic battles, as "tedious." "Not sedulous by nature to indite/Wars, hitherto the only argument/Heroick deem'd," (9.27–29), Milton joins Manilius in mocking the wearisome renditions of epic warfare. This is not to say that Manilius, any more than Milton, is a pacifist. Rather, both poets insist that in their epics there are matters both more difficult to describe and ultimately more important than warfare.

If not military achievements or heroic odysseys or grand empire building, what then is to Manilius truly worthy of celebration through the epic? From the beginning to the end of his epic, Manilius teaches his readers one overriding message: that, however silently, the stars govern human life. This doctrine, at once philosophical, theological, and quasiscientific, is the burden of his poetic argument. Milton and his students would have gleaned that lesson above all from the Latin poet — a lesson, in essence, in natural astrology. An overview of several passages from the *Astronomica* articulating that conviction will clarify Manilius's distinctive view of how the stars influence human lives. The passages share a certain aphoristic, gnomic quality that may have recommended them stylistically to Milton and his students, as they did to at least one other Renaissance thinker, Michel de Montaigne, who in his *Apologie de Raimond Sebond* frequently cites Manilius. Particularly, Montaigne struggles mightily with a single line from the *Astronomica* (3.58) that sums up astrology's determinism: "fata quoque et vitas hominum suspendit ab astris," literally,

"[Nature] also made the fates and lives of men depend on the stars" (48–51).[2]

The very opening lines of the *Astronomica* intimate Manilius's anthropomorphic approach to astrology:

> Carmine divinas artes et conscia fati
> sidera diversos hominum variantia casus,
> caelestis rationis opus, deducere mundo.
>
> By song to draw down from Heaven divine arts and the stars, aware of fate, varying the diverse calamities of men, the work of heavenly reasoning.

The personification of the stars as "aware of fate" ("conscia fati") goes a long way toward characterizing their role throughout the poem. Conscious of what fates await human beings, the stars are the perfect intermediary between heaven and earth. Immediately elaborating on and rationalizing that role, Manilius's next lines link the stars with both the mutability of human fortunes and the contrasting, stabilizing principle of heavenly reason ("caelestis rationis"). The Manilian notion of an overarching divine reason communicated to humankind through the stars supports Milton's poetic theodicy in *Paradise Lost*, however different their sense of what constitutes "divine reason."

Manilius continues by presenting a brief historical sketch of how astrological knowledge has developed. In the beginning, it was the gods who granted to human beings knowledge of heaven, Manilius claims. "For who," he argues, "if the gods wished to conceal it, would have guilefully stolen the secrets from Heaven, by which all things are ruled?" ["quis enim condentibus illis/clepsisset furto mundu, quo cuncta reguntur?"] (1.26–27). As the following verse begins, Manilius attributes the rise of human interest in astrology to the god Mercury, but by sentence's end another deity appears:

> tu princeps auctorque sacri, Cyllenie, tanti;
> per te iam caelum interius, iam sidera nota

> nominaque et cursus signorum, pondera, vires,
> maior uti facies mundi foret, et veneranda
> non species tantum sed et ipsa potentia rerum,
> sentirentque deum gentes qua maximus esset.
>
> (32–37)
>
> You, God of Cyllene [Mercury], are the first founder of this great and holy science; through you has man gained a deeper knowledge of the sky — the constellations, the names and courses of the signs, their importance and influences [*vires*] — that admiration of the firmament might be enhanced, that awe might be roused not only by the appearance but by the force of things, and that the nations might learn wherein lay God's greatest power.

At this point, modern editions of the *Astronomica*, following the best manuscripts, leave a gap of three lines and proceed to line 41. Renaissance editors of the text, however, closed that lacuna with three lines that identify the ultimate power in the universe. Thus those lines complete a quasi-historical account of revealed religion from the messenger god Mercury through the "deum . . . maximus esset" to a single, unchanging, all-powerful deity.[3] I give the spelling and orthography of the Aldine edition: "Idem semper erit, quoniam semper fuit idem./Non alium videre patres, alium ue nepotes/Aspiciunt. Deus est, qui non mutatatur in aevo" (38–40). In a copy of Manilius now in the Newberry Library, Chicago, a marginal hand depicted in ink points to that gnomic final sentence, which is heavily underlined. Early readers apparently took "Deus" to refer to something other than the Stoic doctrine that the universe (*Mundus*) was sacred. Taking the subject of the verbs beginning with "erit" to refer to their proper antecedent, the "greatest God" in line 37, a Renaissance humanist scholar would logically translate the lines into English in this fashion: "He will always be, as He has always been the same. None other did our fathers see; none other do our offspring behold. He is God, who is unchanged throughout eternity." This way of reading is of course reminiscent of Christian interpretations of Roman texts such as Vergil's fourth eclogue. Such a hermeneutic, emphasizing the Christian theological or moral significance of the pagan text, may exist in some tension with the text's overt subject matter, here a history of astrology. Because Manilius treats astrology as a prophetic art, however, his urgency to reveal one all-powerful, eternal God easily yields to Christian allegorical reading. The principle that the pagan poem, indeed that every text, points beyond itself to a greater truth in the matter of Christianity, is a powerful hermeneutic, returning the humanist reader again and again to classical texts in order to seek their partial, indirect revelation of God.

The final stage of astrology's development according to Manilius amounts to a confirmation of the art by the cognoscenti:

> per varios usus artem experientia fecit
> exemplo monstrate viam, spectulataque longe
> deprendit tacitis dominantia legibus astra,
> et totum aeterna mundum ratione moveri,
> fatorumque vices certis discernere signis.
>
> (1.61–65)

> Through repeated practices experience built the art, with the example showing the way, and having long observed, revealed that by silent laws the stars rule, and that the entire cosmos moves by eternal reason, and that by sure signs they point out the Fates' changes.

"The eternal spirit of reason" that Manilius finds in harmony with heaven corresponds to the Miltonic notion of right reason. In *Of Reformation*, Milton's first public prose work, he had described it in astronomical terms: "that intellectual *ray* which God hath planted in us" (YP 1:566).[4] Milton would vigorously deny, however, the Roman's claim that the stars' power is "sovereign" over the free human will. Milton seems to have taken Ptolemy's position, echoed for example by Francis Bacon in *De augmentis scientiarum* and by Robert Burton in the *Anatomy of Melancholy* that there is no necessity in the stars; that they rather incline than compel (*Works*, 2.275–76; 1.2.1.4.130). For Manilius, in contrast, the power of the stars is complete: Human deeds and lives depend upon the stars.

Not only individuals, but kingdoms, empires, and all things in the world below move in step with the slightest movements of the heavens, Manilius argues (1.57–58; 4.14–19). Even the shapes of worldly institutions find their sources and determinants, their ultimate patterns, in the heavens. Thus in the poem's concluding passage, Manilius even depicts the Roman republic as an ideal reflection of the heavens (5.734–45). Manilius's conceit anticipates both Milton's anthropological interest in how communities develop and his political commitment to a theocratic commonwealth. In explaining the development of human society, Manilius charts the transition from self-interest to common good:

> sed cum longa dies acuit mortalia corda
> et labor ingenium miseris dedit et sua quemque
> advigilare sibi iussit fortuna premendo,
> seducta in varias certarunt pectora curas
> et, quodqumque sagax temptando repperit usus,
> in commune bonum commentum laeta dederunt.
> (1.79–84)

> But long ages sharpened human wits, the struggle for survival endowed the wretched with ingenuity, and the burden of each individual's lot forced them to look to themselves for improvement, then they gave thought to divide their tasks and vied with each other in performing them, and whatever wise experience found out by trial, they joyfully gave to the common good.

Manilius's final phrase echoes and emulates Lucretius's formulation in *De rerum natura* that our ancestors, being selfish, agreed to contribute to the common good, but only out of desperate need, and only as a kind of social contract. E. E. Sikes explains: "Taking the actual words of Lucretius — *commune bonum* — he insists on the influence of society as a natural and not merely a conventional bond. The wild and selfish caveman of Epicurean fancy is replaced by the 'noble savage,' who is led upwards to civilization through the providence of God" (176). Manilius's rewriting of Lucretius points toward, and is consistent with, Milton's commitment to the Commonwealth as a political order sanctioned both by nature and by God.

The great surprise in Manilius's poem is the intimation, grounded upon but transcending the Stoic creed, that knowledge of the heavens indicates humankind's celestial nature. This idea creates a dynamic tension for the reader of Manilius to gain knowledge of the stars and, like a god, make one's own destiny. Built into the argument of *Paradise Lost* in a powerful, double way, this dynamic is variously and repeatedly articulated in the *Astronomica*, (cf. 4.886–910), though nowhere with such sublimity as in book 2:

> quis dubitet post haec hominem coniungere caelo,
> cui, cupiens teras ad sidera surgere, munus
> eximium natura dedit linguamque capaxque
> ingenium volucremque animum, quem denique in unum
> descendit deus atque habitat seque ipse requirit? ...
> quis caelum posset nisi caeli munere nosse,
> et reperire deum, nisi qui pars ipse deorum est?
>
> (2.105–16)

> Who after this can doubt that humanity is linked with heaven, to whom, in the desire for earth to rise to the stars, nature gave extraordinary gifts, the power of speech and the spirit of understanding and a wing-swift mind, and into whom alone indeed has God come down and dwells, and seeks himself in man's seeking of him? ... Who could know heaven save by heaven's gift and discover God save one who shares himself in the divine?

Within the context of Manilius's didactic epic, the flattering appeal to readers to use their heavenly gifts to rise to the stars would inspire the astrological acolyte. God is in the details of our art, Manilius whispers. He offers his initiates the ultimate flattery: they can know God because they are part of God ("pars ipse deorum"). To Christian readers such as Milton's "fit audience," however, the language of an indwelling deity and of links between heaven and earth, human and divine, would almost inevitably suggest a different theological dynamic. For such readers, the *Astronomica* echoes the Genesis account of human beings made in the image and likeness of God. For such fit readers, too, its tale of a descending and indwelling God adumbrates the theology of the Incarnation. Manilius promises in the *Astronomica* to make his pupils into magi. Confident that the most enlightened of such "star-led wizards" discovered the true God in a lowly manger, Milton is pleased to do the same for the fit audience of *Paradise Lost*.

The Conjunction of the Stars

Renaissance scholars have recently joined syndicated astrologers in searching the stars for answers to the mysteries of love, sex, and marriage. For example, Charles Trinkaus explains Giovanni Pontano's analogies of human sexual intercourse for the creation of the cosmos as a way of interweaving astrology, biology, and theology (451–53). Lauren Kassell demonstrates how Simon Forman used astrology to guide his medical and sometimes sexual practice with his women patients. In the wake of such erudite studies, my own proposal in this regard is quite modest: that John Milton, composing a creative mixture of science, rhetoric, and theology in *The Doctrine and Discipline of Divorce*, uses astrology to support his arguments for divorce on grounds of incompatibility.

Scholars have convincingly documented John Milton's extensive knowledge of astrology. Lawrence Babb lays out two vital pieces of evidence for Milton's apparent belief in astrology: "His horoscope exists. In the *Logic* he gives, as examples of evidence that is relatively dependable 'signs of physiognomy, and the prognostics of astrologers and physicians'" (30–31). Clay Daniel is surely right when he maintains that, for our understanding of Milton's works, more important than Milton's personal belief in astrology is the poet's familiarity with the subject (96). That familiarity is extensive — even if measured against the norm of astrological interest in Milton's time. D. C. Allen has documented the pan-European controversy, extending from fifteenth century Italy to Augustan England, over stellar influence in a cosmos putatively ruled by Providence. Allen divides Renaissance writers into three broad groups: the first, those who believed in judicial astrology, that given knowledge of the stars one could predict specific events; the second, an opposing group denying that the stars have any particularized and predictable influence; and a third group who, while admitting that current astrological practice was often erroneous, believed that the science might soon be perfected. In other words, virtually all of Milton's contemporaries believed in some form of stellar influence. "There were no opponents of natural astrology," Allen claims, "no deniers of the general influence of the heavens" (*Star-Crossed*, 147–48). John Dee, in his 1570 preface to Euclid's *Elements*, defines natural astrology as an "Art Mathematicall, which demonstrateth reasonably the operations and effects of the naturall beams of light and secret influence of the Stars and Planets in every element and elementall body at all times in any Horizon assigned" (sig. G3).

One way Milton gained awareness of natural astrology was through his tutorial of his nephews Edward and John Phillips during the 1640s. John Phillips eventually entered the debate on stellar influence in 1660 with *Montelion*, an attack upon the astrological claims of William Lilly (Allen, *Star-Crossed*, 243; Daniel, 96–97). Phillips draws upon Manilius at several points to refute Lilly's claims, and it stands to reason that Phillips was recalling his reading under his uncle's tutelage. Finally, in a careful examination of the scene of Satan charting the Son's horoscope in *Paradise Regained*, David Renaker has provided abundant evidence for Milton's endorsement of astrology by aligning Milton's view with that of Johannes Kepler, whose discussion of the supernova of 1604 Milton draws upon in his brief epic. Well before the Restoration or *Paradise Regained*, however, Milton puts natural astrology to work in his divorce tracts.

As Kester Svendsen demonstrated in 1952, Milton refers extensively to at least one branch of natural philosophy in his *Doctrine and Discipline of Divorce* (1643; rev. ed., 1644), namely, medicine ("Science and Structure"). Svendsen persuasively relates Milton's use of medical material to the tract's argument. The tract's aim is itself cast in medical metaphors: as Milton's preface explains, it "undertakes the cure of an inveterate disease crept into the best part of humane societie: and to doe this with no smarting corrosive, but with a smooth and pleasing lesson, which receiv'd hath the vertue to soften and dispell rooted and knotty sorrowes" (YP 2:241). According to this medical metaphor, unnatural and unhealthy compounds, whether of marriage partners or their tempers or humours, should be dissolved. A large portion of the pamphlet's medical imagery specifically targets canon lawyers, mere defenders of custom in Milton's view, who oppose his revolutionary approach to divorce. "Milton's fundamental comparison, carried all through the tract," Svendsen writes, "amounts to this: Canon law impediments to divorce have created diseases in human society which result in a distortion of nature; Milton's proposals are remedies drawn from nature and natural law" (437). In summary, then, Milton uses medical imagery in the tract in two ways. Negatively, it castigates as harmful both his detractors' adherence to custom and the acceptance of unhealthy marriages by the orthodox. Positively, it figures the healthy alternative that Milton's proposal offers, amounting to a virtual "cure." Given this persuasive demonstration of the structural use of medical lore in the pamphlet,

I aim to explore the function of Milton's astrological references. Although Svendsen calls them "central" to the divorce tract (439), his article is silent about what the role of the references to the stars might be.

By analogy with the structural use of medical imagery, a pattern of astrological references added to the revised edition of *The Doctrine and Discipline of Divorce* supports Milton's argument of what constitutes a true marriage and what should lead to a dissolution of an unfortunate one. The fact that these allusions were added to the revised edition of 1644 suggests that Milton found appropriate to his discussion of divorce astrological lore from Manilius's *Astronomica* that he would have been teaching then in his private academy. If one adopts the principles of natural astrology, according to which light and stellar influence can be shown to affect every "elementall body," then a good marriage is essentially made in heaven. For the natures of both partners are essentially fixed at birth in their elemental composition, so that the "fit conversation" Milton regards as the basis of marriage can occur only between those partners who are temperamentally compatible from the start. In a bad marriage, one in which the participants fail to satisfy each other and thus defeat the institution's God-given purposes, malign astrological images — of opposing planets, diagonal contraries, eclipses, and so forth — figure the unnatural, literally dis-astrous, pairing of irreconcilable partners. As he had done with medical references, Milton associates unnatural stellar imagery with his benighted opponents, principally those theologians and canon lawyers who defend merely customary, unreformed views of marriage and divorce. Lastly, Milton ventures a new reading of Genesis that finds sanction for divorce in a surprising place: God's original act of creating the heavens.

Milton's positive use of astrological imagery to characterize a sound marriage, often in tandem with negative imagery associated with an irreconcilable union, is straightforward and clear. Early in the tract Milton contrasts the traditionalists' view of marriage as instituted merely to satisfy the fleshly appetite with his claim of its divinely appointed intellectual and social ends. His opponents "place more of mariage in the channell of concupiscence, then in the pure influence of peace and love," Milton writes, "wherof the souls lawfull contentment is the onely fountain" (YP 2:249). "Influence" here retains its Latinate, astrological meaning, of the supposed flowing or streaming from the heavens of an ethereal fluid acting upon human lives, and affecting sublunary things generally (OED 2). Accordingly, Milton finds ludicrous the customary reading of 1 Corinthians 7.9, in which Paul allows that "it is better to marry than to burn," as recommending marriage to prevent one from burning in lust. Why this urgency "only to remedy a sublunary and bestial burning" (269), Milton objects, when the divine institution of marriage clearly aims to remedy the burning of human loneliness? Milton's astrological distinction between the traditional focus on "sublunary" burning versus spiritual desire castigates his opponents' gloss as inherently corrupt and mortal, deriving from the infected region of creation beneath the moon. In Milton's view, their reading reduces the spiritual partnership of marriage to a brutal means of satisfying the parties' lust. This view of marriage reduces it to what John Donne in "A Valediction: Forbidding Mourning" called "[d]ull sublunary lovers love (whose soule is sense)."

The use of astrological references to challenge orthodoxy may be Milton's most sophisticated use of star lore in the tract. In chapter 1, Milton attacks the traditional interpretation of "uncleanness" in Deuteronomy 24.1 as adultery. Milton calls this reading either "sin muffled in the robe of Law, or Law disguis'd in the loose garment of sin." Milton's comment on that pusillanimous interpretation involves an extended astronomical metaphor: "Both which are too foule *Hypotheses* to save the *Phaenomenon* of our Saviours answer to the Pharises about this matter. And I trust anon by the help of an infallible guide to perfet such *Prutenick* tables as shall mend the *Astronomy* of our wide expositors" (243). As Ernest Sirluck notes (YP 2:, note), Milton's use of the expression "to save the *Phaenomenon*" has a striking precedent in Francis Bacon's essay "Of Superstition": "It was gravely said by some of the prelates in the council of Trent that the schoolmen were like astronomers, which did feign eccentrics and epicycles, and such engines of orbs, to save the phenomena; though they knew there were no such things; and in like manner, that the schoolmen had framed a number of subtle and intricate axioms and theorems, to save the practice of the church" (*Works*, Spedding ed., 12:136). Milton uses the metaphor of saving the appearances for rhetorical effect, as Bacon had done. For Bacon, scholasticism was doomed to fail, for it supported the ultimately insupportable practices of the Roman church, just as defenders of the Ptolemaic system put forward bad science to "save the phenomena" of geocentric motion.

In Milton's case the phenomenon to be saved is the Savior's reply to the Pharisees in Matthew 19.8–9. A narrow, literal reading of this passage, depending on a physical view of marriage, however, will not save it: "He saith unto them, Moses because of the hardness of your hearts suffered you to put away your wives: but from the beginning it was not so. And I say unto you, Whosoever shall put away his wife, except it be for fornication, and shall marry another, committeth adultery: and whoso marrieth her which is put away doth commit adultery" (Authorized Version). To most expositors, Jesus' words seem to retract the Mosaic dispensation allowing for divorce. Indeed, Milton's burden of proof in *The Doctrine and Discipline of Divorce* is to overturn commonly accepted understandings of certain words in this passage — chiefly "fornication" — that contradict his sense of their true meaning. Given this ponderous burden, his allusion to the paradigm shift of the Copernican revolution, though grandiose, is appropriate. Certainly Milton's challenge to orthodox exegesis of this passage uses the intellectual currency of Copernicanism to highlight the revolutionary, forward-looking cast of his new doctrine. But the contemporary vehicle of Milton's metaphor paradoxically belies its ancient, backward-looking tenor, its return to the original meaning, as Milton sees it, of Jesus' words. The tract's subtitle indicates its progressive yet backward-glancing approach: *The Doctrine and Discipline of Divorce, Restor'd to the good of both Sexes.*

Yet Milton's use of "saving the Phenomena" stands Bacon's phrase on its head: Milton believes that Jesus absolutely meant those words as a declaration of a new discipline of divorce, and he sets about to save this new doctrine. Milton has been accused of being less than current in his tract for mentioning the *Prutenick* rather than the Rudolphine tables to correct his opponents' errant astronomy (Banks, 272–73). Such criticism gets the passage the wrong way around. Rather than the latest astronomical calculations, Milton steers by an older, and in his words an "infallible guide." The words of Scripture constitute the ultimate authority for his doctrine of divorce. It is not a better science that Milton offers, it is the ultimate science. Moreover, with the help of this "infallible guide," he trusts that he shall "perfet" — not merely, in the way of the new science, to correct — "such *Prutenick* tables." In this goal of perfecting earlier authorities with his divorce tract, Milton draws an analogy between his purpose and Christ's. As Jesus says, according to Matthew 5.17, "Think not that I am come to destroy the law, or the prophets: I am not come to destroy, but to fulfil." This is not the most humble way to proceed, but it seems to be Milton's. Throughout his career Milton opposes false humility and endorses the classical virtue of proper pride, as Richard Strier has argued (258–85). The passage from Matthew on the law, one should note, sets the agenda for Jesus' remarks on divorce which follow a few verses later.

In the revised version of chapter 10 of *The Doctrine and Discipline of Divorce,* Milton again embarks on a lengthy sequence of stellar imagery, but this time with a twist. Using astrological terms, Milton attempts to explain why one person will be drawn to cleave to another in marriage. In contrast to the previous examples, Milton here constructs a chain of references to astrology as an autonomous science or art, rather than as before proceeding to ground astrology on spiritual authority. Thus this discussion seems to grant astrology a logic and authority of its own:

> *A man*, saith he [the author of *Ecclesiasticus*], *will cleave to his like*. But what might be the cause, whether each ones alotted *Genius* or proper Starre, or whether the supernall influence of Schemes and angular aspects or this elementall *Crasis* here below, whether all these jointly or singly meeting friendly, or unfriendly in either party, I dare not, with the men I am likest to clash, appear so much a Philosopher as to conjecture. (271)

Milton's diction shows far more than a casual acquaintance with astrological terminology. Centering on the concept of stellar influence, his terms offer in intricate detail a range of reasonable possibilities, which as Milton suggests might work individually or in some combination, to explain the mystery of personal attraction. "Genius" is the first of these terms with a rich astrological meaning. According to the OED, "in astrological use the word survived, with some notion of its original sense [that is, relating to a person's genesis or begetting] passing into a symbolical expression for the combination of sidereal influences represented in a person's horoscope" (1.d). The setting of a horoscope is also implied by Milton's distinctive use of "schemes" as sources of influence, since a scheme refers in astrological usage to "a diagram representing the position of the planets at the hour of a person's birth" (OED 2.b). "Aspects," as Bacon tells us in his essay "Of Envy," are what "Astrologers call the evill Influences of the Starrs, Euill Aspects" (OED). The term "crasis" refers to "the blending or combination of elements, 'humours,' or qualities" — specifically as an innate condition, part of one's "temperament, [or] 'complexion'" (OED 1.a) Suddenly, mid-sentence, Milton breaks off the astrological speculation. Concerned with his self-fashioning, as Stephen Greenblatt might say, Milton balks at appearing too much of a "Philosopher," in the Renaissance sense of "an adept in occult science, as an alchemist, magician, diviner of dreams, weather-prophet, etc." (OED 2), which might by association weaken his theological credibility in some quarters.[5] Rather than a sign of Milton's skepticism toward or backing down from astrology, however, this move is a shrewd rhetorical strategy, hiding from a potentially hostile audience ("with the men I am likest to clash") speculations about natural astrology that might receive a warmer reception among like-minded thinkers. Still, Milton has aired the notion that astrology might explain how individuals are attracted to their marriage partners, and he has done so in a metaphorically apt manner.

The revised version of Chapter 10 of *The Doctrine and Discipline of Divorce* ends with an unforgettable astrological or cosmological conceit. It was God who gave human beings the authority and precedent for divorce, Milton argues, in the initial act of creation described in the opening verses of Genesis: "God and nature signifies and lectures to us not onely by those recited decrees, but ev'n by the first and last of all his visible works; when by his divorcing command the world first rose out of Chaos, nor can be renew'd again out of confusion but by the separating of unmeet consorts" (YP 2:273). In Milton's astonishing phrase, God's calling Creation out of Chaos becomes "his divorcing command." This divine command compels human emulation: The only way for human marriage partners to create a new world for themselves, and following the divine command "to be renewed again out of confusion," Milton implies, lies through separating from "unmeet consorts." Svendsen finds this argument, in a word, "outrageous" (444). While it is so inventive as to raise hackles, it is nonetheless consistent with Milton's attempt throughout the divorce tracts to relate natural phenomena to divine decrees.

Not only is a good marriage made in heaven, as astrology claims, divorce too has heavenly precedent in God's original, creative separation of unnatural bedfellows.

A Place among the Stars

With an understanding of how Milton has in his divorce tracts used astrological imagery to advance and support his doctrinal argument, I return to that puzzling linkage between Adam and Eve's relationship and the stars in *Paradise Lost*. The names of 14 constellations appear in *Paradise Lost*: alphabetically, Andromeda, Aries, Astrea, Centaurus, Cancer, Capricornus, Gemini, Leo, Libra, Ophiuchus, Orion, Scorpio, Taurus, and Virgo (Orchard, 91–92). Of these, nine correspond with zodiacal signs. Because the action of the epic takes place in a cosmic setting, this might mean nothing more than that Milton has included the signs as the traditional markers by which to chart the paths of the sun and other bodies through the heavens. Upon examination, however, Milton's allusions to some of the signs have structural and thematic uses as well.

Three of the astrological signs — Virgo, Libra, Scorpio — appear together in one passage toward the end of book 4, in which Satan prepares for battle against Gabriel and his squadron:

> now dreadful deeds
> Might have ensu'd, . . . had not soon
> Th' Eternal to prevent such horrid fray
> Hung forth in Heav'n his golden Scales, yet seen
> Betwixt *Astrea* and the *Scorpios* sign,
> Wherein all things created first he weigh'd,
> The pendulous round Earth with balanc't Air
> In counterpoise, now ponders all events,
> Battles and Realms: in these he put two weights
> The sequel each of parting and of fight;
> The latter quick up flew, and kickt the beam.
> (4.991–1004)

Clay Daniel reads the astrological signs as an allegorical representation of Eve, Gabriel, and Satan, with extensively allusive associations of innocence, justice, and lust (92–98). One need not accept this allegorical reading to credit Daniel's essential point: that Milton uses the astrological signs to reflect upon and extend the significance of his narrative. The astrological connotations of the scales, scorpion, and virgin are relevant so long as they correspond with both Milton's poetic argument and the apposite scriptural passages, principally Isaiah 40.12: "Who has measured the waters in the hollow of his hand and marked off the heavens with a span, enclosed the dust of the earth in a measure,and weighed the mountains in scales and the hills in a balance?" and Daniel 5.27: "TEKEL, you have been weighed on the scales and found wanting." What makes Manilius's discussion of Libra relevant to Milton is that the Roman poet argued that beneath this sign was founded the sovereignty of the world:

> Hesperiam sua Libra tenet, qua condita Roma
> orbis et imperium retinet discrimina rerum,
> lancibus et positas gentes tollitque premitque,
> qua genitus Caesar melius nunc condidit urbem
> et propriis frenat pendentem nutibus orbem.
> (4.773–77)

> Libra holds the balance, her rightful sign: beneath it Rome and her sovereignty of the world were founded, Rome, which decides the issue of events, exalting and depressing nations placed in the scales. Beneath this sign was born the emperor, who has laid a better foundation of the city and who now governs a world which hangs on his command alone.

As Kepler had shown, Jesus was born under Libra under the imperial reign of Caesar. Relevant in this context is Jesus' role as judge of humankind described in John 5.22: "The Father judges no one but has given judgment to the Son." The verse enables Christian readers easily to transfer Manilius's tableau of Caesar weighing all events and nations to Jesus as judge. Consistent with this verse, a definite inference of Milton's image is God's ownership of the scales, clearly showing the subordination of stellar influence to divine determination. As Aratus maintains in the opening of *Phaenomena*, Zeus set the signs in heaven and marked out the constellations as a help to humankind: "For we are also his offspring" (τοῦ γὰρ καὶ γένος εἰμέν), a verse that Paul remembered when, according to Acts 17.28, he stood in the Areopagus and defended Christianity to the Athenians: "For in him we live, and move, and have our being; as certain of your own poets have said, for we are also his offspring." Rather than ruling out the predictive power of the stars, Milton's narrative casts God as the source of stellar predictions, with the angels and readers as obligatory readers of those heavenly signs.

Other references to the constellations in *Paradise Lost* likewise show that they are precisely that — signs but not causes — and that members of Milton's "fit audience" are well advised to read them as such. Milton's simile comparing Satan to a Comet that appears in the northern constellation Ophiuchus, known as the "serpent-bearer," does more than link the infernal serpent with a heavenly one. The comparison arises at the moment of confrontation between Satan and Death in book 2:

> So spake the grisly terror, and in shape,
> So speaking and so threat'ning, grew tenfold
> More dreadful and deform: on th' other side
> Incens't with indignation *Satan* stood
> Unterrifi'd, and like a Comet burn'd,
> That fires the length of *Ophiucus* huge
> In th' Artic Sky, and from his horrid hair
> Shakes Pestilence and War.
>
> (704–11)

Kepler's *De stella nova* had echoed the prediction by a number of astrologers that a devastating comet would appear in

Ophiuchus in 1604; what actually appeared, according to Kepler's observation, was a supernova occupying six minutes of arc as seen from the Earth (Renaker, 226–28). Milton's simile may, as Renaker suggests, indicate that Milton read Kepler's analysis and appropriately associated Satan with "the astrologers' fiery delusion" (228). William B. Hunter likewise reads Ophiuchus as the supernova of 1604, and emphasizes that it was considered at the time a dire portent of evil (19–21).

What Manilius's account adds to the particular, historical appearance of Ophiuchus as Kepler's supernova of 1604 is the perpetual sense of struggle with the serpent:

> serpentem magnis Ophiuchus nomine gyris
> dividit et torto cingentem corpore corpus,
> explicet ut nodoe sinuataque terga per orbes.
> respicit ille tamen molli cervice reflexus
> et redit effusis per laxa volumina palmis.
> semper erit, paribus bellum quia viribus aequant.
> (1.331–36)

> One called Ophiuchus holds apart the serpent which with its mighty spirals and twisted body encircles his own, that so he may untie its knots and back that wind in loops. But, bending its supple neck, the serpent looks back and returns; and the other's hands slide over the loosened coils. The struggle will last for ever, since they wage it on level terms with equal powers. (Loeb, 31)

Manilius's Ophiuchus is a kind of Laocoön figure whose fate is not to be crushed by a serpent but to be locked in an endless struggle with one. Thus, after Manilius, to mention Ophiuchus is to call to mind a perpetual, cosmic struggle with the serpent, which is precisely the struggle between Death and Satan that Milton describes. Death, Milton's counterpart for Ophiuchus, is accordingly enormous and powerful but also '"dreadful and deform." Especially apposite to the problem of satanic heroism in *Paradise Lost* is the way Manilius treats Ophiuchus's struggle with the serpent as grand in scope, enduring, but not necessarily heroic. Their struggle is rather a sign of their mutual doom.

Whereas Milton's comparison with Ophiuchus intensifies the struggle in his epic's plot, the simile also reflects a detailed description of comets that is indebted to Manilius. The reflection upholds the power of comets to predict impending disaster. The first book of Manilius's epic concludes with the fascinating appearance of comets, the doom they predict, and the hope that violence and war will now cease. To begin with, he describes the fiery hair comets seem to possess: "nam modo, ceu longi fluitent de vertice crines,/flamma comas imitata volat, tenuisque capillos/diffusos radiis ardentibus explicat ignis" (1.835–37). [For sometimes, as though long tresses were flowing down from a person's head, the flame flies in the guise of hair, and the slender fire lets loose its streaming locks in brilliant rays] (Loeb, 71). Milton accordingly describes the hair of the satanic comet as burning, while "horrid" in his account is a Latinism from *horreo*, to stand on end or bristle: "from his *horrid* hair" Satan "[s]hakes Pestilence and War." At the same time, the appearance of the comet's hair is horrid in the modern sense, too, as it portends a variety of disasters that Manilius tallies — chiefly blight (874–79), plague (880–95), and war (896–921). Milton's precise wording, by which Satan "[s]hakes Pestilence and War" from his comet-like hair, makes the devil's appearance a harbinger of those impending horrors on Earth.

A final, contrasting constellation's appearance reinforces the portentous power of the stars in *Paradise Lost*. Adam's explanation that the heavenly bodies shed influence in a beneficent way is confirmed by Milton's inclusion of the Pleiades during his account of Creation in book 7. That constellation appears at the initial appearance of the sun. The Pleiades accompany the sun's inaugural and "jocund" progress:

> First in his East the glorious Lamp was seen,
> Regent of Day, and all th' Horizon round

> Invested with bright Rays, jocund to run
> His longitude through Heav'n's high road: the gray
> Dawn, and the *Pleiades* before him danc'd
> Shedding sweet influence.
>
> (7.370–75)

Though brief, the mention of the Pleiades and their "sweet influence" is remarkable. Not surprisingly, Milton mentions the influence of those stars on the fourth day of the hexameron, following but expanding upon the Priestly account in Genesis 1.14–19 of God's creating all the lights in the firmament. Yet the Genesis account makes no mention of stellar influence. For the "sweet influence" of the Pleiades, Milton could claim the support of two authorities. Manilius writes:

> quibus aspirantibus almam
> in lucem eduntur Bacchi Venerisque sequaces
> perque dapes mensasque super petulantia corda
> et sale mordaci dulcis quaerentia risus.
>
> (5.142–45)

> Beneath their [the Pleiades'] influence followers of Bacchus and Venus are born into the nurturing light, and those who run free at feasts and banquets and who strive to provoke sweet [*dulcis*] laughter with biting wit.

Manilius thus describes the sort of convivial scene that Milton imagines in the Pleiades dancing before the jocund sun. Both poets link stellar influence with birth scenes: Manilius tells how the influence of the Pleiades brings revelers into the light; Milton makes the Pleiades, shedding their influence as flower girls do their petals, part of the the train of the newly emergent sun. If a severe reformed reader found anything untoward in this association with Bacchus and the lower Venus, Milton's "fit audience" could supply the unquestionable authority of Job for the overflowing sweetness of Milton's scene: "Canst thou bind the sweet influences of Pleiades, or loose the bands of Orion?" (Job 38.31). God's answer to Job out of the whirlwind admits of no reply. One can only hope to avoid, if a human speaker can, Job's error of darkening counsel by words without knowledge. One can say with some confidence, however, that the God of Job, while manifestly the master of stellar influence, has apparently delegated it to the mythological sisters whom astrologers are left free to chart.

When, therefore, Adam in book 8 of *Paradise Lost* echoes Eve's earlier question with a question beginning: "*reasoning* I oft admire,/How Nature wise and frugal could commit/Such disproportions, with superfluous hand/So many nobler Bodies to create,/Greater so manifold to this one use" (8.25–29, my italics), readers have been prepared to see his question as narrow-minded and thus inadequate. The intricate, multiple layering of epistemologies that Milton's epic has worked to incorporate shows that such a monolithically rational approach is bound to prove self-defeating. The angel Raphael's response, with its series of "what ifs" and its inclusion of aspects of no less than five astronomical systems, attempts to restore Adam to a balance of rational speculation, faith, and a sense of the human observer's inescapable conditions and limitations. Neither Raphael nor Milton is opposed to intellectual curiosity: "To ask or search I blame thee not," the angel tells Adam (66). The opposition is not to questioning but only to questions that contain built-in assumptions and presume knowledge.

To underscore the difference, Milton concludes Adam's dialogue with Raphael by showing a properly oriented Adam once more questioning the angel, this time on the subject of love among the spirits. Adam's final question echoes the word "blame" that Raphael had used in his earlier response:

> To Love thou blam'st me not, for Love thou say'st
> Leads us to Heav'n, is both the way and guide;
> Bear with me then, if lawful what I ask;
> Love not the heav'nly Spirits, and how thir Love
> Express they, by looks only, or do they mix
> Irradiance, virtual or immediate touch?
>
> (8.612–17)

We need not read Raphael's immediate reaction — "with a smile that glow'd/Celestial rosy red" — as an angelic blush to see that Adam's question, unlike his earlier one, arises from an open and respectful curiosity. Adam's innocent speculation about the operation of love among the heavenly spirits receives the instructive reply that indeed the angels are happy, and "without Love no happiness" (621). In this regard, one might recall Milton's argument from *The Doctrine and Discipline of Divorce* that some readers "place more of mariage in the channell of concupiscence, then in the pure influence of peace and love." In wondering about love's power in spheres beyond his own, Adam is tracing influence back along a celestial path linking the human couple and God, in language happily drawing from the Manilian discourse of natural astrology. Adam's notion that love leads to heaven, with the Manilian background that stellar influence contributes to that ascent, also echoes and reformulates Edmund Spenser's appeal to the heavens for a large posterity in the final stanza of his *Epithalamion*:

> And ye high heavens, the temple of the gods,
> In which a thousand torches flaming bright
> Doe burne, that to us wretched earthly clods
> In dreadful darknesse lend desired light;
> And all ye powers which in the same remayne,
> More then we men can fayne,
> Poure out your blessing on us plentiously,
> And happy influence upon us raine,
> That we may raise a large posterity,
> Which from the earth, which they may long possesse,
> With lasting happinesse,
> Up to your haughty pallaces may mount,
> And for the guerdon of theyr glorious merit
> May heavenly tabernacles there inherit,
> Of blessed Saints for to increase the count.
> So let us rest, sweet love, in hope of this,
> And cease till then our tymely joyes to sing,
> The woods no more us answer, nor our eccho ring.
>
> (409–26)

Adam and Eve's conversation about stellar influence contains within it all of the above discussed elements. The fact that they *are* conversing indicates that they are fulfilling Milton's sense of the purpose of marriage: "fit conversation." They not only delight each other sensually, as Eve's celebration of the sweetness she finds in Adam's company indicates. The question that Eve raises, together with Adam's reply, shows that they give each other the higher delight of intellectual exchange through conversation. As "fit conversing souls," Adam and Eve demonstrate that before the Fall they are mutually compatible by nature, which is to say in harmony with divine will. In that sense, their marriage was indeed made in heaven. The turn in their conversation to the stars may appear to be casual, but in light of Manilius's didactic epic, that shift in conversation is revealing. Human beings show their link with heaven by inquiring into the stars, Manilius writes, and that is precisely what Eve does with her teacher-husband in book 4, and what Adam does in book 8 with Raphael. Like Manilius, Adam teaches that the stars shed their influence upon every being and event on earth. To the extent that inquiring into the stars enables one to understand God, creation, or oneself, Milton shares Manilius's epic estimate of the distinctive value of astrology. Unlike the Roman astrologer, however, Adam does not maintain that the stars have "sovereign" or absolute control. For however strong the inclination by the stars, Adam and Eve determine their own fate, developing their nature according to their own wills. As Adam reminds Eve immediately before their separation,

> within himself
> The danger lies, yet lies within his power:
> Against his will he can receive no harm.
> But God left free the Will, for what obeys
> Reason, is free, and Reason he made right,
>
> (9.348–52)

To link the beginning and ending of this passage, the danger for human beings lies in abandoning the freedom of the will. That can all too easily happen, the sequel demonstrates, if reason is deceived by "some specious object" and falls into error. That is, of course, Eve's path. For Adam, desire for Eve is that "specious" object — in the double sense of glittering and false — that he exchanges for loving obedience to God.

In a curious way, the doctrine at the heart of Manilius's *Astronomica* — that human beings can reclaim their divinity in the stars — is just such a "specious object," one anticipating Satan's temptation to Eve to gain divine knowledge by eating the fruit. Reading Manilius, then, amounted to a most useful lesson for Milton, with both scientific and ethical significance. In terms of science, Manilius's text provides a way of reconciling the theory of stellar influence with a seventeenth century view of nature as God's second book. Considered from a poetic or ethical viewpoint, the central premise of Manilius's text provided Milton with an eloquent and usefully ambiguous precedent for satanic seduction. Finding one's place among the stars can mean either growing in awareness of one's proper place in the universe or reaching for forbidden fruit. Milton recast the urgency of scientific speculation, embodied in the ancient stargazers and rekindled in his own day, into the poetics of choice that confronts Satan, Eve, Adam, and indeed every reader of *Paradise Lost*.

FIVE

The Wounded Earth in *Paradise Lost*

Mysterious Mingling

At the critical moment in *Paradise Lost,* Milton introduces a puzzling personification, which appears immediately after Eve eats the forbidden fruit:

> So saying, her rash hand in evil hour
> Forth reaching to the Fruit, she pluck'd, she eat:
> Earth felt the Wound, and Nature from her seat
> Sighing through all her Works gave signs of woe,
> That all was lost.
>
> (9.780–84)

The personification, elaborated, reappears immediately after Adam eats the forbidden fruit:

> Earth trembl'd from her entrails, as again
> In pangs, and Nature gave a second groan,
> Sky low'r'd, and muttering Thunder, some sad drops

> Wept at completing of the mortal Sin
> Original.
>
> (9.1000–04)

The fundamental question can be simply put: What is the personification of the Earth doing at this pivotal moment in *Paradise Lost*? For all its originality and importance, the significance of this figure has virtually escaped critics' attention.[1]

At first glance, one might see this double personification essentially as rhetoric, as the Miltonic narrator's way of intensifying readers' response to a human tragedy. In other art forms, intensification would be precisely the purpose that such a device would serve. The rising strains of film soundtracks, for example, typically intensify audiences' reactions to important scenes. Certainly the moment in Milton's narrative is emotionally tense, for it is the climax of the tragic plot. In the opening proem of book 9, Milton explicitly identifies the generic mode of this portion of his narrative as tragedy. In the present passage, terms associated with pathos ("[s]ighing," "woe") reinforce emotions proper to Aristotelian tragedy.

The timely appearance of the personified Earth, with the parallel personification of nature, however, does more than merely intensify our experience of a human tragedy. Essentially, the figure extends the scope of the Fall from a human to a cosmological event. Milton suggests that the Fall corrupts both human and physical nature, beginning with the Earth itself. In developing these notions, Milton adapted literary and scientific traditions recorded in a variety of Latin texts, including several from his pre-university curriculum along with others. What is especially remarkable is that this cluster of implications is made possible by Milton's economical poetic utterance: "Earth felt the Wound."

No such personification, of course, appears in the scriptural account of the Fall. In Genesis 3.6 the biblical narrator describes Eve and Adam eating the fruit, then proceeds directly to the following verse, in the Authorized Version: "And the eyes of them both were opened, and they knew that they were naked; and they sewed fig leaves together, and made themselves aprons." With its notorious fig leaves indicating the sinners' shame, the Bible tells a story of human action and human consequences. The narrator of Genesis focuses exclusively on the change in human consciousness during the Fall. Milton's personification, in contrast, shifts the focus away from the immediate human drama to show that human sin somehow injures the natural world. While shifting attention away from Adam and Eve, personification by its nature indicates that injury in a way palpable to human beings.

Scripture elsewhere, however, does hint at a personified Earth. Most significantly, Matthew 27.51 describes how "the earth did quake" at the death of Jesus. Milton may have relied upon the principle of typology to connect Adam and Eve's fatal act with Christ's death. Supporting both the typological reading and the personification of the Earth, Psalm 68.8 amounts to an intermediate Hebraic account: "The earth shook, the heavens also dropped at the presence of God: even Sinai itself was moved at the presence of God, the God of Israel" (Authorized Version). The fourth century Christian apologist, Arnobius of Sicca, who was well versed in Epicurean philosophy, makes the quasi-scientific observation on Matthew 27.51 that "all the elements of the universe were thrown into confusion."[2] Arnobius thus demonstrates one way of mingling scriptural commentary and ancient science. As biblical metaphors, the personifications from Psalms and Matthew provided Milton with scriptural authority for employing the device in *Paradise Lost*. Moreover, they may have suggested to the poet ways in which theology and natural history are inevitably intertwined.

My first conclusion, then, can be simply put: The sin of Adam and Eve has a palpable, harmful effect on nature. In Milton's poem, we are shown immediately what Adam and Eve will realize only later: that the choices of human beings intimately affect the entire scale of being. Chiefly, yet still rather mysteriously, Adam and Eve's choice wounds the Earth.

Again in Pangs

In attempting to explain the Earth's appearance at the moment of the Fall, we need to examine the larger pattern of the Earth's role in *Paradise Lost*. A numerical analysis indicates that the Earth's prominence at the climax matches her persistent appearance throughout the poem. Milton refers to the Earth by name in every book of *Paradise Lost*; the word *earth* in its substantive form appears a total, according to the Ingram and Swaim concordance, of 204 times (141–43). That number puts *earth* in the same league — at least in terms of frequency — with *all*, which William Empson isolated as the epic's preeminent "complex word" (*Structure*, 101–04). Surprisingly, earth is named twice as often as any other major character including Adam (105), Death (118), and Eve (98). Of course, many appearances of the word are distinct from the personified figure we are discussing. Laura Lockwood has analyzed the variety of meanings of the word *earth* into five categories: (1) soil, (2) the world in which we live, (3) regarded as planet or heavenly body, (4) the inhabitants of the planet, (5) one of the four elements. Among the second category, Lockwood describes a subset in which the Earth is "more or less clearly personified," and lists seven passages from *Paradise Lost*: 1.687ff., 5.338ff., 7.453ff., 7.501ff., 9.782ff., 9.1000ff., 9.1041. Although one might arrive at a different total of personifications, Lockwood's list comprises what is unquestionably a meaningful, coherent sequence. Retracing that sequence goes a long way toward explaining the Earth's appearance during the Fall.

The first example of the personified Earth in *Paradise Lost* appears in book 1, amid the scene of the devils building Pandaemonium. Reflecting in miniature the epic's double plot, the passage recapitulates the spread of sin from demonic to human agents:

> *Mammon* led them on,
> *Mammon*, the least erected Spirit that fell
> . . . .
>   by him first
> Men also, and by his suggestion taught,
> Ransack'd the Center, and with impious hands
> Rifl'd the bowels of thir mother Earth
> For Treasures better hid. Soon had his crew
> Op'n'd into the Hill a spacious wound
> And digg'd out ribs of Gold.
>
>   (1.678–90)

Carolyn Merchant associates this passage with the late sixteenth and early seventeenth century debate over mining.[3] Milton's poetic argument goes deeper, locating the ethics of mining in the long history of universal abuse of the Earth. Chronologically, of course, the devils' digging must precede that of human beings. Yet Milton complicates that expected order by interpolating human digging before completing his account of Mammon's digging. A further complication arises from Milton's deployment of a Janus-faced adverb "first," which may attach itself either to Mammon (taught by him first) or to the verbs (men first "Ransack'd," "Rifl'd").

The passage's account of ransacking some abstract "Center" seems at first to describe a simple case of burglary. As Milton's sentence goes on to specify "rifl[ing] the bowels of thir mother Earth," however, the crime is compounded. With the Earth cast as "their mother," the impious men are, at least metaphorically, guilty of assault, and assault of a vicious and universally condemned kind. From the perspective of the Law, attacking Mother Earth grossly parodies the Mosaic commandment to "Honor thy Father and Mother." Milton's graphic description of their assault makes it even more disgusting and damnable. The sinners "rifle" the bowels of Mother Earth: as the root sense of that verb, the *Oxford English Dictionary* gives "to scratch, to scrape." Transferred from that violent and violating act are the OED's other definitions of "to rifle" as "to plunder" and "to affect strongly or injuriously." This horrible scraping of Mother Earth's "entrails," a term Milton later in the poem associates with the birth canal, amounts to a sickeningly palpable simulacrum of an abortion. Appropriately, anthropomorphic images conclude Milton's scene. The devils' opening of a "spacious wound" may recall the wound opened in Christ's side during the Crucifixion. Certainly the devils' plunder of "ribs of Gold" echoes the Yahwistic account of Eve's creation from Adam's rib. Either way, the passage affirms a ringing ethical imperative: Violating the Earth amounts to a desecration of the female, and of divine creation in general.

As so often in *Paradise Lost*, Milton parallels that negative, demonic scene with a positive, ideal one. The audience first meets the personified Earth in its healthy, creative form as part of our introduction to Edenic life in book 5. Upon the arrival of the archangel Raphael in Eden, Eve brings to their repast a cornucopia of fruits and grains, "whatever Earth allbearing Mother yields" (5.338). At first glance, this epithet may appear merely decorative. On reflection, it is thematically crucial. It links the Earth's fecundity, already well known to Eve and Adam, with the angel's ontological analogy of the universe as a flowering, fruitful plant (5.469–503). That analogy makes possible Adam and Eve's understanding of the scale of being. The dialogue with the angel also shows Adam and Eve the power of their choice to affect their place in the created order — indeed to disturb the created order itself.

The positive picture of the Earth as life-bearing mother is developed in great detail in Milton's rendition of the hexameral Creation account. In book 7 of *Paradise Lost*, the angel tells of the Earth's part in the creation of animals:

> The Sixt, and of Creation last arose
> With ev'ning Harps and Matin, when God said,
> Let th'Earth bring forth Soul living in her kind,

> Cattle and Creeping things, and Beasts of the Earth,
> Each in their kind. The Earth obey'd, and straight
> Op'ning her fertile Womb teem'd at a Birth
> Innumerous living Creatures, perfet forms,
> Limb'd and full grown.
>
> (7.449–56)

Citing this passage, Stephen Fallon argues that Milton's animated imagery reflects his commitment to animist materialism, the belief that matter can possess the traits of mind.[4] Indeed Milton depicts the Earth as both animate and mindful. In Milton's version, day six of the hexameron results not simply in the creation of animals, but in their parturition from the already living, personified Earth. Perhaps to account for that personification, Milton includes in his Creation narrative a description of the Earth's formation as an embryo hidden in the womb of waters: "The Earth was form'd, but in the Womb as yet/Of Waters, Embryon immature involv'd,/ Appear'd not" (7.276–78). And before Milton's sentence ends, the Earth conceives and is first named "the great Mother":

> Over all the face of Earth
> Main Ocean flow'd, not idle, but with warm
> Prolific humor soft'ning all her Globe,
> Fermented the great Mother to conceive,
> Satiate with genial moisture.
>
> (278–82)

In this stunning passage, Milton has mingled the cosmic waters said to surround the biblical firmament with the waters of life surrounding human childbirth. This is definitely a case of a positive cosmic womb image in *Paradise Lost*, associated, as Mary Adams suggests, with the created world (169). In discussing Milton's Creation account, Barbara Kiefer Lewalski has recently demonstrated Milton's emulation of Lucretius's description of various flora and fauna springing to life from the earth in *De rerum natura* 2.992–95 and 5.781–924.[5] Milton's personifications of the Earth are consistent, both mutually coherent and logically developed throughout his epic.

As part of the sequence of passages personifying the Earth in *Paradise Lost*, this one at Creation marks several major conceptual advances over the others. The anthropomorphic Earth is obedient to God's creative word, but Milton's emphatic focus on her compliance, reinforced by the unusual caesura — "The Earth obey'd" — at least raises the question of whether the Earth *can* will to disobey God. Certainly this focus on the Earth's obedience heightens our awareness of human obedience, a process which has been underway since Adam's question in book 5: "What meant that caution joined, 'if ye be found/Obedient'?" (513–14). As a counter to the sterile digging into the Earth's womb by Mammon and men, this passage shows what the fertile Earth properly brings forth. Complementing her sheer fertility (she "teem'd at a birth" with "Innumerous living Creatures"), the Earth is productive in an orderly manner, with creatures produced according to their kinds, in perfect forms, yet without the dangers of human childbirth and maturation ("limb'd and full grown"). Milton sums up this positive phase of the productive Earth by depicting her as happily wearing the living creatures she has brought forth: "Earth in her rich attire/Consummate lovely smil'd" (7.501–02).

In the midst of the sequential passages developing the personified Earth, the personifications during the Fall cast the Earth as a consciously changed being. Because Milton depicts the Earth as a sentient, responsive being, her suffering at the Fall would seem to be no mere reflection or extension of a human problem. The Earth herself is damaged by human sin, and she is moreover well aware of that injury: "Earth felt the wound." Because the injuries to the Earth by mining depicted in book 1 have been shown to be abuses of the Earth's creative force, Adam and Eve's sin likewise seems to involve a violation of Mother Earth's creative power. Earth's response to Adam's fall — "Earth trembl'd from her entrails, as again/In pangs" — specifically characterizes the Earth's response to the Fall as a perverse, forced reenactment of her part in Creation.

In the last frame of Milton's sequence of scenes describing the personified Earth in *Paradise Lost*, we are shown conclusively that the Earth's sufferings are no mere reflection or intensification of the human situation. The Earth is physically afflicted by the dual shifts of irregular solar movement and tilted axes, as God physically effects the plagues of extreme seasons and temperatures. The sun:

> Had first his precept so to move, so shine,
> As might affect the Earth with cold and heat
> Scarce tolerable, and from the North to call
> Decrepit Winter, from the South to bring
> Solstitial summer's heat.
> . . . .
> Some say he bid his Angels turn askance
> The Poles of Earth twice ten degrees and more
> From the Sun's Axle; they with labor push'd
> Oblique the Centric Globe.
>
> (10.651–71)

The physical re-positioning of astronomical bodies shows that the injury to the Earth is neither whimsical nor a case of the pathetic fallacy, Ruskin's term for the poetic projection of human emotion onto physical nature. Rather, in contrast with the passages on the Earth wounded by us during the Fall, this passage reverses cause and effect, with the Earth damaged first and human affliction to follow. What affects the Earth immediately will eventually affect human beings on Earth: extremes of temperature and irregular seasons. The lack of witnesses who can corroborate this cataclysmic change prompts the uncertain pronouns: "Some say." One thing is certain, however. The Fall has irreversibly damaged the living Earth.

Stoical Outrage

Milton, as we have seen, presents the Earth in *Paradise Lost* as a living being, not a mere reflection of humankind, who brings life to all terrestrial creatures and who is injured by the Fall. In short, Milton describes the Earth as a living organism. His chief precursors in this belief were the Roman Stoics. [6]

As Edward Phillips writes, Milton was reading and teaching the works of several Romans during the 1640s when, as Phillips also recalled, Milton began to compose what would eventually become *Paradise Lost*. Six of those Latin authors, all of whom Milton recommends in *Of Education*, made distinct contributions to the view of the Earth in *Paradise Lost*. Collectively, they provided Milton with precedents to authorize his distinctive personification.[7]

In the *Georgics* 4.147–48, Vergil challenged his poetic successors to complete what he had left undone: a versified description of the cultivation of gardens. Lucas Junius Columella (d. A.D. 70) takes up that challenge in book 10 of his *De Re Rustica*. In depicting a complete growing season of the Earth as mother or stepmother of all plants (10.94–214), Columella's poem anticipates Milton's representation of the Earth as nurturing Mother:

> Flagitat ecce suos genetrix mitissima fetus,
> Et quos enixa est partus iam quaerit alendos,
> Privignasque rogat proles. Date nunc sua matri
> Pignora, tempus adest; viridi redimite parentem
> Progenie, tu cinge comam, tu dissere crines.
>
> (10.161–65)

> Behold! Gentlest mother, Earth demands her young
> And longs to nurse the offspring she has borne
> And her step-children. To the mother give —
> The time is come — the pledges of her love;
> With her green progeny the parent crown,
> Bedeck her hair, in order to set her locks.
>
> (Loeb, 21)

Columella's inventive playfulness with the basic notion of Earth as Mother anticipates Milton's poetic elaboration of that image. Columella writes that the Earth may have stepchildren as well as children, a witty stroke comparable to Milton's doubling of womb images (7.276, 454). Columella's wit elicited the longest of Baptistus Pius's comments on Columella's garden poem, a comment found in annotated Renaissance collections of *De Re Rustica*. Essentially, the commentator explains, a stepmother Earth could account for transplanting.[8]

As a relative latecomer to Stoic theory concerning the Earth, Columella depended heavily in his garden poem upon the work of Stoic philosophers and natural historians. In book 2 of *De natura deorum*, Cicero adduced arguments from both Greek philosophy and physics to demonstrate that the Earth is sentient, animate, and rational. The logical argument derives from Zeno:

> "Nullius sensu carentis pars aliqua potest esse sentiens; mundi autem partes sentientes sunt; non igitur caret sensu mundus." Pergit idem et urget angustius: "Nihil," inquit "quod animi quodque rationis est expers, id generare ex se potest animantem conpotemque rationis; mundus autem generat animantis compotesque rationis; animans est igitur mundus composque rationis." (2.8.22)

> "Nothing devoid of sensation can have a part of itself that is sentient; but the world has parts that are sentient; therefore the world is not devoid of sensation." He [Zeno] also proceeds to press the argument more closely: "Nothing," he says, "that is inanimate and irrational can give birth to an animate and rational being; but the world gives birth to animate and rational beings; therefore the world is animate and rational." (Loeb, 145)

Milton's personified Earth is certainly depicted as animate; in its sympathetic response to the Fall it might reasonably be seen as exemplifying Zeno's proof. For present purposes, Cicero adds two crucial notions to Stoic theory of the Earth: its rationality and its hegemony over all of nature. The former we have found to be implicit in Milton's lines during the Fall. The latter is implicit in the syntax of Milton's personification: "Earth felt the Wound, and Nature from her seat/Sighing through all her Works gave signs of woe/That all was lost." Earth responds to the Fall first, then nature in general follows. Moreover, while the Earth acts or at least reacts, nature signifies. It may be, as Alastair Fowler suggests (484), quoting Romans 8.22 ("For we know that the whole creation groaneth and travaileth in pain together until now"), that nature here indicates all the woe that will happen in the future. Certainly Milton's verse is arranged so that whereas Earth reacts to the Fall, nature proclaims that dire event.

In the generation after Cicero and before Columella, that is, roughly contemporary with Jesus, Seneca developed Stoic thought about the Earth along anthropomorphic lines. In his *Natural Questions*, Seneca argues that the Earth has veins and arteries, much like the human body:

> Placet natura regi terram, et quidem ad nostrorum corporum exemplar, in quibus et venae sunt et arteriae, illae saguinis, hae spiritus receptacula. In terra quoque sunt alia itinera per quae aqua, alia per quae spiritus currit; adeoque ad similitudinem illa humanorum corporum natura formavit ut maiores quoque nostri aquarum appellaverint venas. (3.15.1–2)

> The idea appeals to me that the earth is governed by nature and is much like the system of our own bodies in which there are both veins (receptacles for blood) and arteries (receptacles for air). In the earth also there are some routes through which water runs, others through which air passes. And nature fashioned these routes so like human bodies that our ancestors even called them "veins" of waters.
>
> (my translation)

Seneca's notion that the Earth's "veins" are like those of human bodies may reduce to an ancient commonplace, as the nod to "our ancestors" suggests. Nonetheless, that basic comparison underlies Milton's depictions of the abusive digging into the Earth's "bowels" in book 1, as we have seen.

Seneca's comparison seems to have inspired Milton in another way as well. In addressing the dispute over the cause of earthquakes, Seneca relies on the analogy of the Earth as human body. He endorses the theory that the Earth possesses the breath of life:

> Etiamnunc dicendum est quo plerisque auctoribus placet et in quod fortasse fiet discessio. Non esse terram sine spiritu palam est, non tantum illo dico quo se tenet ac partes suid iungit, qui inest etiam saxis mortuisque corporibus, sed illo dico vitali et vegeto et alente omnia. hunc nisi haberet, quomodo tot arbustis spiritum infunderet non aliunde viventibus et tot satis? Quaemodum tam diversas radicas aliter atque aliter in se mersas foveret, quasdam summa receptas parte, quasdam altius tractas, nisi multum haberet animae tam multa tam varia generantis et haustu atque alimento qui educantis? (6.16.1)

> And now I must state a theory which many experts prefer and on which perhaps formal approval will be given. It is obvious that the Earth is not without air. I speak not only of the air by which it holds itself together and joins the parts of itself, which exists also in rocks and dead bodies, but also of that air which is vital and active, nourishing all things. Unless the Earth had this, how could the Earth infuse air into the many trees and plants which derive life from no other source? How could the Earth nurture the many different roots plunged into herself in various ways, some penetrating only the upper part of the Earth, others sunk deeper, unless the Earth had an abundance of the breath which generates so many and such varied growth and nourishes them with food and drink?
>
> (my translation)

Seneca's rhetorical questions not only support the fundamental Miltonic notion that the Earth is a living being, endowed with the breath of life, they also provide a physical explanation of what Milton describes as happening during the Fall. The Earth can feel a wound and "sigh" at the Fall, for the same reason that the Earth can nurture all things, that is, because the Earth's vital air or breath derives from divine inspiration during the act of creation. The author of the *De doctrina christiana* articulates the compatible view that the scriptural terms "Spirit of God" and "Holy Spirit" mean "particularly that divine breath or influence by which every thing is created and nourished" (YP 6:282). Seneca's organic account of the Earth's breath is perfectly consistent with Milton's insistence on the Spirit's material substance.

Completed in A.D. 77, Pliny's *Natural History* presents a view of the Earth which sums up many of the points gleaned thus far: the image of Earth as mother, the detailed anatomical analogy between the Earth and the human body, the underlying sense that the Earth is a living, breathing being:

> Sequitur terra, cui uni rerum naturae parium eximia propter meritia cognomen indidimus maternae venerationis. sic hominum illa ut caelum dei, quae nos nascentes excipit, natos alit, semelque editos sustinet semper, novissime conplexa gremio iam a reliqua natura abdicatos tum maxime ut mater operians, nullo nagis sacra merito quam quo nos quoque sacros facit, etiam monimenta ac titulos gerens nomenque prorogans nostrum et memoriam extendens contra brevitatem aevi, cuius numen ultimum iam nullis precamur irati grave, tamquam nesciamus hanc esse solam quae numquam irascatur homini. (2.63.154–55)

> Next comes the Earth, the one division of the natural world on which for its merits we have bestowed the venerable title of mother. She belongs to human beings as the sky belongs to God: she receives us at birth, she gives us nurture after birth, and when once brought forth she upholds us always, and at the last when we have finally been disinherited by the rest of nature she embraces us in her bosom and at that very time gives us her maternal shelter; sanctified by no service more than that whereby she makes us also sacred, even bearing our monuments and epitaphs and prolonging our name and extending our memory against the shortness of time; whose divinity is the last which in anger we invoke to lie heavy on those who are now no more, as though we did not know that she is the only element who is never wroth with man. (Loeb, 291)

The encyclopedic nature of Pliny's project explains the cumulative style of this and many other sections of *Natural History*. Pliny is far more concerned with inclusive coverage than with originality. Throughout Pliny's entry about the Earth, nonetheless, one feature stands out: the unique sympathy, figured as maternal care, on the part of the Earth toward humankind.

Logically, then, Pliny bristles with moral outrage over humankind's abuse of the Earth. Expanding Seneca's notion of the Earth's veins, Pliny particularly directs his anger at mining practices which invade the Earth's "entrails":

> penetramus in viscera auri argentique venas et aeris ac plumbi metalla fodientes, gemmas etiam et quosdam parvolos quaerimus lapides scrobibus in profundum actis, viscera eius extrahimus, ut digito gestetur gemma petitur. quot manus atteruntur ut unus niteat articulus! (2.63.158)

> We probe her entrails [*viscera*], digging into her veins of gold and silver and mines of copper and lead; we actually drive shafts down into the depth to search for gems and certain tiny stones; we drag out her entrails, we seek a jewel merely to be worn upon a finger! How many hands are worn away with toil so that a single knuckle may shine resplendent! (Loeb, 293)

Here Pliny mocks the perverse action of scraping away Mother Earth's entrails, and in the process scraping away the diggers' knuckles, all in order to adorn another human knuckle.[9] As we have seen, Milton shares Pliny's righteous indignation over humankind's perverse mistreatment of the beneficent Earth. Moreover, Milton's language that at the Fall "Earth trembled from her entrails" echoes this Plinian passage. Pliny's irony reappears in oxymoronic form in the Miltonic narrator's comment on gold as "precious bane": "Let none admire/That riches grow in Hell; that soil may best/Deserve the precious bane" (1.690–92). For Milton, humanity's abuse of the Earth is not merely perverse but ultimately self-destructive. Whereas the devils conclude the council in Pandaemonium peacefully, men, alone among rational creatures, "[y]et live in hatred, enmity, and strife/Among themselves, and levy cruel wars,/Wasting the Earth, each other to destroy" (2.500–02).

Epic Forbears and the Return to Mystery

Because Lucretius and Vergil shaped personifications of the Earth in their epics, Milton's poetic representation of the Earth in *Paradise Lost* seeks comparison with those epic precursors. While Milton's treatment of the Earth does indeed echo both Lucretius and Vergil, the manner of Milton's imitation is sharply corrective. Milton practices what Thomas Greene has termed "heuristic imitation." In this process, Greene writes, the later writer insists upon qualifying the true value of the precursor text (40–43). Milton emulates his epic precursors' accounts of the Earth in order to show that his poem refutes their mistaken arguments and overgoes their relatively inconsequential concerns. Phillips, possibly mimicking his uncle, called Lucretius an "egregious" poet. That epithet means "outstanding" in modern English, but its literal and punning meaning, "away from the herd," is also apt.[10] As the chief Roman exponent of Epicurean philosophy, Lucretius (99–55? B.C.) stands apart from the herd of Stoics with their assertion of a living, sacred Earth. In his didactic epic, *De rerum natura*, Lucretius aims to dispel all such superstitious views of the gods, which serve ultimately in his view to trouble and degrade humanity. As an antidote to *turpi religione*, or base superstition, Lucretius articulates his poetic exposition of the Epicurean theory of atoms underlying all things. That lesson in atomic physics is the tenor behind all Lucretian images. At the same time, Lucretius the poet depends to a great extent on fables, including fables about the Earth.

Such dependence amid denial occurs in his discussion of the Earth in book 2, lines 589–643. Lucretius repeatedly insists that the Earth deserves its honorific titles as *magna mater* (great mother) and *mater ferarum* (mother of wild beasts):

"quare magna deum mater materque ferarum/et nostri genetrix haec dicta est corporis una" (2.598–99) [Therefore she was called great mother of the gods, and mother of the wild beasts, and maker of our bodies, even she alone]. Further, Lucretius meticulously records the Phrygian rituals celebrating Mother Earth, including the armed group known as Curetes who escort the Great Mother, and thus prevent the curse of ancient legend: "ne Saturnus eum malis mandaret adeptus/aeternumque daret matri sub pectore volnus" (2.638–39) ["That Saturn, having caught him [Jupiter], might not compel him to torments and plant an everlasting wound in the mother's heart"]. Finally, however, Lucretius denies that such legends have any basis in truth — the truth, that is, of atomic physics:

> Quae bene et eximie quamvis disposta ferantur,
> longe sunt tamen a vera ratione repulsa.
> . . . .
> hic siquis mare Neptunum Ceremque vocare
> constituis fruges et Bacchi nomine abuti
> mavolt quam laticis proprium proferre vocamen,
> concedamus ut his terrarum dictitet orbem
> esse deum Matrem, dum vera re tamen ipse
> religione animum turpi contingere parcat.
> terra quidem vero caret omni tempore sensu,
> et quia multarum potitur primordia rerum,
> multa modis multis effert in lumina solis.
>
> (2.644–60)

But well and excellently as all this is set forth and told, yet it is far removed from true reasoning. . . .
Here if anyone decides to call the sea Neptune, and corn Ceres, and to misapply the name of Bacchus rather than to use the title that is proper to that liquor, let us grant him to dub the round world Mother of the Gods, while he forbears in reality himself to infect his mind with base superstition. The earth indeed lacks true sensation at all times, and only because it receives into itself the first beginnings of many things does it bring forth many in many ways into the sun's light. (Loeb, 145–47)

Essentially, as Bailey explains, Lucretius insists that the Earth is not only devoid of divinity but also of sense, for it is a collection of atoms working by their own laws.[11]

Now Milton's account of the Earth in *Paradise Lost* stands as a denial of Lucretius's denials. In short, Milton reasserts the personification and mythic legends of the Earth that Lucretius tried to debunk. Contra Lucretius, Milton's poem vigorously asserts three major points. First, the deity is concerned about and responsive to human troubles. Milton's dialogue in heaven is one sign of that concern; God's response to Adam and Eve's prayers at the end of book 10 is a sign of divine propitiation. Second, "Earth *felt* the Wound" (my emphasis). That is, the Earth indeed possesses the true power to sense spiritual truth, and to respond accordingly. By displaying the physical alterations to the Earth in book 10, Milton suggests that what we see in book 9 is likewise a physical affliction. In other words, at the Fall Milton's Earth registers both sympathy with human suffering and sentience of its own injury. Thus it possesses a double capacity for sensation, in opposition to Lucretius's philosophy. Third, "Earth felt the *Wound*" (my emphasis). Some kind of eternal injury, echoing Lucretius's rejected "aeternum volnus" from the Phrygian legend, actually befell the Earth. Thus, the ancient legend, however exaggerated, embodies an essential though dimly seen Judeo-Christian truth. This process, whereby scripture realizes pagan poetry and legend, is elsewhere evident in *Paradise Lost*, most notably whereby pagan accounts of a perfect paradise gesture toward the true Eden. For Milton, as Brooks and Hardy maintain, pagan myths "may *foreshadow* the final truth, but no more" (229).

Not surprisingly, it is the mightiest of Latin poets whom Milton most closely imitates in his treatment of the Earth. Of all the precedents we have examined, Vergil's moving portrayal of the Earth in book 4 of the *Aeneid* has the greatest affinities with Milton's account. The Earth appears at the pivotal moment when Aeneas and Dido have lost their fellows in the hunting party and together have reached the fatal cave:

> prima et Tellus et pronuba Iuno
> dant signum; fulsere ignes et conscius Aether
> conubiis, summoque ululae[r]unt vertice Nymphae.
> ille dies primus leti primusque malorum
> causa fuit.
>
> (4.166–70)

> Primal Earth and nuptial Juno give the sign; fires flashed, and Heaven was aware of their nuptials, and on the mountain-top screamed the Nymphs. That day was the first day of death, that first the cause of woes.
>
> (my translation)

The Earth appears as a sentient, sacred force, at a moment which is, like Milton's, described as the beginning of tragedy. Commenting on "dant signum," Servius the Grammarian noted that Earth and Juno give the sign "ut dei nuptiales," that is, as the proper nuptial deities (Servius, 2:493). In his edition of the *Aeneid*, R. D. Williams maintains that the goddesses conspire to produce "a parody of a wedding, a hallucination by which the unhappy Dido is deceived" (346). The role of Vergil's Tellus as a nuptial goddess in this context points to marital discord and deception, both of which carry over for Adam and Eve. It is perfectly fitting that Milton's Earth should be represented in the same manner as Vergil's "prima Tellus," that is, as the oldest of divinities celebrated among the Romans. All Milton's descriptions of the Earth as the original mother point that way. It is also perfectly appropriate that Milton should link the woeful, tragic drama of Adam and Eve's fall with the intimate personal losses Dido and Aeneas suffer. In both cases, too, the domestic tragedy points to global discord.

In contrast with Milton's refutation of Lucretius, however, Milton's emulation of Vergil takes the form of displacement. In his presentation of the Earth at the Fall, Milton quietly asserts that a much greater event than the Roman poet described has occurred. Granted, Vergil had brilliantly telescoped the international tragedy of Rome's wars with Carthage into the "cause of woes" ("causa malorum") stemming from Aeneas's affair with Dido. The signs of woe given by Milton's Earth and nature, however, far exceed Vergil's, and do so in two crucial ways. First, they signal, as Milton simply puts it, "That all was lost." To begin with, that loss refers to the immortal, innocent life Adam and Eve had previously enjoyed in paradise. At the same time, Adam and Eve, along with all their descendants, become mortal. In contrast, Vergil's orotund assertion that "ille dies primus leti" [That day was the first of death] makes sense only in a limited, rhetorical way. That day in the cave was indeed the beginning of Dido's, and by extension Carthage's, tragedy. On the other hand, the day of the Fall in Milton's narrative was literally "the first day of death" entering the world. Though lamentable, the suffering Vergil foresees is parochial by comparison.

Second, Milton's Earth signals a woeful shift in human possibility. Through the visions and dreams of the future in books 11 and 12, Milton shows Adam and Eve that their disobedience is the foundation of "all" human suffering to come, including worldwide warfare and generations of suffering for all humankind. Their descendants remain responsible for their actions, of course, but Adam and Eve's fall, as the angel explains, brings with it a deterioration in free will and right reason along with the doom of mortality. In short, the humanity of Adam and Eve's descendants is permanently damaged by their choice.

Overall, Milton's emulation of Vergil insists that forces beyond human beings are affected by the Fall. It might be seen as to Vergil's advantage that primal Earth and Juno *actively* signal a wedding, whereas Milton's Earth *reacts* in response to sin. Upon closer inspection, however, one sees the logic of Milton's variation. In the *Aeneid*, Earth and Juno conduct business as usual, for the elemental powers of nature and the gods are essentially unchanged by Dido's impending tragedy. On the contrary, Milton's description of a reactive, wounded Earth indicates that natural forces are themselves permanently damaged by the human fall. Mother Earth can only react in pain because of her human children's damaging action. The "wound" the Earth feels upon Eve's sin is at first unlocalized, but after Adam eats, Milton specifically locates it in the vital, creative part of Mother Earth, her womb: "Earth trembl'd from her entrails, as again/In pangs" (9.1000–01). In her anguished response to the Fall, the Earth shows the bitter consequences of the act. As a mother, the Earth is forced to repeat the painful process of labor, but this time without the joyful outcome of new life. Moreover, human sin damages the creative capacity of our "all-bearing Mother": hereafter, her offspring will be tainted with mortality. Despite Lucretius's denial, the ancient Earth remains alive in Milton's poem. She remains vital though wounded — if only to give evidence of sin's power to reverse, for an interim, divine creation.

Dissolving Borders

In discussing the "drift towards allegory" he saw in post-Vergilian poetry, C. S. Lewis adduced the "strange borderline position" that a notion such as "Nature" occupies in modern usage: "It is something more than a personification and less than a myth, and ready to be either or both as the stress of argument demands" (49). Unlike allegory, Lewis insists, such a figure does not point to some other frame of reference (history, theology, psychology) for its meaning; it is already significant in itself.

Milton's treatment of the Earth in *Paradise Lost* occupies just such a border zone. Out of the legendary and quasi-scientific accounts by Epicurean and Stoic writers, Milton crafted a story of the Earth that complements and extends the significance of the biblical Fall story. Cast in the traditional figure of the original mother, the Earth brings forth living creatures and sustains them by her continuing bounty. As a mother, Earth fits perfectly well with the elementary forces of fecundity celebrated by Columella and the natural historians. Just as Milton's angels are surprisingly material, so too is Milton's Earth. In her cosmic awareness and association with marriage, Milton's Earth closely resembles the goddess Tellus — whom Lucretius had shouted down and Vergil had regarded as luring Dido into a fatal union with Aeneas. Milton, however, rejects the Earth's role as the scheming goddess of epic machinery; his Earth is a living organism expressly obedient to God's will. All the while, Milton insists that the ancient Roman writers, with their moral and scientific concerns, had embodied an essential element of Judeo-Christian truth. What Milton preserves of the Stoic Earth in *Paradise Lost* is her fecundity, her sentience, and above all her capacity to signal a tragic change at once human and cosmic. Milton's depiction of the wounded Earth at the pivotal moment of his epic narrative argues that human beings and other living creatures are inescapably, if invisibly, united.

CONCLUSION

Regenerating Rome

Milton on Learning and Wisdom Yet Once More

In the ode *Ad Joannem Rousium*, dated 23 January 1646 but first printed in his 1673 *Poems*, Milton directly addresses one of his books. He had sent John Rouse a copy of his 1645 *Poems* along with 11 of his prose works; somehow the book was either lost or stolen (lines 14–15). When Rouse requested a replacement copy, Milton took the occasion to pen the ode to accompany it. Speaking directly to the lost volume, Milton tells it, despite its wandering, to rejoice ("Laetare felix") in its distinguished fate ("egregiam sortem"), for Rouse will place a new copy of the book in the Bodleian:

> Illic legeris inter alta nomina
> Authorum, Graiae simul et Latine
> Antiqua gentis lumina et verum decus.
>
> (70–72)

> There you shall be read among the lofty names of authors, the ancient lights and true glory of both the Greek and Roman peoples.
>
> (my translation)

A narrow reading might hold that being "read among" the great names means simply that Milton imagines his book on the same shelves as the ancients, somewhere between, say, Manilius and Ovid. This hope is patently appropriate to the 1645 volume, comprising as it does both English and Latin poems, with separate title pages and pagination ("gemina fronde") for each part. In this narrow sense, Milton's hope has been realized: The replacement volume remains in the Bodleian, and the manuscript of the ode remains where he placed it, between the English and Latin poems (Hughes, 146).

Milton's prophecy that his book shall be read among the Greek and Roman classics projects, I claim, a much bolder vision. In this vision, Milton's fondest hope for his 1645 poems is that they be read among the classics as the work of their newest peer. Just as Raphael painted himself conversing with Plato and his followers in the "The School of Athens," Milton imaginatively joins company with the great authors of classical antiquity through his book. His poetic conceit celebrates the ancient authors as at once national treasures, the true glory ("verum decus") of the Greek and Roman people, and as enduring exemplars of literary worth, the lofty names ("alta nomina") of living authors. Placing his own name among them, John Milton, Englishman, lays claim to both distinctions. For a belated English poet to be read among the ancients, however, involves a mixed blessing. While it means sharing in the glory of the ancients, it demands submission to their artistic canons. There is both celebration and anxiety, as Harold Bloom has taught us, in the encounter. "The poem," as the contemporary poet and Latin translator J. V. Cunningham writes, "is the trial."

To be read among the classics was, I maintain, Milton's

fondest hope for his major poems as well. This is especially the case for *Paradise Lost*. Unlike the 1645 volume, with its separate English and Latin sections, the conversation with the Romans occurs implicitly within Milton's diffuse epic. The previous chapters, explicating Milton's conversation with the Latin authors of the tutorial, have sifted and presented the evidence for this dialogue. Two related questions arise concerning the overall significance of Milton's engagement with his Latin mentors. First, how are we to take the alleged rejection of the Roman Empire — and of the pagan classics generally — in *Paradise Regained*? Second, what difference does a grasp of the Latin tutorial make to our understanding of Milton? Addressing these questions helps us assess the importance of Milton's engagement with the Roman authors on two fronts: the difference it makes for an interpretation of Milton's works, chiefly *Paradise Lost*, and the difference it makes to Milton's literary standing, his place among the lofty names of authors, ancient and modern.

Conquering Well, Governing Ill

Stella Revard has urged Miltonists to take seriously the denunciation of Rome that takes place in the fourth book of *Paradise Regained* ("Classical," 409). While she points out that it is the empire and not the republic that is being denounced and that it is not Milton but a literary character (albeit the Son) who makes the charge, these distinctions do not invalidate the denunciation, she concludes. They do, however, direct us to examine Milton's scene closely, to determine precisely what it is that is being rejected and why. Does the Son's denunciation of Rome imply a devaluation of Roman literature? Specifically, to what extent does the Son's rejection of certain parts of the Roman legacy diminish Milton's estimate of the Latin authors included in the tutorial?

We need, first of all, to see the Son's response to Satan within its immediate narrative context. Satan's offer of Rome to the Son is part of the so-called "temptation of the kingdoms" that stretches between the second and fourth books *of Paradise Regained*. Thus, Satan's presentation of Rome is explicitly political: "The City which thou seest no other deem/Than great and glorious *Rome*, Queen of the Earth/So far renown'd, and with the spoils enricht/Of Nations" (4.44–47). In response, the Son points out that the Roman Empire's apparent "grandeur and majestic show/Of luxury" are hollow, thus leaving him unmoved (4.109–11). Tales of rich Roman feasts, the fasting Son replies with delicious irony, "to me shoulds't tell who thirst/And hunger still" (120–21). Worst of all, the Romans, masters of others, are themselves not free:

> That people victor once, now vile and base,
> Deservedly made vassal, who once just,
> Frugal, and mild, and temperate, conquer'd well,
> But govern ill the Nations under yoke.
> . . . .
> What wise and valiant man would seek to free
> These thus degenerate, by themselves enslav'd,
> Or could of inward slaves make outward free?
>
> (4.132–45)

In asserting Milton's advocacy for the colonial imperative, Paul Stevens has cogently demonstrated that this "rejection" of Rome turns out to be highly ambiguous on several grounds. For one, the Son's critique of Tiberian Rome advances a traditional, humanist argument for restraint and civility. These are virtues that are well taught by the Romans themselves and their Renaissance heirs. For another, Jesus makes it clear that while the state of Rome has fallen into corruption, it actually *began* well: the Romans "who once just,/Frugal, and mild, and temperate, [had] *conquer'd well*" (Stevens's emphasis). "Thus presumably," Stevens argues, "for a state or people bound by the civil imperatives of justice, frugality, mildness, and temperance, it was still possible to conquer well"

("Colonial," 16). As it was Roman authors within Milton's tutorial, notably Cato, Varro, Lucretius, Pliny, and Manilius, together with Cicero and others who teach and exemplify these civic virtues, no rejection or diminution of their worth is indicated. Quite the contrary. Political power is inescapable; some will conquer, others will be conquered. This political lesson is as urgent in Restoration England as it was in Rome under Tiberius. Only those who practice self-rule can oppose the corruption of the current regime, Milton indicates. For those few, training in the art of civility is essential, and the old Romans, who still speak to readers in Milton's Restoration England and beyond, remain irreplaceable mentors.

Egyptian Gold

Granted that ancient Rome remains a positive political model for Milton at least as late in his career as *Paradise Regained* (1671), we still need to assess the difference the Latin tutorial makes to our understanding of Milton. Because England never achieved the reformers' hope articulated by Milton in *The Readie and Easie Way* (1660) to be "another Rome in the west," might not the recurrent allusions to the Roman classics exemplify Ralegh's critique of *Paradise Lost* as "a monument to dead ideas"? Even for readers who are willing to grant Milton his données, do the Roman authors do any essential and distinctive work in the epic? Does Milton's Romanizing finally amount to an irrelevancy, or, what is perhaps worse, a mere pedantic display, and thus an aspect that a finer aesthetic would have purged?

"Purged" recalls Aristotle's account of the emotional experience appropriate to tragedy. One recent appropriation of Aristotle's κάθαρσις argues that elements or discourses contrary to the dominant ideology espoused by a text exist to be purged. Certainly this use of Aristotle fits with the 21-year-old Milton's treatment of the pagan gods in his Nativity ode, in which Christ's fleshly incarnation routs the pagan deities. In response to Charles Diodati's question, Milton explains in Elegy 6 (December 1629):

> At tu si quid agam scitabere (si modo saltem
>   Esse putas tanti noscere siquid agam)
> Paciferum canimus caelesti semine regem,
>   Faustaque sacratis saecula pacta libris;
> Vagitumque Dei, et stabulantem paupere tecto
>   Qui suprema suo cum patre regna colit;
> Stelliparumque polum, modulantesque aethere turmas,
>   Et subito elisos ad sua fana Deos.
>   (lines 79–86)

> But if you will know what I am doing (if only you consider
>   it important to know whether I am doing anything)
> I am singing the Bringer of Peace, the King descended from heaven,
>   and the blessed times promised in the sacred books,
> the infant cries of our God, his stabling under a poor roof
>   who with his Father rules the heavenly kingdom,
> the star-studded sky and the hosts singing hymns in the air,
>   and the gods suddenly destroyed in their own shrines.
>   (my translation)

Without question, Christ at his birth triumphs over the pagan gods, as the elegy makes clear. In the Nativity ode itself, at the apotheosis of the infant Jesus, the pagan gods flee their temples. The routed are said to include, among others, the Roman household gods ("The *Lars*, and *Lemures*"), "mooned *Ashtaroth*," and "sullen Moloch."

Yet these very same gods appear again a generation later in *Paradise Lost*, a fact that suggests that their scattering in the Nativity ode reflected divine power over them but not their annihilation. Whereas the Christ child could silence and put to flight the pagan gods, the mature John Milton felt that he had good reasons, as a teacher and poet, to let them return and speak once more.

As an illustrative analogy, consider the approach to pagan learning taken by an early Christian apologist among the

Romans. The author of the *Confessions* surely understood the clash between pagan and Christian cultures. In Book 2, chapter 40 of his *De doctrina christiana*, Augustine of Hippo paused to answer a question that had plagued early Christian leaders, how best to deal with the writings of the learned non-Christians, particularly the Platonists. Whatever they have said that is true and useful, Augustine exhorts, we ought not to shrink from but put to our own better use. To illustrate, he elaborates upon the story, told in Exodus 3.21–22 and 12.35–36, of how the Israelites brought Egyptian gold and silver vessels with them when they escaped captivity:

> Situ enim Aegyptii non tantum idola habebant et onora gravia, quae populus Israhel detestaretur et fugeret, sed etiam uasa atque ornamenta de auro et argento et uestem, quae ille populus exiens de Aegypto sibi potius tamquam ad usum meliorem clanculo uindicauit, non auctoritate propria, sed praecepto dei ipsis Aegyptiis nescienter commodantibus ea, quibus non bene utebantur, sic doctrinae omnes gentilium non solum simulata et superstitiosa figmenta grauesque sarcinas supervacanei laboris habent, quae unusquisque nostrum duce Christo de societate gentilium exiens debet abonimari atque vitare, set etiam liberales disciplinas usui ueritatis aptiores et quaedam morum praecepta utilissima continent deque ipso uno deo colendo nonnulla vera inueniuntur apud eos, quod eorum tamquam aurum et argentum, quod non ipsi instituerunt, sed de quibusdam quasi metallis divinae prouidentiae, quae ubique infusa est, eruerunt et, quo peruerse atque iniuriose ad obsequia daemonum abutuntur. (2.40.60)

> For, as the Egyptians had not only idols and heavy burdens which the people of Israel hated and fled from, but also vessels and ornaments of gold and silver, as well as clothing, which the same people going out of Egypt put to their own better use, not doing this on their own authority but by the command of God — the Egyptians thus unknowingly providing them with things that they themselves were not putting to good use. In the same way, all branches of pagan learning have not only deceptive and superstitious illusions and heavy burdens of useless toil, which every one of us, when leaving the fellowship of

the heathen under Christ's leadership ought to abhor and avoid, but they also contain liberal instruction which is better adapted to the use of the truth, as well as extremely useful moral precepts. Even some truths reverencing the one true God are to be found among them. These are, so to speak, their gold and silver, which they did not fabricate themselves, but dug out as it were from the mines of divine providence which are everywhere scattered about, and which they have perversely and unlawfully abused in the service of the devils.

A cluster of images familiar to readers of Milton appear in this passage: escape from Egyptian bondage, gold implanted by divine Providence, liberal learning adaptable to the pursuit of truth, demonic prostitution of the divine. In Augustine's judgment, the value of the pagan material far outweighs any danger of contamination from it. David J. Bradshaw maintains that Augustine's image of Egyptian gold aptly describes Milton's cautious appropriation of Vergil in the conclusion of *Paradise Lost* (189–90). Selectively yet effectively, Milton carried the liberal learning of the Romans into his classical curriculum, and eventually into his poetry. In doing so, Milton literally creates a tradition, a handing across, in which the Latin authors serve new purposes within Milton's poetic narratives.

Undermining Mammon

What did Milton carry away from the Romans into his poetry that is unlike anything else? What gold vessels from their pages did he transmute within his? The scope of this conclusion allows us to revisit only one, but a seminal proof text. With the image of Egyptian gold in mind, one place surely worth revisiting is the mining operation led by Mammon in book 1 of *Paradise Lost*. Mammon's vision exemplifies the perversity and immorality Augustine excoriates, "for even in heaven," Milton points out, "his looks and thoughts/Were always downward bent" (1.680–81). Milton's approbation of the devil is patently clear. What is less apparent may be more revealing. In the following passage, Milton places his narrative describing Mammon in dialogue with several Roman texts, expressions, and ways of thought. What, one must wonder, is he up to?

> Mammon led them on,
> Mammon, the least erected Spirit that fell
> From Heav'n, for ev'n in Heav'n his looks and thoughts
> Were always downward bent, admiring more
> The riches of Heav'n's pavement, trodd'n Gold,
> Then aught divine or holy else enjoy'd
> In vision beatific: by him first
> Men also, and by his suggestion taught,
> Ransack'd the Center, and with impious hands
> Rifl'd the bowels of thir mother Earth
> For Treasures better hid. Soon had his crew
> Op'n'd into the hill a spacious wound
> And digged out ribs of gold. Let none admire
> That riches grow in Hell; that soil may best
> Deserve the precious bane. And here let those
> Who boast in mortal things, and wond'ring tell
> Of *Babel*, and the works of *Memphian* kings
> Learn how thir greatest Monuments of Fame,
> And Strength and Art are easily outdone
> By spirits reprobate.
>
> (1.678–92)

A small thing, on which larger things depend, is the Latinate syntactic looseness of "first," enabling it to refer both backward and forward. Backward: "By him first" men worked this wonder, which is to say that Mammon was the first to teach the doctrine of mining. Back further, to the opening proem, our "first disobedience" was proclaimed as the epic subject, moreover, the phrase "first taught" was applied to the exemplary teacher and leader Moses, "who first taught the chosen Seed" (8). Are we not to compare that teacher with this one? At the same time, the syntax points forward: "By him first" men were taught one dark art (mining), then the next (metallurgy), and so forth. This syntactic richness due to ambiguity is a staple feature of ancient Latin poetry, particularly of Lucretius, Ovid, and Vergil; by adapting this device to English poetry, Milton is expanding the syntactic resources of his mother tongue.

Editors of *Paradise Lost* have observed that Ovid, *Metamorphoses* 1.125–42, is the *locus classicus* for the commonplace that digging in the earth for human gain is evil. Certainly Milton's passage makes that point, in part by recalling Ovid's account of the historical and moral descent from the Golden Age to the Silver, then the Bronze, to the Iron, with which this passage deals. This is another way in which Milton places his narrative in dialogue with the Romans. Ovid's poetic linking of gold, iron, and earth, presented in high epic style, is moving:

> nec tantum segetes alimentaque debitaque dives
> poscebatur humus, set itum est in viscera terrae,
> quasque recondiderat Stygiisque admoverat umbris,
> effodiuntur opes, inritimenta malorum;
> iamque nocens ferrum ferroque nocentius aurum
> prodierat.
>
> (1.137–42)

> Not only did human beings demand of the rich fields the crops and sustenance they produced, but they delved as well into the entrails [*viscera*] of the Earth; and brought forth the wealth which the creator had hidden away and buried deep among the Stygian shades — wealth that incites men to crime. For now noxious iron had come, and gold more noxious even than iron.
>
> (my translation)

No one, to my knowledge, has credited Milton's witty variation on Ovidian wit here, in linking Mammon's perverse pursuit of gold with the Iron Age, the last and most degenerate of human epochs. Given Milton's insistence that Mammon "first" led men to mining, the allusion to the last of the ages in Ovid's account surely casts in doubt the goodness of *all* first things. Readers who recognize Milton's allusion to Ovid must sort out the various narrative strands that Milton has interwoven. The formal pattern of echo with reversal, in other words, seems designed not for its own sake but to lead the reader to evaluate the relative veracity of the various strands. In other words, Milton's allusion has the effect of inviting the reader to undertake hermeneutic and epistemological labor. Thus, Milton's multilayered narrative is designed not merely as a brilliant aesthetic composition but as a pragmatic means of cultivating virtue in the fit reader.

Yet Ovid is by no means the only Roman alluded to in the Mammon passage. With its sharp oxymoron ("precious bane") and admixture of wonder with condemnation, Milton's passage recalls other Latin texts dealing with the violation of the Earth, principally Pliny's *Natural History*, as I have argued in chapter 5. Pliny had summarized the Stoic view of the Earth as mother while presenting a detailed analogy between her body and that of a human mother. Pliny lashes out at the paradoxical folly of human miners violating the sacred, personified Earth:

> Ut tamen quae summa patitur atque extrema cute tolerabilia videantur, penetramus in viscera auri argentique venas ac plumbi metalla fodientes, gemmas etiam et quosdam pervolos quareimus lapides scrobibus in profundum actis, viscera eius extrahimus, ut digito gestetur gemma petitur. Quot manus atteruntur ut unus niteat articulus! (2.63.158)

> Yet in order to make the sufferings inflicted on her surface and mere outer skin seem endurable, we probe her entrails, digging shafts down into the depth to search for gems and certain tiny stones; we drag out her entrails, we seek a jewel merely to be worn upon a finger. How many fingers must be worn away so that a single knuckle may shine resplendent!

Pliny's anatomy of the Earth's entrails (*"viscera"*) violated by senseless mining provides an imaginative precedent for Milton's narrative. In particular, the clinical diction of the Roman's quasi-scientific account informs Milton's graphic description of mining as a sequence involving "[r]ifling the bowels of thir mother Earth" (687), opening a "wound" (689), and digging out golden "ribs" (690). Even the trenchant irony of Pliny's final sentence reappears in Milton's pejorative oxymoron for gold as "precious bane" (692). Perhaps most important, the devils' plunder of "ribs of Gold" is a perverse echo of the Yahwistic account of Eve's creation out of Adam's rib. Indeed, the account Adam gives Raphael of Eve's creation from his side recapitulates the story of Mammon's mining:

> methought I saw
> Though sleeping, where I lay, and saw the shape
> Still glorious before whom awake I stood,
> Who stooping *open'd* my left side, and took
> From thence a *rib*, with cordial spirits warm,
> And life-blood streaming fresh, wide was the *wound*,
> But suddenly with flesh filled up and healed.
> (8.462–68; my italics)

Fowler calls this a "sensitive" echo of the Mammon episode, and justifies its appropriateness by arguing for the congruity between Eve's role as universal mother and the epithet phrase "Mother Earth" (83). The Roman material serves a crucial role in negotiating between these passages. It helps readers distinguish between the self-serving, senseless desecration of the Earth that Pliny describes and the compassionate, providential creativity using Adam's rib that Milton associates with God. The Mammon episode, in other words, inaugurates a pattern that Milton's epic narrative will go on to complete. When, crucially, at the moment of Eve's fall in book 9, we hear that "Earth felt the wound" (9.782), the Mammon episode has well prepared readers for the long descent into the history of humankind's selfish and destructive environmental choices, with irreparable damage to our innocent mother Earth.

The passage describing Mammon's mining unfolds three specific moments of teaching: the human mimicry of Mammon's destructive mining, "by his example taught" (685); the narrator's interruption of the narrative, urging readers to cease admiration for gold (690–91); and a summary directive admonishing "those/Who boast in mortal things" to "learn" to see how even the greatest human achievements are passing things, "easily outdone/By spirits reprobate" (695–97). In brief, readers are offered a choice of lessons: the perverse destructiveness exemplified by Mammon, or the radical humility — etymologically rooted in Latin *humus*, the earth — that the narrator urges. With its recurrent emphasis on education in humility, Milton's poetic episode rehearses the daily practice of Milton's Latin tutorial no less than its pedagogical aims. One particular stylistic link with Latin epic poetry deserves mention. The unusual presence of an epic narrator who interrupts the narrative to offer corrective commentary has a clear precedent in Marcus Manilius's *Astronomica*. Manilius in particular adopts the unusual device of the second person negative imperative to keep readers on track. For example, "But the principle of the Earth's suspension should cause you no surprise" ["Nec vero admiranda tibi natura videri pendentis terrae debet"] (1.194–95). Frequent deployment of this device makes sense on several counts: the didactic nature of Manilius's task overall; his attempt to win converts to his belief that the stars control human destiny; the technical dimension of his subject, requiring focused mental attention. Milton's urgency to convey his instructive narrative demands no less attention. Surely Milton would not hesitate to use in his epic a teaching device well deployed by Manilius. In *Milton Unbound* John Rumrich urges Miltonists to reconsider the dominant critical picture of the sharply corrective, deceptive poet posited by Stanley Fish who lays traps for the reader to stumble into error (32–36). No doubt Fish's account is in several ways overstated: Not every reader of *Paradise Lost* feels harassed and humiliated by the Miltonic narrator's control. The portrait of Milton gleaned from the Latin tutorial supports not so much an entrapping teacher as a delightfully entangling one, as Fish elsewhere observes. At the same time, my study reasserts the central place of effective teaching within Milton's vision of poetry.

In the ensuing description of the building of Pandaemonium, Milton goes on to allude to yet another text from the Latin tutorial, Vitruvius's *De architectura*. The allusion to Vitruvius is signaled by an unusual epic simile, comparing the means of filling "each hollow nook" within the subterranean foundation of Pandaemonium with a pipe organ: "As in an Organ from one blast of wind/To many a row of Pipes the soundboard breathes" (708–09). Milton's simile is transitional, or like the adverb "first," Janus-faced: it refers equally well to the distribution of the molten ore comprising Pandemonium's foundation described previously (700–07) as to following account of the structure's harmonious rising "with the sound/ Of dulcet Symphonies and voices sweet" (711–12). In book 5 of *De architectura*, Vitruvius had adopted virtually the same image, using the notion of an organ's sounding board to argue that ancient architects carefully designed the acoustics of public theatres. Like Milton, Vitruvius uses the simile transitionally, between one section on choosing the ideal building site and another on maximizing a theater's sound qualities:

> Uti enim organa in aeneis laminis aut corneis echeis ad chordarum sonitum claritatem perficiuntur, sic theatrorum per harmonicen ad augendam vocem ratiocinationes ab antiquis sunt constitutae. (5.3.8)

> For just as organs which have bronze plates or horn sounding boards can be tuned to the clear sound of strings, so by designing theatres in accordance with the science of acoustics the ancients augmented the actor's voice.

Milton and Vitruvius share a vision that all arts and sciences are related. Indeed, Vitruvius's book opens with an inspiring, if demanding, sketch of the ideal architect:

> Et ut litteratus sit, peritus graphidos, eruditus geometria, historias complures noverit, philosophos diligenter audierit, musicam

> scierit, medicinae non sit ignarus, responsa iuris- consultorum noveret, astrologiam caelique rationes cognitas habeat. (1.1.3)
>
> He or she should be highly literate, skilful at drafting, learned in geometry, familiar with history, a diligent student of philosophy, musically knowledgeable, not ignorant of medicine, aware of the legal precedents, familiar with astrology and the rational study of the heavens.

This Vitruvian ideal would accurately describe a student who had completed with distinction Milton's Latin tutorial. When one holds Pandaemonium up to this ideal, however, the faults begin to show. Rather than being attuned to celebrate the human voice, Pandemonium is said to rise "like an Exhalation" (711), in an apparent parody of divine creation by inspiration. By applying Vitruvius's simile to the hollow foundation of Pandaemonium, Milton implies that the magnificent edifice that the devils build is erected on a hollow foundation. Nonetheless, Pandaemonium remains impressive, even humbling to human architects. The enduring vision of Vitruvius, whose principles also gave rise to the magnificent church designs of Leonardo da Vinci, is a fit medium for the impressive if misdirected ambition Pandaemonium embodies.

Milton's methods and motives for conversing with the Romans have by this point been well established. The Roman authors teach readers — in a lapidary yet richly ambiguous style laden with recognized authority in Milton's day — to be wary of the ends their inventions serve, and mindful of the ethical implications of every human activity. Masters of technical achievement, the Romans were also masters of themselves — or they were, as the Son reminds Satan in *Paradise Regained*, until their own moral failings eroded their self-government, their moral authority, and their imperial ambition. So with the talented yet misguided builder of Pandaemonium: "nor did he scape/By all his Engines, but was headlong sent/With his industrious crew to build in hell" (749–51).

Civilizing Labor

When Milton considers in his prose works the effect of reading books of all kinds, he insists upon the hermeneutic discrimination — and ultimately the ethical cultivation — that occur in the process. In *Areopagitica,* Milton addresses the question "whether be more the benefit, or the harm that thence proceeds" from reading books, "what ever sort they be." His answer comes in a familiar passage:

> Good and evil we know in the field of this World grow up together almost inseparably; and the knowledge of good is so involv'd and interwoven with the knowledge of evill, and in so many cunning resemblances hardly to be discern'd, that those confused seeds which were impos'd on *Psyche* as an incessant labour to cull out, and sort asunder, were not more intermixt. It was from out the rinde of one apple tasted, that the knowledge of good and evill as two twins cleaving together leapt forth into the World. And perhaps this is that doom which *Adam* fell into of knowing good and evill, that is to say of knowing good by evil. As therefore the state of man now is; what wisdome can there be to choose, what continence to forbeare without the knowledge of evill? . . . Since therefore the knowledge and survay of vice is in this world so necessary to the constituting of human vertue, and the scanning of error to the confirmation of truth, how can we more safely, and with lesse danger scout into the regions of sin and falsity then by reading all manner of tractats, and hearing all manner of reason? And this is the benefit which may be had of books promiscuously read. (YP 2:514)

Here Milton's distinctive blending of the Hebraic story of Adam's fall with the Latin narrative by Apuleius, the Romanized African, embodies the "promiscuous" reading he advocates. More than that, the allusion to Psyche's "*incessant labour*" (my italics) in Milton's passage is revealing. In *The Golden Ass* of Apuleius, Venus gives her daughter-in-law Psyche the task of separating a heap of grains into their various kinds before she returns at dusk (134); even then, helpful ants help her complete the work. In other words, Milton makes of this temporary punishment given to the mythic figure an unending duty — but a beneficial, humanizing one as well — for Adam's sons and daughters. Our constant labor in sorting out good from evil, Milton argues, is at least as difficult as Psyche's temporary curse: "those confused seeds... were not more intermixt." Greater, too, is our reward: nothing less than the "constituting of human vertue" and the "confirmation of truth."

This argument, in which Milton makes the epistemological "doom" of fallen readers the ground of human virtue, is writ large within the epic *Paradise Lost*. In that single work we encounter Milton's promiscuous reading on a prodigious range of subjects, and in sorting among these many seeds we are set on our own hermeneutic labor. The poem's mixture of darkness and light aims to do for the reader what it does for its blind poet: "what in me is dark/Illumine; what is low, raise and support" (1.22–23). Just as the surveying of vice was seen as necessary to the cultivation of the reader's virtue in *Areopagitica*, in *Paradise Lost* Milton's encounter with the unregenerate yet civic-minded Romans has the power to cultivate personal and public virtues, as the autobiographical digression of *The Reason of Church Government* claims: "These abilities... are of power beside the office of a pulpit, to imbreed and cherish in a great people the seeds of vertu, and publick civility, to allay the perturbations of the mind, and set the affections in right tune, to celebrate in glorious and lofty Hymns the throne and equipage of Gods Almightinesse" (YP 1:816–17). Here the seed image, appropriate both to the implanting of virtue and to the "fruit of that forbidden tree," recurs. With its rich biblical and agricultural associations, the image is brilliantly fused with Milton's Republican values: "the seeds of vertu, and publick civility." As Milton turns from the reader's competence to the poet's, the careful tending of those seeds — drawing out their personal and political potential — becomes the focus of his civilizing labor.

Yet Milton's epic poetry aims not only to "imbreed and cherish" vertue, but in its metrical and generic choices to exemplify it. As Milton's headnote on "The Verse" appended to the second edition of *Paradise Lost* claims, the abandonment of rhyme "is to be esteem'd an example set, the first in *English*, of ancient liberty recover'd to Heroic Poem from the troublesome and modern bondage of Riming" (Hughes, 210). Such liberty, at once artistic and political, Milton credits to his imitation of ancient exemplars in their own tongues: "Homer in Greek and of Virgil in Latin." The liberation is unthinkable without the precedent set by the ancient poets. In his final personal utterance within his epic, the proem to book 9, Milton asserts that his epic argument is superior to those of his ancient precursors. It is so, Milton insists, precisely because the interiorized virtues, as much Stoic as Christian — "the better fortitude/Of Patience and Heroic Martyrdom" — that his poetry inculcates surpass the martial virtues and emotional excesses Homer and Vergil described:

>   the wrath
> Of stern *Achilles* on his Foe pursu'd
> Thrice Fugitive about Troy Wall; or rage
> Of Turnus for Lavinia disespous'd,
> Or Neptune's or Juno's, that so long
> Perplex'd the Greek and Cytherea's Son.
>   (9.14–19)

In his classroom teaching, as we have seen, Milton avoided teaching works based upon martial exploits, preferring instead texts exploring subjects from agriculture to physics and astrology. Inspired by ancient exemplars including Lucretius and Manilius, Milton never abandoned his vision of the teaching power of the poet. He articulates that power in *The Reason of Church Government*: "Teaching over the whole book of sanctity and vertu through all the instances of example with such delight to those especially of soft and delicious temper as will not so much as look upon Truth herselfe, unlesse they see her elegantly drest" (YP 1:817–18). Milton's "delicious" phrasing adds a further measure of delight to Lucretius's famous simile of poetry as a honeyed cup delivering healthful but initially bitter doctrine to an unsuspecting patient, who gulps down useful medicine with the sweet potion (*De rerum natura* 4.11–25). Milton's conversation with the Latin authors of the tutorial, overflowing within his epic poetry, certainly serves the end of delightful teaching.

APPENDIX

Overview of the Texts in the Latin Curriculum

The agricultural works of Cato, Varro, Columella, and Palladius were frequently published together in Renaissance compendia; hence Phillips's collective designation of those authors as the "four grand authors *De Re Rustica.*" In concise yet comprehensive fashion, Cato sets out in his little book to explain how to design, outfit, and manage a farm. Expanding upon the base provided by Cato, Varro devotes the three sections of his work on rustic matters to agriculture, animal husbandry, and management of a villa. Along with practical advice about farming, Varro, who also wrote a treatise on the origin and development of the Latin language, offers observations of an archaeological or historical kind. For example, tilling the earth is not only more ancient but also nobler than commerce and manufacturing, he claims. Varro repeatedly contrasts the piety and useful nature of farm life, celebrated by the most ancient authorities, with the greed and corruption surrounding him in Augustan Rome. With ten books on rustic matters, Columella greatly increases the detail and coverage provided by his precursors. Several of those details reemerge at pivotal moments of Milton's epic, including the transplanting of the flower amaranth in the dialogue in heaven; and the harvesting of grain in the "careful Ploughman" simile in book 4. Most important for Latin literature and for Milton, Columella, after nine books of prose, took a dramatic new approach in his tenth book. Taking up Vergil's challenge to his literary heirs in the *Georgics*, Columella composed his final book on the cultivation of gardens in dactyllic hexameter verse, the metrical form of the epic. The creation of a Garden poem raised to epic status is itself a high achievement and one of obvious but neglected importance for Milton. Beyond that general concept, key details of Columella's poem hold particular relevance for Milton. Milton's panegyric of the productive Earth during the Creation account in *Paradise Lost* alludes to Columella's elaborate description (10.140–230) of the Earth as mother or stepmother of all plants, beginning with her impregnation and concluding, as does Milton, with parturition. Writing in the fourth century, Palladius cast his book on agriculture in the form of a calendar or farmer's almanac. Such an arrangement has practical value, of course, describing the appropriate tasks farmers must do throughout the year. For poets including Spenser and Milton, the calendar format also serves as a way of perceiving and organizing time, of relating human labor to cosmological order.

Phillips's next work, the *De medicina* of Cornelius Celsus, is an invaluable distillation of Greek and Roman medical practice. Celsus's eight books on medicine comprised but one part of an encyclopedia of knowledge, of which only fragments survive. In his opening remarks, Celsus creates a link between agriculture and medicine: "Ut alimenta sanis corporibus agricultura, sic sanitatem aegris Medicina promittit" [Just as agriculture promises nourishment for healthy bodies, Medicine promises health to the sick]. Following Hippocrates, Celsus divides the art of medicine into three parts: dietetics, pharmacology, and surgery. Throughout his text, Celsus strikes a tone of concern for patients as much as for the medical profession. In his first book, Celsus argues that dissection of human cadavers is useful and humane, while he vigorously condemns experimentation on living bodies. An observant practitioner should learn about interior organs when chance presents them to view (40–43, 74), he maintains. That argument reappears centrally in *Paradise Lost* during Milton's account of heavenly warfare; we learn about angelic biology when the combatants are wounded. After the Fall, Celsus's *De medicina* contributes most prominently to a chilling scene in a "Lazar house," or leper colony, in which Adam confronts an array of ghastly diseases, all in Milton's phrase "inductive to his sin."

Filling 30 Roman books, Pliny the Elder's *Natural History* is the longest work on Milton's syllabus. Pliny describes it as an encyclopedia in the Greek sense, that is, as a comprehensive round of studies essential to a student's education. While Phillips's remark that the tutorial covered "a great part" of Pliny's work leaves open precisely what of Pliny Milton taught, the *Natural History* certainly stands at the center of Milton's tutorial. Reading Pliny's compilation in its entirety, sequentially, would be wearying to say the least; fortunately, Pliny provides a useful table of contents that fills the entire first book. The beginning of Pliny's history proper provides a significant link with Milton's encyclopedic epic: a description of the "Mundus," or the Earth as our point of perspective on the cosmos. Continuing from that auspicious beginning, Pliny discusses various aspects of the natural world. Beyond its wealth of detailed observations, what makes reading his work fascinating and rewarding are the frequent flashes of feeling and insight that show its author's humane spirit. In discussing mining in book 2, for example, Pliny deplores the waste of human potential along with the damage to the Earth mining entails. Milton incorporates this notion into *Paradise Lost* by ascribing the invention of mining to the demon Mammon, by whose suggestion, Milton asserts "men also . . . [r]ifl'd the bowels of thir mother Earth/For Treasures better hid" (1.685–88).

The *De architectura* of Vitruvius both explains and celebrates the architectural marvels of the ancient world. Vitruvius held an official post in Augustus's campaign to rebuild Rome (Granger, xiv); not surprisingly, the architect's ten books contain a wealth of practical details about building materials and methods. At the same time, Vitruvius often pauses, in the manner of a master builder on site, to offer theoretical observations about his art. The principle of single-point perspective perfected by Renaissance designers derives from one such Vitruvian observation; so does the putatively Renaissance concept of designing buildings according to geometric figures coinciding with the human body. Like Celsus, Vitruvius interweaves connections among various fields of knowledge. In the design of amphitheaters, he maintains that the best acoustics result from logarithms based on musical fifths. Several Vitruvian principles appear early in *Paradise Lost*, when the devils build their temple of self-worship, Pandaemonium. Designed according to harmonic proportions, Pandaemonium arises to the sound of a pipe organ, in an epic simile emulating a like simile in Vitruvius. Moreover, throughout *Paradise Lost* the Miltonic narrator's comments on Edenic and fallen societies frequently reflect Vitruvian sentiments. Sir Henry Wotton, who supplied Milton with a letter of introduction for his continental travels of 1638, perhaps showed Milton the way by paraphrasing Vitruvius in his *Elements of Architecture*. Given Milton's aim of "justifying God's ways," the appeal of Vitruvius's manual would be heightened by its unorthodox combination of a scientific temper with a rational respect for the numinous (Granger, xiv).

Early printed versions of Vitruvius frequently include the writings of the engineer Sextus Julius Frontinus. Milton may have moved in his tutorial from Vitruvius to Frontinus for that textual reason. Known chiefly for his description of the imperial system of aqueducts, Frontinus served both as consul and provincial governor of Britain in the late first century. The edition of Frontinus by Scriverius (Leyden, 1607), the first printed text to unite Frontinus's works in a single volume, contains not only *De aquis* but the work Phillips mentions, four books on military science entitled *Stratagemata*. The *Stratagemata* relates a variety of successful battle plans and tactical maneuvers, many derived from Frontinus's own experience. In the preface, Frontinus expresses his hope that his work might furnish commanders with specimens of wisdom and foresight (*providentiae*) enabling them to conceive and execute successful stratagems. What makes Frontinus fascinating for nonspecialists is his attention to the psychological aspects of warfare, to factors including how a general motivates his troops and takes advantage of surprise. With Milton's aims in mind, Frontinus's work is most relevant to the war in heaven in *Paradise Lost*. During that campaign, Satan follows to the letter Frontinus's advice about concealing one's battle plans and arousing a weaker unit's spirits for battle. At the same time, God the Father in Milton's epic enjoys the strategic advantages of "eternal providence" and a kind of force, in the Son, that his enemies grossly underestimate.

Lucretius's *De rerum natura* is at once the most familiar and the most challenging of all the texts in Milton's tutorial. The title translates *Peri physeos*, the lost masterwork of Epicurus, and thereby indicates Lucretius's commitment to Epicureanism. The *De rerum natura* divides into three units or groups of two books each. A summary can give only the most superficial sense of Lucretius's subtle and powerful epic argument. Following the epic convention of invoking the muse, the poem opens with an invocation to Venus, which both celebrates the potency of natural generation and begins Lucretius's attack on superstitious beliefs in celestial gods. The first unit also attacks the doctrines of other natural philosophers including Heraclitus, Empedocles, and Anaxagoras. Book 2 contains Lucretius's distinctive contribution to atomic physics: the notion of the *clinamen*, the unexpected swerve atoms take on their paths that accounts for free will. Books 3 and 4 expound atomic anthropology. Like Milton, Lucretius argues that both body and soul are material, and that therefore the soul dies with the body. This central unit also introduces the theory of *simulacra*, thin membranes of atoms which create sense impressions, and Lucretius's treatment of love as a phantasm based solely on physical attraction. In the final section Lucretius extends his argument to cosmology. Again, eschewing mythology and superstition, he offers strictly physical explanations for phenomena including stellar movement, earthquakes, and plagues.

The *Astronomica* of Marcus Manilius, too, is remarkable for blending the practical business of astrology with theoretical reflections on spiritual and intellectual affairs in a new form of epic. Whereas other astronomical texts available to Milton, for example, William Lilly's *Christian Astrology*, were devoted almost exclusively to star charts and horoscopes, Manilius's text discusses fundamental philosophical and spiritual issues relevant to *Paradise Lost*. In Eden before the Fall, Milton describes the "benign" influence of the stars upon Adam and Eve's actions. How, one wonders, can stellar influence work without coopting human freedom or divine foreknowledge — two fundamental principles of Milton's theodicy? In the first of the five books of his didactic epic, the *Astronomica*, Manilius describes the awakening of the human intellect brought about by speculation about the heavens. Moreover, he repeatedly points out the order and immutability of celestial motions, despite their apparent randomness. As Matt Neuberg has argued, Manilius ambiguously addresses Caesar in his poem in order to develop a paradox central to the work: Caesar as the ideal ruler controls events in such a way as to give citizens of the republic maximum freedom. This paradox of freedom within the strict bounds of control applies equally well to the control of human liberty by an all-knowing God in Milton's poem. The didactic approach adopted by Manilius, who employs an unprecedented use of the second person singular form of address, enables the epic bard to counter readers' mistaken assumptions about fate and destiny. Manilius concludes the *Astronomica* by describing the stars as forming a celestial city or commonwealth, an analogy underlying Milton's portrayal of politics in the post-fallen world in his epic's conclusion.

NOTES

Introduction

1. Phillips continues by listing several Greek authors and scriptural books, in the original languages, along with French and Italian texts, through which Milton led his students. Among the scholarship dealing with Milton's reading and teaching of Greek literature, I have found the following especially useful: Allen, *Mysteriously Meant*; Bush; Greene; Lewalski, *Rhetoric of Literary Forms*; Low; Parker; Patrides; Radzinowicz, *Toward "Samson Agonistes"*; Revard, *Tangles of Neaera's Hair*; Shuger. On how Milton read Greek texts, Mulder and Patterson are especially illuminating. Budick, Fish, Haskin, Lieb, and Radzinowicz, *Book of Psalms*, along with Schwartz, Shawcross, *Self and the World*, and Wittreich, have informed me about Milton's distinctive ways of reading scripture. For biographical accounts of the tutorial, see Parker, 1:186, 192–94, 248–49; French, 2:6–10; and Masson, 3:253–54. Unless otherwise indicated, all references to Milton's poetry are to Hughes, while all references to Milton's prose are to YP.

2. Ernest Sirluck, editor of the Yale edition of the tract *Of Education*, introduced the view that "Milton's conception of a good educational system was fundamentally opposed to that of Comenius" (YP 2:186ff). With Timothy Raylor ("New Light"), I find little evidence for that alleged opposition. Milton's alleged slight of Comenius's *"Januas and Didactics"* reads more like a confession of Milton's hesitance to speak authoritatively on the Comenian corpus than an insult to Hartlib or his circle. Moreover, Milton and Hartlib remained in friendly communication until the later 1650s (Stocker and Raylor).

3. For the view that Milton's phrase "subsequent or indeed precedent" raises the question of "whether the laws of discourse are immanent in the particular examples from which they are induced, or logical in the Platonic and Thomistic sense of being prior to, and enabling of,

176

discourse as such," see Marshall Grossman, "Milton and the Rhetoric of Prophecy," in CC, 168–69; and Grossman, "*Authors to Themselves.*"

4. See DuRocher 36–37.

5. While noting some important differences in approach, Conte associates his emphasis on literary systems with the work of the Tel Quel group, especially that of Julia Kristeva, with Gerard Genette's *Palimpsestes* (Paris, 1982), and with the rhetorical view of allusion advanced by Michael Riffaterre in "Syllepsis," *Critical Inquiry* 6 (1980): 625–38.

6. See Jerry Weinberger's discussion of *vincitur* in his edition of *New Atlantis and The Great Instauration*, 21, note 40. While using Spedding's translation of *vincitur* as "command" in his text, Weinberger argues in his note that "conquer" is a more accurate translation.

Chapter One. Conning the Creature

1. Beginning with William B. Hunter's essay, "The Provenance of the *Christian Doctrine*," Milton scholarship has witnessed a lively debate over the authorship of *De doctrina christiana*. Proving or disproving Milton's authorship of the theological compendium lies beyond the scope of my present argument. My working assumption is that the tract is "Miltonic," in that it is generally — though not entirely — compatible with John Milton's ideas and expressions in his canonical works. The possibility of multiple authorship of the compendium, with contributions by Milton along with an amanuensis or student, best accounts in my view for the work's inconsistencies yet overall Miltonic tenor. See further Hunter's most recently published conclusions about the issue in "*Visitation Unimplor'd*," 146, 156.

2. D. C. Allen's magisterial historical sketch in *The Legend of Noah* remains unsurpassed in tracing the variety of attempts, from Scotus to Boyle, to reconcile faith and science. In "Milton and the Beasts of the Field," Frank Manley posits that Milton "realized the limits of reason" (403) in attempting to reconcile science and religion. I strongly disagree, however, with Manley's characterization of Milton's attitude as that of "a seriously disturbed student," unable to resolve intellectually the putatively competing truths of science and faith.

For valuable scholarship on Milton's use of the new science, particularly on post-Copernican astronomy, see in particular the essays by Grant McColley, Judith Scherer Herz, Donald Friedman, and Harinder Singh Marjara. Marjara presents an especially insightful discussion of the use of analogy, by both Milton and Renaissance scientists, in describing natural phenomena (*Contemplation of Created Things*, 31–37). Galileo, it has often been observed, is the only contemporary of Milton's who appears in *Paradise Lost*. Yet Marjara admits that Milton rejects heliocentrism, the central tenet of the new astronomers. Marjara's thesis is that

Milton strategically adopts whatever paradigm for understanding Creation best fits his aims in a particular episode. This approach shrewdly applies Thomas Kuhn's terminology to the epistemological shifts in scientific systems during Milton's day (*Structure*, 10–22).

The most recent study of Milton and the new science, Karen Edwards's *Milton and the Natural World*, argues that Milton's representation of nature in *Paradise Lost* is "experimental" in a double sense: "It is based on Milton's devotional practice, his 'experimental' reading of the Bible; and this practice, applied to the natural world (God's 'other scripture'), is parallel to and cognizant of the scientifically experimental rendering of the natural world evident in the style of Browne, Boyle, and other new philosophers" (17). For Edwards, this experimentalism is reflected in the "ceaseless interpretive activity" that she sees demanded by Milton's style. Edwards is particularly concerned to dispute the findings of Kester Svendsen, who after weighing the scientific allusions in the epic concludes that it is "the old science which looms largest in Milton's thought" (*Milton and Science*, 7). Edwards's insistence on placing Milton in the vanguard of his experimental contemporaries, however, has some unfortunate side effects. One of these is her unsubstantiated claim that Milton treats the old science as boring and unreliable, the new, fascinating and sound: "The old science is invariably invoked for the less interesting, and less demanding, interpretive option. Its presence in the poem is often marked by sly humor; its inclusion carried out in such a way as to incorporate an acknowledgement of its unreliability. At the same time, the poem consistently makes available new representational possibilities suggested by the experimental philosophy, and it does so with excitement, wit, and creative relish" (10). On the contrary, one of Milton's astonishing achievements in *Paradise Lost* is his ability to assimilate a prodigious range of materials to his argument. As Samuel Johnson observed of the epic: "Here is a full display of the united force of study and genius; of a great accumulation of materials, with judgment to digest and fancy to combine them: Milton was able to select from nature or from story, from ancient fable or from modern science, whatever could illustrate or adorn his thoughts" (438). Roy Flannagan cogently reasserts Svendsen's emphasis on the conservative cast of Milton's science: "The science of *Paradise Lost* is not innovative" (325). My study, however, is not a contest for preeminence among Milton's source materials. Rather than seeking to distinguish old from new science in Milton's poetry, or to discount one or the other, I aim to document the blended, eclectic epistemological outlook contained in his poetry. The Latin authors of the tutorial vitally contribute to that outlook.

3. In a thorough and valuable discussion, Haskin traces the interpretive history of Psalm 19 through Jewish, early Christian, and Reformation commentators in order to explain how the heavens were understood to "declare" God's glory (202–16). Haskin concludes that

Milton's narration of Adam's inquiry amounts to a "depiction of a physical world that does not 'declare' clearly and simply in plain language all that the first parents desire to know about the divine 'Author'" (204). Perhaps Haskin's concluding qualifiers limit his claim about what he calls the silence of creation in Milton's account. While the creatures do not literally declare God's presence, they nevertheless prompt Adam to conclude a great deal about their powerful and beneficent Creator.

4. The discussions of Milton's serpent lore that I have examined are the following: Frank Manley, "Milton and the Beasts of the Field"; John M. Steadman, "Sin, Echidna, and the Viper's Brood"; Mother Mary Christopher, O.S.U., "'O Foul Descent!'," which points out that Satan's reluctance to assume the lower corporeal form of the serpent directly contrasts the Son's willingness to assume human form to redeem our race; Leslie Brisman, "Serpent Error," which refers to Newton's suggestion that Pliny's description of snakes shedding their skins underlies Milton's simile "as the snake with youthful Coat repaid"; Lawrence W. Hyman, "A Note on Satan as Serpent"; David S. Berkeley, "Dalila as Amphisbaena"; King-Kok Cheung, "Beauty and the Beast," which draws upon Peter Comestor's commentary on Genesis to argue that the serpent that Satan chose for the temptation resembled Eve.

Steadman's article supports my argument in several ways. First, Steadman shows that Milton derived his viper lore directly from the "pseudo-scientific tradition," that is, from ancient and medieval authors including Hesiod, Dio Chrysostom, Pliny, and Albertus Magnus as well as seventeenth century authors such as Pierius and Topsell (62–63). Moreover, Steadman demonstrates that Pliny's account of vipers bursting open their mothers' sides provided a crucial account undergirding the way Sin's offspring gnaw her bowels and burst violently forth from her womb (64). Finally, Steadman argues that in Milton's account of Sin — as in several Renaissance authors — a fusion of mythological and scientific traditions occurs (62, 66). A similar fusion occurs, I maintain, in Milton's depiction of Amaranth and serpents.

5. On bees in mid-century England see Timothy Raylor's, "Samuel Hartlib and the Commonwealth of Bees." Raylor demonstrates Hartlib's virtually unprecedented, groundbreaking stance of avoiding moral or spiritual applications based on his scientific observations of bees. Despite Milton's high regard for Hartlib, the epic bee simile in book 1 of *Paradise Lost*, with its pointed significance for politics and church government, shows that the poet was unwilling to follow Hartlib in refraining from such applications of natural history.

Chapter Two. Careful Plowing

1. See the majestic discussion of fruit in Alastair Fowler's introduction to his edition of *Paradise Lost*:

> When Milton's exploitation of the semantic field of *fruit* is reviewed, it is found to account for no small proportion of the poem's content. It extends not only to immediate concrete and abstract uses of *fruit* itself (as well as of *fruitless* and *fruition*) but also to almost every other reference to vegetable nature. Thus Eve is herself a "fairest unsupported flower" (ix 432) and Christ's promise is to her seed; the fallen angels lie like leaves in Vallombrosa (i 302); the serpent is a shoot of fraud (ix 89); and under the Covenant mankind proceeds "as from a second stock [trunk]" (xii 7). But none of these images would have half so much force were it not for the actual presence of the trees that dominate the physical landscape of the poem. The sacred Biblical Trees of Life and of Knowledge, the emblematic trees and plants of virtue, the ordinary wild natural trees that complete the grotesque surrounding frame — everywhere in Paradise vegetation burgeons luxuriantly. It is natural and inevitable that the universe itself should be thought of as a plant whose "bright consummate flower" is breathed in heaven (v 481). Mankind is as naturally both part and guardian of a plant; and a plant's desecration must inevitably have cosmic repercussions. (18–19)

For a rare discussion of Milton's poetic use of both fruit and seed imagery, see Swaim, 62–66. Swaim traces a shift in these images away from natural and toward spiritual signification. Swaim's primary concern in that discussion, however, is to locate the image patterns within Raphael's and Michael's contrasting modes. Thus Swaim views the "recollection" of seed passages as characteristic of the postlapsarian mode in the epic.

2. For the literary kinship of Milton and George Eliot, see Postlethwaite, 197–222.

3. For the alternate reading that Milton's fruit is merely an apple and a "completely arbitrary sign," see R. A. Shoaf, 31, and Satan in *Paradise Lost* 10.485–89. John Leonard relates those readings of "fruit" — along with others by C. S. Lewis, Cleanth Brooks, and Christopher Ricks — to the continuing debate over natural language in Eden (7–9).

4. For further discussion of the various biblical translations of this verse available to Milton, see Fowler's note to *Paradise Lost* 8.320–22 (413).

5. Rosenmeyer, *The Green Cabinet*, 20–23. For pastoralism in *Paradise Lost*, see especially Knott, *Milton's Pastoral Vision*. Annabel Patterson claims that Milton knowingly said goodbye to pastoral in his 1645 volume of poems (160).

6. Lewalski, *Rhetoric of Literary Forms*, 173–219; and "Milton on Women — Yet Again," esp. 55: Adam and Eve "are expected to grow, change, and develop in virtue by properly pruning and directing their own impulses as well as their garden"; Radzinowicz, "Man as a Probationer of

Immortality," 31–51, and *Toward "Samson Agonistes,"* esp. 244–45. Diane McColley, in *Milton's Eve*, focuses on the relation of floral and psychosocial growth in *Paradise Lost*.

7. The Varro, Cato, and Columella editions cited in my text are, unless otherwise indicated, from the Loeb Classical Library. Unless otherwise indicated, the English translations of Cato, Varro, and Columella in my text are those of the Loeb editions.

8. On the publication history of the Roman agricultural manuals, see Hooper and Ash, xx–xxiii, and Thirsk, "Making a Fresh Start," 18–19.

9. The resemblance of Cato's aphorism to Franklin's style is noted by Hooper and Ash in their edition of Cato (12).

10. Richard Bentley insists that the Plowman is afraid of losing his crop in a storm, a reading which Fowler labels "erroneous" (251). Bentley's "error," however, may have already existed in Milton's imagination and that of his readers, because of Vergil's emphasis on the danger of devastating storms during harvesting in *Georgics* 1.311–34. Given England's northern latitude, that danger would be even more acute than in Rome. In *Milton's God*, William Empson reads the simile as a sign that either God is lacking omnipotence (if the anxiety is his) or that Satan has assumed his rightful rule over the angels (172).

Eschewing the search for exact point-by-point correspondences between the epic's plot and every detail of the similes, Christopher Ricks finds this simile "beautiful but digressive" (129). As in all great poetry, he maintains, "we cannot do without a sense of disparity as well as of similarity in Milton's similes" (130). Ricks's assumption, which I gratefully acknowledge, underlies my interpretation. My understanding of how metaphors work generally has been shaped by the late Max Black. Particularly I acknowledge Black's notion of interaction in metaphor as set forth in *Models and Metaphors*.

11. Robert Cecil, in Sir Simonds D'Ewes, *The Journals of All the Parliaments During the Reign of Queen Elizabeth* (London, 1682), 674, cited by Andrew McRae, "Husbandry Manuals and the Language of Agrarian Improvement," in Leslie and Raylor, *Culture*, 35.

12. Thirsk, "Enclosing and Engrossing," 237; cf. Robert C. Allen, *Enclosure and the Yeoman*, 277.

13. For the text of the Diggers' song, see Tate, 149. On the Diggers generally, see Brailsford, esp. 56–67.

Chapter Three. Building Pandaemonium

1. Regina M. Schwartz observes that Milton begins the opening proem of *Paradise Lost* with just such a reversal, which has the effect, as she argues, of emphasizing the poet's search for authoritative origins

(2–3). See also my discussion of the reversal of fruit and seed in the epic in chapter 2.

2. Andrew Barnaby argues that the allusion to the Roman republic at once "establishes Rome as a model for England's godly task in history" and "associates Roman *imperium* with ungodly conquest" (81). This notion of Rome's bifurcated status as a successful yet suspect model underlies my argument.

3. See Fink, 105–16. Recent scholarship, most notably the essays gathered by Armitage, Himy, and Skinner, eds., and Norbrook, has extended and particularized this pattern. Dzelzainis constructively challenges Fink's claim of the primacy of Polybius, and his theory of the mixed state, in Milton's republican principles after *Of Reformation*. Dzelzainis proposes Cicero as Milton's main authority on republicanism, but adds that "when examining the political consequences of a classical education, one should cast the net as widely as possible" (8–9).

4. For a summary of Vitruvius's life and work in the context of the Augustan age, see Kenney and Clausen, eds., 493–94; and Frank Granger's introduction to Vitruvius *On Architecture*, The Loeb Classical Library edition, xiii–xvi. Unless otherwise indicated, all references to the Latin text of Vitruvius are to this edition and are cited parenthetically in my text.

5. Anthony Johnson's *Ben Jonson* could serve as a useful precedent for such a comprehensive study.

6. This copy is in the private collection of Jeffrey Jahns. I am happy to acknowledge his generosity in allowing me to examine the book.

7. Paul Stevens, "Milton and the Icastic Imagination," 43–73; Budick, esp. 7–8; Loewenstein; Cable, "Milton's Iconoclastic Truth," 135–51; Cooley, "Iconoclasm and Self-Definition," 23–36; Lieb; and Cable, *Carnal Rhetoric*.

In *Ceremony and Community from Herbert to Milton*, Achsah Guibbory argues that Milton attempts to distinguish *Paradise Lost* as an act of true worship from the idolatrous inventions of Satan, in particular, the building of Pandaemonium. Guibbory rightly points out that "Pandemonium is a derivative imitation, an attempt to imitate heaven" (193). Yet she admits that there is something heroic about Pandaemonium mingled with its decadence: "But it is also monumental, glorious, and embodies Milton's fear that his glorious structure could rival and violate divinity" (193). This sense of mingled grandeur and anxiety in Pandaemonium supports my claim of its double nature.

8. In the introduction to *De architectura* 1.1.3, Vitruvius argues that the master architect should be a man of letters, a skillful artist, a sound mathematician, familiar with scientific studies, a diligent student of philosophy, acquainted with music, not ignorant of medicine, learned in the writings of jurists, and familiar with astronomy. Such encyclopedic

learning is the aim of Milton's educational scheme, as well as a corollary of his own ambition as an epic poet, in accord with the notion in the *Apology against a Pamphlet* "that he who would not be frustrate of his hope to write well hereafter in laudable things, ought himself to be a true poem, that is, a composition and pattern of the best and honorablest things" (YP 2:354).

9. Browne's argument goes as follows: "In our study of Anatomy there is a masse of mysterious Philosophy, and such as reduced the very Heathens to Divinitie; yet amongst all those rare discoveries, and curious pieces I finde in the fabricke of man, I doe not so much content myselfe as in that I finde not, that is, no Organ or instrument for the rationall soule; for in the braine, which we tearme the seate of reason, there is not any thing of moment more than I can discover in the cranie of a beast: and this is a sensible and in inconsiderable argument of the inorganity of the soule, at least in that sense we usually so receive it" (43). For this reference I am indebted to William Howard of the University of Washington.

10. McClung refutes the notion that Pandaemonium is a monstrous mélange of styles, a notion advanced by A. L. Turner in "Milton and the Arts of Design," and by Roland Mushat Frye, *Milton's Imagery and the Visual Arts*, 134–35. But Pandaemonium is not Chaos. That notion depends upon two misreadings: of "Roof" in line 717 as excluding the ceiling; and "arched" in line 726 as implying Gothic vaulting. Essentially, Pandaemonium is constructed in the Doric order, with some reasonable departures considering its supernatural context.

11. Cesariano, ed., Vitruvius, *De architectura*, 3.1, fol. xliii. The translation is mine.

12. See Alastair Fowler's edition of *Paradise Lost*, 527.

Chapter Four. A Marriage Made in Heaven

1. Milton certainly read, consulted, and taught other works concerning the stars. Thomas Orchard explores the ways Milton used the *De Sphaera Mundi* of John Holywood (the same Johannes Sacro Bosco named by Phillips; see Hughes, 1030), a thirteenth century epitome of Ptolemy's *Almagest*, as a textbook to teach astronomy to his pupils. David Masson writes that Milton may have owned a Paris 1559 edition of Aratus's *Phaenomena* and *Diosemeia* as early as 1631 (1.268), and Edward Phillips lists those works among the Greek texts that Milton included in his tutorial (Hughes, 1029). Moreover, the precedent of Saint Paul in citing a verse from Aratus while preaching at the Areopagus (Acts 17.28) — "for we also are his [God's] offspring," Paul tells the Greeks, citing what "your own poet" wrote in *Phaenomena*, 5 — may have served to authorize Milton's didactic epic practice. The humanist

compendium of star lore in *Astronomi veteres* included Aratus together with Manilius, Proclus, and several other authors and commentators.

My working assumption is that Milton owned and used a copy of *Astronomi veteres* during his tutorial and the composition of *Paradise Lost*, that is, from the 1640s through the 1660s. At the same time, the Latin text of Manilius first edited by Joseph Scaliger in 1579 and frequently reprinted (1590, 1600, 1655) contains a patently superior text and apparatus: G. P. Goold quotes A. E. Housman's remark that the Scaliger edition constitutes "the only avenue to a study of the poem" (Goold, cxiii). Accordingly, I cite the Latin text of Manilius from this edition throughout my essay. Except where otherwise indicated, I give the English translation of Manilius from the Loeb edition. In my reading of the *Astronomi veteres* in its entirety, the sheer bulk of Manilius's text (five Roman books of Manilius compared with the other fragments and brief commentaries) and its distinctive emphasis on natural astrology incline me to regard Manilius as Milton's primary, though by no means his only, authority on the subject. By the way, I find no definite prognostications deriving from judicial astrology in *Paradise Lost*. Thus a popular book such as William Lilly's *An Easie and Plain Method*, which is predominantly concerned to draw nativities and chart horoscopes, seems not to have directly influenced Milton's epic. Nonetheless, the popularity of such books together with the revival of the ancient texts indicates a widespread fascination with the stars among Milton's contemporaries that was not lost on the poet.

2. I am indebted to Catherine Yandell of Carleton College for pointing out Montaigne's use of Manilius.

3. Housman logically relocates the lines to 1.521–23. In that context, they clarify the exposition in the preceding lines of something like the Einsteinian law of conservation of matter and energy: "at manet incolumis mundus suaque omnia servat,/quem neque longa dies auget minuitque senectus/nec motus puncto curvat cursusque fatigat" [The firmament, however, conserving all its parts, remains intact, neither increased with length of time nor diminished by old age; it is neither the least bit warped by its motion nor wearied by its speed] (Loeb, 45). The three lines placed in that context read like a summary of the Stoic doctrine of the world-soul, a variation on Pliny's notion at the start of book 2 of the *Natural History* that the *mundus* is a sacred, living organism. Housman's solution is impeccable; one must recall, however, that it was not known to readers before 1903.

4. Accordingly, in *Milton and the Puritan Dilemma*, Arthur E. Barker entitles his chapter on right reason "That Intellectual Ray" (48–59). Barker cites Lord Brooke, who, in his *Discourse Opening the Nature of ... Episcopacie* (London 1641), defined reason as a "ray of the divine

nature, warming and enlivening the creature, conforming it to the likeness of the Creator" (58). Thus we see that disputants on church government of both Anglican and Nonconformist convictions cast theological questions in the language of astrological influence.

5. As Allen explains (*Star-Crossed*, 71–73), Calvin's *Contre l'astrologie* not only linked judicial astrology with known heresies but cited many biblical passages as a way of heaping scorn upon the practice. Vigorous applications of Calvin's arguments — whether or not logically relevant to Milton's position — would be likely to undermine his authority as a biblical exegete in the tract. Possibly Milton broke off the astrological discussion with that consideration in mind.

Chapter Five. The Wounded Earth in Paradise Lost

1. Editors of *Paradise Lost* have been more concerned with Milton's personification of the Earth than have critics. For example, of book 9, lines 782–84, the Romantic editor Henry John Todd remarked: "I need not observe to the reader with what conciseness and energy, with what beauty and judgement, Milton's sense of *completing the mortal sin original* [his italics] is drawn." Of the parallel passage at 9.1000, Todd, after noting the relevance of book 4 of the *Aeneid*, observed that the "sublimity and pathos" of Milton's passage are nonetheless unmatched in ancient and modern poetry. See Todd's edition of *The Poetical Works of John Milton*, 3.206.

For assurance that the figure is indeed a case of personification, see Abrams, *A Glossary of Literary Terms*, where Milton's lines are cited to define the term.

2. Arnobius, 1:53. The comments of Arnobius on Lucretius are included in the edition of *De rerum natura* edited by Dionysius Lambinus, among others.

3. See Merchant, 33–39. Merchant compares Milton's passage with Spenser's image of "sacrilegious" digging in the Earth in *Faerie Queene* 2.7.17, and she cites Walter M. Kendrick's article, "Earth of Flesh, Flesh of Earth," for Spenser's association of lust with mining. According to Kendrick, Spenser's Mother Earth is an emblem of "mindless fecundity," and thus a far different entity than Milton's. The conclusion of Kendrick's essay emphasizes Spenser's Calvinist view: "man's chief task, which is the central preoccupation of *The Faerie Queene*, is to rule and vanquish the earth in his flesh before the earth reclaims it" (548). Milton's agenda, as we shall see, is quite different.

4. Fallon, 125; For Fallon's definition of animist materialism, 111. Fallon regards the animism of Milton's Creation account as a counterstatement to Cartesian mechanism and dualism. Both my discussion of

the living Earth here and my association of mechanism with satanic architecture in chapter 3 support Fallon's view. My further suggestion is that the animism implicit in Milton's poetic argument consistently supports an ecological ethic.

5. For a discussion of Lucretian epic as a generic frame for Milton's Creation account, see Lewalski, *Rhetoric of Literary Forms*, 133–35; and an expanded version in "Generic Multiplicity," 176–78. Lewalski also notes, as does Hughes, the resemblance of Milton's Creation account to Ovid's in *Metamorphoses* 1.1–51.

6. For a summary of the Stoic view of the cosmos, see Merchant 23–24; see also Verbeke, 11–15.

Roman Stoicism, like most Roman institutions, had its roots in Greece. For the roots of the Roman Stoics' belief in a living Earth, see Plato's *Timaeus* 30.b, where the κοσμος is said to be a living creature; and especially the life of Zeno in Diogenes Laertius's *Lives of the Eminent Philosopher*, 7.142, where the Earth is described as an animate substance endowed with sensation.

Turning to the reception of Stoicism, scholars have explored seventeenth century works that sometimes transmit and sometimes alter ancient notions. Stephen M. Fallon discusses several of Milton's contemporaries, chiefly Gassendi, who revived Stoic and Epicurean theories of matter. Kester Svendsen, who in *Milton and Science* traces Milton's scientific thought through contemporary encyclopedias and handbooks, nonetheless concludes: "It is the old science, rather than the new, which bulks the larger in Milton, despite his spectacular allusions to Galileo and his interest in some elements of the new cosmology" (3). Likewise, William Kerrigan asserts that Milton's universe is "unmistakably terracentric; we look through the telescope of Galileo (the only contemporary named in the epic) at the universe of Ptolemy" (195). In *The Theory of the Earth* (London, 1684), Thomas Burnet, basing his arguments on Scripture and deductive reasoning, argues that the Earth's surface, swamped by waters from below, became, in his term, "Terraqueous" as a result of the Flood. Burnet's work appeared too late to influence Milton. As Basil Willey suggests in his introduction to Burnet's *Sacred Theory of the Earth*, however, Burnet's physico-scriptural approach may owe something to Milton's poetry (5).

7. Jonathan Bate (83–117) describes the Renaissance mode of using antiquity as precedent to authorize sixteenth century poetic practice.

8. See, for example, the Paris, 1533 edition of *Libri de re rustica* published by Iehan Petit, which contains Baptistus Pius's comment on 10.161–62:

> *Privignasque rogat.* Solet ambigi quidem quid in eo versiculo velit Columella quod ut intelligas scito privignum eum vocari qui filius

est eius de matris, sed non patris. Victricus maritus meae matris, sed non genitor meus. Sunt enim relativa victricus & privignus. Herbae quae transferentur in alium terram, dicuntur illius Privignae.

She calls for her stepchildren. Generally it is uncertain what Columella intends in this short line. For you would think he would be called a stepson who is of the same mother but not of the same father. For a stepfather may wed my mother, but not be my father. To be sure, a stepfather and a stepson are related. Herbs which will be transplanted into another soil may be called these "stepchildren."

9. Whiting points out Milton's indebtedness to Pliny for these vivid accounts of humankind's perversity in torturing the Earth (92–93).

10. See Hughes, 1029. For the translation of "egregious" as "out of the herd," I am indebted to William J. Kennedy of Cornell University.

11. See Cyril Bailey's edition of *De rerum natura*, 2:898–99. Curiously, when Lucretius returns in 5.783–836 to consider the age of the world, he not only characterizes the primal Earth as a fecund mother (in contrast with her putative present sterility) but offers several arguments to prove that the Earth generates as a mother does. For a useful analysis of that passage, see West, "Two Notes on Lucretius."

Works Cited

Primary Sources

Apuleius. *The Golden Ass.* Trans. Jack Lindsay. Bloomington, Ind.: Indiana University Press, 1962.

Aratus. *Phaenomena* and *Diosemia.* Paris, 1559.

———. *Phaenomena.* The Loeb Classical Library. Cambridge, Mass.: Harvard University Press, 1955.

Arnobius. *Adversus Gentes.* Trans. as *The Case against the Pagans.* 2 vols. Westminster, Md.: Newman Press, 1949.

Astronomi veteres. Venice: Aldus, 1499.

Augustine. *De doctrina christiana.* Vol. 32, Corpus Christianorum Series Latina. Brepolis: Turnholti, 1962.

———. *On Christian Doctrine.* Trans. D. W. Robertson, Jr. New York: Macmillan, 1958.

Bacon, Francis. *Works.* 18 vols. Eds. Robert L. Ellis and James Spedding. London: Longman, 1857–60.

———. *The Advancement of Learning and New Atlantis.* Ed. Arthur Johnston. Oxford: Clarendon Press, 1974.

Boyle, Sir Robert. *The Works of the Honourable Robert Boyle.* Ed. Thomas Birch. London, 1744.

———. *Considerations Touching the Usefulness of Experimental Natural Philosophy.* London, 1663. In Marie Boas Hall, *Robert Boyle on Natural Philosophy: An Essay with Selections from His Writings.* Bloomington, Ind.: Indiana University Press, 1965.

Browne, Sir Thomas. *Religio medici.* In *Selected Writings.* Ed. Sir Geoffrey Keynes, 1–89. London: Faber and Faber, 1968.

Burton, Robert. *The Anatomy of Melancholy*. Philadelphia: J. W. Moore, 1847.

Calvin, Jean. *Contre l'astrologie*. Trans. as *An Admonicion against astrology iudiciall*. London, 1563.

Cato, Marcus Porcius. *On Agriculture*. Varro, Marcus Terentius. *On Agriculture*. Trans. William Davis Hooper. Revised by Harrison Boyd Ash. Cambridge, Mass.: Harvard University Press, 1934; rpt., 1979.

Cato, Varro, Columella, Palladius. *De Re Rustica Scriptores*. Paris: Robert Stephanus, 1543.

———. *Libri de re rustica*. Ed. Phillipus Iunta. With the exposition of Nicolas Angelio. Venice, 1515.

———. *Libri de re rustica*. Paris: Iehan Petit, 1533.

———. *Rei Rusticae Auctores Latini Veteres, M. Cato, M. Varro, L. Columella, Palladius*. Ed. Hieronymus Commelinus. Heidelberg, 1595.

Celsus, A. Cornelius. *De medicina*. 3 vols. Loeb Classical Library. Trans. W. G. Spencer. Cambridge, Mass.: Harvard University Press, 1935; rpt. 1971.

Cicero. *De natura deorum*. Trans. and ed. H. Rackham. London: Heinemann, 1933.

Clement of Alexandria. *The Exhortation to the Greeks; The Rich Man's Salvation; The Fragment of an Address Entitled "To the Newly Baptized."* Trans. G. W. Butterfield. London: William Heinemann, 1919.

———. *The Ante-Nicene Fathers*. Volume 2. Ed. Alexander Roberts and James Donaldson. Revised with notes by A. Cleveland Coxe. New York: Charles Scribner's Sons, 1899.

Columella, Lucius Junius Moderatus. *On Agriculture*. 3 vols. Eds. Harrison Boyd Ash, E. S. Forster, and Edward H. Heffner. Cambridge, Mass.: Harvard University Press, 1941–79.

Comenius, Jan Amos. *A Reformation of Schooles*. London, 1642; rpt. Menston, England: The Scolar Press, Ltd., 1969.

Dee, John. *The Mathematicall Preface to the Elements of Geometrie of Euclid of Megara*. Ed. Allen G. Debus. New York: Science History Publications, 1975.

Diogenes Laertius. *Lives of the Eminent Philosophers*. Trans. R. D. Hicks. Cambridge, Mass.: Harvard University Press, 1925; rpt. 1958.

Dury, John. *The Reformed School and The Reformed Library Keeper*. London, 1651; rpt. Menston, England: The Scolar Press Ltd., 1972.

French, J. Milton. *The Life Records of John Milton*. 5 vols. New Brunswick, N.J.: Rutgers University Press, 1950; rpt. New York: Gordian Press, 1966.

Frontinus, S. Julius. *Strategemata. The Stratagems and Aqueducts of Rome*. Trans. Charles E. Bennett. Ed. Mary B. McElwain. Cambridge, Mass.: Harvard University Press, 1925.

Homer. *The Iliad*. Trans. Richmond Lattimore. Chicago: University of Chicago Press, 1961.

Horace. *Epistles, Book II, and Epistle to the Pisones ('Ars Poetica')*. Ed. Niall Rudd. Cambridge: Cambridge University Press, 1989.

Hume, Patrick. *Annotations on Mr. Milton's "Paradise Lost."* London, 1695.

Johnson, Samuel. *Life of Milton*. In *Samuel Johnson: Selected Poetry and Prose*. Ed. Frank Brady and W. K. Wimsatt. Berkeley: University of California Press, 1977.

The Journals of All the Parliaments during the Reign of Queen Elizabeth. Ed. Sir Simonds D'Ewes. London, 1682.

La Primaudaye, Pierre de. *The French Academie*. London: T. Adams, 1618.

Lilly, William. *Christian Astrology*. London, 1647.

———. *An Easie and Plain Method Teaching How to Judge Upon Nativities*. London, 1658.

Lucretius Carus, Titus. *De rerum natura libri sex*. Venice: Aldus, 1515.

———. *De rerum natura libri sex*. With commentary by Dionysius Lambinus. Paris: Philippus G. Rouillius, 1563.

———. *De rerum natura libri vi*. 3rd ed. Commentary by Dionysius Lambinus. Frankfurt: Andreas Wechelus, 1583.

———. *De rerum natura libri sex*. 3 vols. Ed. and trans. Cyril Bailey. Oxford: Clarendon Press, 1947.

———. *In carum Lucretium poetam commentarii a Joanne Baptista Pio editi*. Bologna: Hieronymus de Benedictis, 1511.

Manilius, Marcus. *Astronomica*. Trans. G. P. Goold. Cambridge, Mass.: Harvard University Press, 1977.

———. *Astronomicon*. 4 vols. Ed. A. E. Housman. London: Grant Richards, 1903; 2nd ed. Cambridge: Cambridge University Press, 1937.

———. *Astronomicon libri quinque*. Ed. Joseph Scaliger. Heidelberg, 1590.

Marvell, Andrew. *The Poems and Letters of Andrew Marvell*. 2 vols. Ed. H. M. Margoliouth. 3rd ed., rev. by Pierre Legouis with E. E. Duncan-Jones. Oxford: Clarendon Press, 1971.

Masson, David. *The Life of John Milton*. 7 vols. London: Macmillan, 1859–94; rpt. New York: Peter Smith, 1946.

Milton, John. *The Complete Prose Works of John Milton*. 8 vols. Gen ed. Don M. Wolfe. New Haven, Conn.: Yale University Press, 1953–85.

———. *John Milton: Complete Poetry and Major Prose*. Ed. Merritt Y. Hughes. Indianapolis: Odyssey Press, 1957.

———. *The Manuscript of Milton's "Paradise Lost," Book I*. Ed. Helen Darbishire. Oxford: Clarendon Press, 1931.

———. *Paradise Lost*. Ed. Alastair Fowler. London: Longman, 1971.

———. *Paradise Lost, A New Edition*. Ed. Richard Bentley. London, 1732.

———. *The Poetical Works of John Milton*. 6 vols. Ed. Henry John Todd. London, 1826.

———. *The Riverside Milton*. Ed. Roy Flannagan. Boston: Houghton Mifflin, 1998.

———. *The Works of John Milton*. Ed. Frank Allen Patterson et al. 18 vols. New York: Columbia University Press, 1931–40.

Montaigne, Michel Eyquem de. *Apologie de Raimond Sebond*. Ed. Samuel Sylvestre de Sacy. Paris: Gallimard, 1967.

More, Henry. *Enchiridion Metaphysicum*. London, 1671.

———. *Immortality of the Soul*. London, 1659.

Mouffet, Thomas. *The Theater of Insects: Or, Lesser Living Creatures*. London: E. Cotes, 1658.

Ovid. *P. Ovidii Nasonis. Metamorphoses*. Ed. William S. Anderson. Leipzig: Teubner, 1977.

Pascal, Blaise. *Pensées*. Trans. A. J. Krailscheimer. London: Penguin, 1966.

Patrides, C. A., ed. *The Cambridge Platonists*. Cambridge, Mass.: Harvard University Press, 1970.

Pauw Pieter. Pietri Pauw Amsteldamensis. *Succenturiatus Anatomicus. Continens Commentaria in Hippocretem, de Capiis Vulneribus. Addite in aliquoto Capita libri VIII C. Celsi Explicationes*. London: Ioducum a Colster, 1616.

Plato. *Timaeus, Critias, Cleitophon, Menexenus, Epistles*. Ed. and trans. R. G. Bury. London: William Heinemann, 1919.

Pliny the Elder. *The Historie of the World: Commonly Called, The Naturall History of C. Plinius Secundus*. 2 vols. Trans. and ed. Philemon Holland. London: Adam Islip, 1635.

———. *Natural History*. 10 vols. Ed. Arthur Rackham. Cambridge, Mass.: Harvard University Press, 1938.

Seneca. *Natural Questions*. Trans. Thomas H. Corcoran. Cambridge, Mass.: Harvard University Press, 1972.

Servius. Servii Grammatici (Servius Honoratus Marcus), *Qui Feruntur in Vergilii Carmina Commentarii*. 4 vols. Eds. George Thilo and Herman Hagen. Leipzig: Teubner, 1881–84.

Spenser, Edmund. *The Yale Edition of the Shorter Poems of Edmund Spenser*. Eds. William A. Oram, Einar Bjorvand, Ronald Bond, Thomas H. Cain, Alexander Dunlop, and Richard Schell. New Haven, Conn.: Yale University Press, 1989.

Stillingfleet, Edward. *Origines Sacrae*. London, 1662.

Topsell, Edward. *The History of Four-Footed Beasts and Serpents. Whereunto is Now Added, The Theater of Insects: Or, Lesser Living Creatures*. London: E. Cotes, 1658.

Varro. Marcus Terentius. *On Agriculture*. Trans. William Davis Hooper. Revised by Harrison Boyd Ash. Cambridge, Mass.: Harvard University Press, 1934; rpt., 1979.

Vergil. *Aeneid*. Trans. H. R. Fairclough. Cambridge, Mass.: Harvard University Press, 1937.

———. *Aeneid*. 2 vols. Ed. R. D. Williams. London: Macmillan, 1972.

———. *P. Vergili Maronis Opera*. Ed. R. A. B. Mynors. Oxford: Clarendon Press, 1969.

Vitruvius. [M. Vitruvii Pollionis]. *M. Vitruvius per Iocondum*. Venice, 1511.

———. *Lucio Vitruvio Pollione de Architectura*. Ed. G. Cesariano. Como: Gotardus de Ponte, 1521.

———. *De architectura* and Iulius Frontinus, *De aqueductibus*. Florence: Phillipus Iunta, 1522.

———. *De architectura libri decem*. Cum commentariis Danielis Barbari. Venice, 1567.

———. *On Architecture*. 2 vols. Ed. from the Harleian Manuscript 2767 and trans. by Frank Granger. London: William Heinemann; 1931; rev. ed., Cambridge, Mass.: Harvard University Press, 1931–70.

Winstanley, Gerrard. *The True Levellers' Standard Advanced*. 1649. In *"The Law of Freedom" and Other Writings*. Ed. Christopher Hill. Cambridge: Cambridge University Press, 1983.

Wotton, Sir Henry. *The Elements of Architecture*. London: John Bill, 1624.

Secondary Sources

Abrams, M. H. *A Glossary of Literary Terms.* 5th ed. New York: Holt, Rinehart, and Winston, 1988.

———. *Natural Supernaturalism: Tradition and Revolution in Romantic Literature.* New York: W. W. Norton and Co., 1971.

Adams, Mary. "Fallen Wombs: The Origins of Death in Miltonic Sexuality." *Milton Studies* 29 (1992): 165–79.

Allen, Don Cameron. *The Legend of Noah: Renaissance Rationalism in Art, Science, and Letters.* Urbana, Ill.: University of Illinois Press, 1949.

———. "Milton's Amarant." *Modern Language Notes* 72 (1957): 25–58.

———. *Mysteriously Meant: The Rediscovery of Pagan Symbolism and Allegorical Interpretation in the Renaissance.* Baltimore: Johns Hopkins University Press, 1970.

———. *The Star-Crossed Renaissance: The Quarrel about Astrology and Its Influence in England.* New York: Octagon Books, 1966.

Allen, Robert C. *Enclosure and the Yeoman: The Agricultural Development of the South Midlands, 1450–1850.* Oxford: Clarendon Press, 1992.

Anselment, Raymond A. *The Realms of Apollo: Literature and Healing in Seventeenth-Century England.* Dover: University of Delaware Press, 1995.

Armitage, David, Armand Himy, and Quentin Skinner, eds. *Milton and Republicanism.* Cambridge: Cambridge University Press, 1995.

Babb, Lawrence. *The Moral Cosmos of "Paradise Lost."* Lansing, Mich.: Michigan State University Press, 1970.

Banks, Theodore. *Milton's Imagery.* New York: Columbia University Press, 1950.

Barker, Arthur E. *Milton and the Puritan Dilemma, 1641–1660.* Toronto: University of Toronto Press, 1941; rpt. 1976.

Barnaby, Andrew. "Another Rome in the West?: Milton and the Imperial Republic, 1654–1670." *Milton Studies* 30 (1993): 67–84.

Bate, Jonathan. *Shakespeare and Ovid.* Oxford: Clarendon Press, 1993.

Berkeley, David S. "Dalila as Amphisbaena." *Papers on Language and Literature* 19, no. 1 (1983): 87–92.

Black, Max. *Models and Metaphors.* Ithaca, N.Y.: Cornell University Press, 1967.

Bloom, Harold. *The Anxiety of Influence: A Theory of Poetry*. New York: Oxford University Press, 1973.

Bradshaw, David J. "Egyptian Gold: Milton's Use of Virgil in *Paradise Lost*, Books 11 and 12." In *"All in All": Unity, Diversity, and the Miltonic Perspective*. Ed. Charles W. Durham and Kristin A. Pruitt, 189–99. Selinsgrove, Pa.: Susquehanna University Press, 1999.

Brailsford, H. N. "Diggers." In *The Levellers and the English Revolution*. Ed. Christopher Hill. Stanford, Calif.: Stanford University Press, 1961.

Brisman, Leslie. "Serpent Error: *Paradise Lost* X, 216–18." *Milton Studies* 2 (1970): 27–35.

Budick, Sanford. *The Dividing Muse: Images of Sacred Disjunction in Milton's Poetry*. New Haven, Conn.: Yale University Press, 1985.

Bush, Douglas. *Mythology and the Renaissance Tradition in English Poetry*. Minneapolis: University of Minnesota Press, 1932; rev. ed., New York: W. W. Norton and Co., 1963.

Cable, Lana. *Carnal Rhetoric: Milton's Iconoclasm and the Poetics of Desire*. Durham, N.C.: Duke University Press, 1995.

———. "Milton's Iconoclastic Truth." In *Politics, Poetics, and Hermeneutics in Milton's Prose*. Ed. David Loewenstein, 135–51. Cambridge: Cambridge University Press, 1990.

Cassirer, Ernst. *The Individual and the Cosmos in Renaissance Philosophy*. Trans. Marie Domandi. New York: Barnes and Noble, 1963.

———. *The Platonic Renaissance in England*. Trans. James P. Pettegrove. New York: Gordian Press, 1970.

Cheung, King-Kok. "Beauty and the Beast: A Sinuous Reflection of Milton's Eve." *Milton Studies* 23 (1987): 197–214.

Christopher, Georgia B. *Milton and the Science of the Saints*. Princeton, N.J.: Princeton University Press, 1982.

Christopher, Mother Mary, O.S.U., "'O Foul Descent!': Satan and the Serpent Form." *Studies in Philology* 62 (1965): 188–96.

Clark, Donald L. *John Milton at St. Paul's School*. New York: Columbia University Press, 1948.

Conte, Gian Biagio. *The Rhetoric of Imitation: Genre and Poetic Memory in Virgil and Other Latin Poets*. Trans. and ed. Charles Segal. Ithaca, N.Y.: Cornell University Press, 1986.

Cooley, Ronald W. "Iconoclasm and Self-Definition in Milton's *Of Reformation*." *Religion and Literature* 23, no. 1 (Spring 1991): 23–36.

Daniel, Clay. "Astrea, the Golden Scales, and the Scorpion: Milton's Heavenly Reflection of the Scene in Eden." *Milton Quarterly* 20, no. 3 (1986): 92–98.

Danielson, Dennis. *The Cambridge Companion to Milton*. Cambridge: Cambridge University Press, 1989.

Darbishire, Helen, ed. *The Manuscript of Milton's "Paradise Lost," Book I*. Oxford: The Clarendon Press, 1931.

Darnton, Robert. *The Great Cat Massacre and Other Episodes in French Cultural History*. New York: Basic Books, 1984.

DuRocher, Richard J. *Milton and Ovid*. Ithaca, N.Y.: Cornell University Press, 1985.

Dzelzainis, Martin. "Milton's Classical Republicanism." In *Milton and Republicanism*. Ed. David Armitage, Armand Himy, and Quentin Skinner, 3–24. Cambridge: Cambridge University Press, 1995.

Edwards, Karen L. *Milton and the Natural World: Science and Poetry in "Paradise Lost."* Cambridge: Cambridge University Press, 1999.

Eliot, T. S. *The Sacred Wood: Essays on Criticism and Poetry*. London: Methuen, 1920; rpt. 1960.

Empson, William. *Milton's God*. London: Chatto and Windus, 1961.

———. *The Structure of Complex Words*. London: Chatto and Windus, 1951.

Fallon, Robert Thomas. *Captain or Colonel: The Soldier in Milton's Life and Art*. Columbia, Mo.: University of Missouri Press, 1984.

Fallon, Stephen M. *Milton among the Philosophers: Poetry and Materialism in Seventeenth-Century England*. Ithaca, N.Y.: Cornell University Press, 1991.

Fink, Z. S. *The Classical Republicans: An Essay in the Recovery of a Pattern of Thought in Seventeenth-Century England*. Evanston: Northwestern University Press, 1962.

Fish, Stanley. *Surprised by Sin: The Reader in "Paradise Lost."* 2nd ed. Cambridge, Mass.: Harvard University Press, 1997.

Flannagan, Roy, ed. *The Riverside Milton*. Boston: Houghton Mifflin, 1998.

Foucault, Michel. *Les mots et les choses: Une archeologie des sciences humaines*. Paris: Editions Gallimard, 1966. Translated as *The Order of Things: An Archaeology of the Human Sciences*. New York: Random House, 1970.

Fowler, Alastair. *Time's Purpled Masquers: Stars and the Afterlife in English Renaissance Literature*. Oxford: Clarendon Press, 1996.

Friedlander, Paul. "Patterns of Sound and Atomic Theory in Lucretius." *American Journal of Philology* 62 (1941): 16–34.

Friedman, Donald. "Galileo and the Art of Seeing." In *Milton in Italy: Contexts, Images, Contradictions*. Ed. Mario Di Cesare, 159–74. Binghamton, N.Y.: Medieval and Renaissance Texts and Studies, 1991.

Frye, Northrop. *The Return of Eden: Five Essays on Milton's Epics*. Toronto: University of Toronto Press, 1965.

Frye, Roland Mushat. *Milton's Imagery and the Visual Arts: Iconographic Tradition in the Epic Poems*. Princeton, N.J.: Princeton University Press, 1978.

Geneva, Ann. *Astrology and the Seventeenth-Century Mind: William Lilly and the Language of the Stars*. Manchester: Manchester University Press, 1995.

Goold, G. P., ed. *Manilius. Astronomica*. Cambridge, Mass.: Harvard University Press, 1977.

Grafton, Anthony. *Defenders of the Text: The Traditions of Scholarship in an Age of Science, 1450–1800*. Cambridge, Mass.: Harvard University Press, 1991.

Granger, Frank, ed. *Vitruvius. On Architecture*. Cambridge, Mass.: Harvard University Press, 1931.

Greenblatt, Stephen. *Marvelous Possessions: The Wonder of the New World*. Chicago: University of Chicago Press, 1991.

Greene, Thomas M. *The Light in Troy: Imitation and Discovery in Renaissance Poetry*. New Haven, Conn.: Yale University Press, 1982.

Greengrass, Mark, Michael Leslie, and Timothy Raylor, eds. *Samuel Hartlib and Universal Reformation: Studies in Intellectual Communication*. Cambridge: Cambridge University Press, 1994.

Grossman, Marshall. *"Authors to Themselves": Milton and the Revelation of History*. Cambridge: Cambridge University Press, 1987.

Guibbory, Achsah. *Ceremony and Community from Herbert to Milton: Literature, Religion, and Cultural Conflict in Seventeenth-Century England*. Cambridge: Cambridge University Press, 1998.

Hale, John K. *Milton's Languages: The Impact of Multilingualism on Style*. Cambridge: Cambridge University Press, 1997.

———. "The Pre-Criticism of Milton's Latin Verse, Illustrated from the Ode 'Ad Joannem Rousium.'" In *Of Poetry and Politics: New Essays* on *Milton and His World*. Ed. P. G. Stanwood. Binghamton, N.Y.: Medieval and Renaissance Texts and Studies, 1995.

Hanford, James Holly. "Milton and the Art of War." In *John Milton: Poet and Humanist: Essays by James Holly Hanford*, 185–223. Cleveland: Case Western Reserve University Press, 1966.

Harding, Davis. *Milton and the Renaissance Ovid*. Urbana, Ill.: University of Illinois Press, 1946.

Haskin, Dayton. *Milton's Burden of Interpretation*. Philadelphia: University of Pennsylvania Press, 1994.

Herz, Judith Scherer. "'For Whom This Glorious Sight?': Dante, Milton, and the Galileo Question." In *Milton in Italy: Contexts, Images, Contradictions*. Ed. Mario Di Cesare, 147–57. Binghamton, N.Y.: Medieval and Renaissance Texts and Studies, 1991.

Hill, Christopher. *The English Bible and the Seventeenth-Century Revolution*. New York: Penguin, 1993.

———. "The Religion of Gerrard Winstanley." In *The Collected Essays of Christopher Hill*. Vol. 2. Amherst: University of Massachusetts Press, 1986.

———. *The World Turned Upside Down: Radical Ideas during the English Revolution*. New York: Columbia University Press, 1972.

Hooper, W. D., and H. B. Ash, eds. *Cato and Varro. On Agriculture*. Loeb Classical Library. Cambridge, Mass.: Harvard University Press, 1979.

Hughes, Merritt Y. "Satan 'Now Dragon Grown.'" *Etudes anglaises* 20 (1964): 356–69.

Hunter, William B., Jr. "The Provenance of the *Christian Doctrine*." *Studies in English Literature* 32 (1992): 129–42.

———. "Satan as Comet: *Paradise Lost* 2.708–711," *English Language Notes* 5 (1967): 17–21. Rpt. in *The Descent of Urania: Studies in Milton, 1946–1988*, 63–66. Lewisburg, Pa.: Bucknell University Press, 1989.

———. *"Visitation Unimplor'd": Milton and the Authorship of "De Doctrina Christiana."* Pittsburgh: Duquesne University Press, 1998.

Hyman, Lawrence W. "A Note on Satan as Serpent." *Milton Quarterly* 14 (1980): 62.

Ingram, William, and Kathleen Swaim. A *Concordance to Milton's English Poetry*. Oxford: Clarendon Press, 1972.

Johnson, Anthony W. *Ben Jonson: Poetry and Architecture*. Oxford: Clarendon Press, 1994.

Kassell, Lauren. "How to Read Simon Forman's Casebooks: Medicine, Astrology, and Gender in Elizabethan London." *Social History of Medicine* 12, no. 1 (April 1999): 3–18.

Kendrick, Walter M. "Earth of Flesh, Flesh of Earth: Mother Earth in the *Faerie Queene.*" *Renaissance Quarterly* 27 (1974): 533–48.

Kenney, E. J., and W. V. Clausen, eds. *The Cambridge History of Classical Literature.* 2 vols. Cambridge: Cambridge University Press, 1982.

Kerrigan, William. *The Sacred Complex: On the Psychogenesis of "Paradise Lost."* Cambridge, Mass.: Harvard University Press, 1983.

Knoppers, Laura Lunger. *Historicizing Milton: Spectacle, Power, and Poetry in Restoration England.* Athens, Ga.: University of Georgia Press, 1994.

Knott, John R. *Milton's Pastoral Vision.* Chicago: University of Chicago Press, 1971.

Kuhn, Thomas S. *The Structure of Scientific Revolutions.* Chicago: University of Chicago Press, 1970.

Lanham, Richard A. *The Motives of Eloquence.* New Haven, Conn.: Yale University Press, 1976.

Leonard, John. *Naming in Paradise: Milton and the Language of Adam and Eve.* Oxford: Clarendon Press, 1990.

Leslie, Michael, and Timothy Raylor, eds. *Culture and Cultivation in Early Modern England: Writing and the Land.* Leicester: Leicester University Press, 1992.

Lewalski, Barbara Kiefer. "Generic Multiplicity and Milton's Literary God." In *A Fine Tuning: Studies of the Religious Poetry of Herbert and Milton.* Ed. Mary A. Maleski, 163–86. Binghamton, N.Y.: Medieval and Renaissance Texts and Studies, 1989.

———. "Milton on Women — Yet Again." In *Problems for Feminist Criticism.* Ed. Sally Minogue, 46–69. London: Routledge, 1990.

———. *"Paradise Lost" and the Rhetoric of Literary Forms.* Princeton, N.J.: Princeton University Press, 1985.

Lewis, C. S. *The Allegory of Love: A Study in Medieval Tradition.* London: Oxford University Press, 1936; rpt. 1977.

Lieb, Michael. *Milton and the Culture of Violence.* Ithaca, N.Y.: Cornell University Press, 1994.

Lindberg, David C. *The Beginnings of Western Science: The European Scientific Tradition in Philosophical, Religious, and Institutional Context.* Chicago: University of Chicago Press, 1992.

Lockwood, Laura. *A Lexicon to John Milton's Poems*. London: Macmillan, 1907.

Loewenstein, David. *Milton and the Drama of History: Historical Vision, Iconoclasm, and the Literary Imagination*. Cambridge: Cambridge University Press, 1990.

Low, Anthony. *The Georgic Revolution*. Princeton, N.J.: Princeton University Press, 1985.

MacKellar, Walter. *A Variorum Commentary on the Poems of John Milton*. Vol. 4, *Paradise Regained*. New York: Columbia University Press, 1975.

Majno, Guido. *The Healing Hand: Man and Wound in the Ancient World*. Cambridge, Mass.: Harvard University Press, 1975; rpt. 1982.

Manley, Frank. "Milton and the Beasts of the Field." *Modern Language Notes* 76 (1961): 398–403.

Marjara, Harinder Singh. "Analogy in the Scientific Imagery of *Paradise Lost*." *Milton Studies* 26 (1990): 81–99.

———. *Contemplation of Created Things: Science in "Paradise Lost."* Toronto: University of Toronto Press, 1992.

Martz, Louis. "*Paradise Regained*: The Meditative Combat." *English Literary History* 27 (1960): 223–47.

McClung, William A. "The Architecture of Pandaemonium." *Milton Quarterly* 15, no. 4 (1981): 109–12.

McColley, Diane Kelsey. *A Gust for Paradise: Milton's Eden and the Visual Arts*. Urbana, Ill.: University of Illinois Press, 1993.

———. *Milton's Eve*. Urbana, Ill.: University of Illinois Press, 1983.

McColley, Grant. "The Astronomy of *Paradise Lost*." *Studies in Philology* 34 (1937): 209–47.

Merchant, Carolyn. *The Death of Nature: Women, Ecology, and the Scientific Revolution*. San Francisco: Harper-Collins, 1989.

Milton, Anthony. "'The Unchanged Peacemaker'?: John Dury and the Politics of Irenicism in England, 1628–1643." In *Samuel Hartlib and Universal Reformation: Studies in Intellectual Communication*. Ed. Mark Greengrass, Michael Leslie, and Timothy Raylor, 95–117. Cambridge: Cambridge University Press, 1994.

Mitchell, W. J. T. *Iconology: Image, Text, Ideology*. Chicago: University of Chicago Press, 1985.

Mulder, John R. *The Temple of the Mind: Education and Literary Taste in Seventeenth-Century England*. New York: Pegasus, 1969.

Neuberg, Matt. "Hitch Your Wagon to a Star: Manilius and his Two Addressees." *Materiali e Discussioni per l'analisi dei Testi Classici* 31 (1993): 243–82.

Norbrook, David. *Writing the English Republic: Poetry, Rhetoric and Politics, 1627–1660.* Cambridge: Cambridge University Press, 1999.

Orchard, Thomas. *The Astronomy of Milton's "Paradise Lost."* New York: Haskell House, 1966.

The Oxford English Dictionary. 20 vols. Prepared by J. A. Simpson and E. S. C. Weiner. Oxford: Clarendon Press, 1989.

Parker, William Riley. *Milton: A Biography.* 2 vols. Oxford: Clarendon Press, 1968; 2nd ed., edited by Gordon Campbell, 1996.

Patrides, C. A. *Milton and the Christian Tradition.* Oxford: Clarendon Press, 1966.

Patterson, Annabel. *Pastoral and Ideology, Virgil to Valery.* Berkeley: University of California Press, 1987.

Pigman, G. W., III. "Limping Examples: Exemplarity, the New Historicism, and Psychoanalysis." In *Creative Imitation: New Essays on Renaissance Literature in Honor of Thomas Greene.* Ed. David Quint, Margaret W. Ferguson, G. W. Pigman III, and Wayne Rebhorn, 281–96. Binghamton, N.Y.: Medieval and Renaissance Texts and Studies, 1992.

———. "Versions of Imitation in the Renaissance." *Renaissance Quarterly* 33 (1980): 1–32.

Popkin, Richard H. "Hartlib, Dury and the Jews." In *Samuel Hartlib and Universal Reformation: Studies in Intellectual Communication,* ed. Mark Greengrass, Michael Leslie, and Timothy Raylor, 118–36. Cambridge, Cambridge University Press, 1994.

Postlethwaite, Diana. "When Eliot Reads Milton: The Muse in a Different Voice," *English Literary History* 57, no. 1 (1990): 197–222.

Rackham, H., ed. *Pliny. Natural History.* Cambridge, Mass.: Harvard University Press, 1938.

Radzinowicz, Mary Ann. "Man as a Probationer of Immortality," In *Approaches to "Paradise Lost."* Ed. C. A. Patrides. London: Methuen, 1968.

———. *Milton's Epics and the Book of Psalms.* Princeton, N.J.: Princeton University Press, 1989.

———. "*Paradise Regained* as Hermeneutic Combat." *Hartford Studies in Literature* 15–16 (1983–84): 99–107.

———. *Toward "Samson Agonistes."* Princeton, N.J.: Princeton University Press, 1979.

Rajan, Balachandra. "Simple, Sensuous, and Passionate." *Review of English Studies* 21 (1945): 289–301. Reprint *Milton: Modern Essays in Criticism.* Ed. Arthur E. Barker, 3–20. New York: Oxford University Press, 1965.

Raylor, Timothy. "New Light on Milton and Hartlib." *Milton Quarterly* 27, no. 1 (1993): 19–31.

———. "Samuel Hartlib and the Commonwealth of Bees." In *Culture and Cultivation in Early Modern England.* Ed. Michael Leslie and Timothy Raylor, 91–129. Leicester: Leicester University Press, 1992.

Redondi, Pietro. *Galileo Heretic [Galileo Eretico].* Trans. Raymond Rosenthal. Princeton, N.J.: Princeton University Press, 1987.

Renaker, David. "The Horoscope of Christ." *Milton Studies* 12 (1978): 213–33.

Revard, Stella. "Milton and Classical Rome: The Political Context of *Paradise Regained.*" In *Rome in the Renaissance: The City and the Myth.* Ed. P. A. Ramsey, 409–19. Binghamton, N.Y.: Medieval and Renaissance Texts and Studies, 1982.

———. *Milton and the Tangles of Neaera's Hair: The Making of the 1645 "Poems."* Columbia, Mo.: University of Missouri Press, 1997.

Ricks, Christopher. *Milton's Grand Style.* Oxford: Oxford University Press, 1963.

Rogers, John. *The Matter of Revolution: Science, Poetry, and Politics in the Age of Milton.* Ithaca, N.Y.: Cornell University Press, 1996.

Rosenmeyer, Thomas. *The Green Cabinet: Essays in Pastoral from Theocritus to Milton.* Berkeley: University of California Press, 1969.

Rumrich, John. "Milton's God and the Matter of Chaos." *PMLA* 110 (1995): 1035–46.

Samuel, Irene. "Milton on Learning and Wisdom." *PMLA* 64 (1949): 708–23.

Saurat, Denis. *Milton, Man and Thinker.* New York: The Dial Press, 1925.

Schultz, Howard. *Milton and Forbidden Knowledge.* New York: Modern Language Association of America, 1955.

Schwartz, Regina M. *Remembering and Repeating: Biblical Creation in "Paradise Lost."* Cambridge: Cambridge University Press, 1988.

Shawcross, John T. *John Milton: The Self and the World*. Lexington, Ky.: The University Press of Kentucky, 1993.

———. *"Paradise Regain'd: 'Worthy T' Have Not Remain'd So Long Unsung.'"* Pittsburgh: Duquesne University Press, 1988.

Shoaf, R. A. *Milton: Poet of Duality*. New Haven, Conn.: Yale University Press, 1985.

Shuger, Debora K. *Sacred Rhetoric: The Christian Grand Style in the English Renaissance*. Princeton, N.J.: Princeton University Press, 1988.

Sikes, E. E. *Roman Poetry*. London: Faber and Faber, 1923.

Sims, James H. "A Greater than Rome: The Inversion of a Virgilian Symbol From Camões to Milton." In *Rome in the Renaissance: The City and the Myth*. Ed. P. A. Ramsey, 333–44. Binghamton, N.Y.: Medieval and Renaissance Texts and Studies, 1982.

Smith, Nigel. *Literature and Revolution, 1640–1660*. New Haven, Conn.: Yale University Press, 1994.

Smith, Rebecca W. "The Sources of Milton's Pandemonium." *Modern Philology* 29 (1931): 187–98.

Steadman, John M. *Milton and the Renaissance Hero*. Oxford: Clarendon Press, 1967.

———. "Sin, Echidna, and the Viper's Brood," *Modern Language Review* 56 (1961): 62–66.

Stein, Arnold. *Heroic Knowledge: An Interpretation of "Paradise Regained" and "Samson Agonistes."* Hamden, Conn.: Archon Books, 1965.

Stevens, Paul. "Milton and the Icastic Imagination." *Milton Studies* 20 (1984): 43–73.

———. "*Paradise Lost* and the Colonial Imperative." *Milton Studies* 34 (1996): 3–21.

Stocker, Margarita and Timothy Raylor. "A New Marvell Manuscript: Cromwellian Patronage and Politics." *English Literary Renaissance* 20 (1990): 106–62.

Strier, Richard. "Milton against Humility." In *Religion and Culture in Renaissance England*. Ed. Claire McEachern and Debora Shuger, 258–86. Cambridge: Cambridge University Press, 1997.

Summers, Joseph H. *The Muse's Method: An Introduction to "Paradise Lost."* Cambridge, Mass.: Harvard University Press, 1962; rpt. Binghamton, N.Y: Medieval and Renaissance Texts and Studies, 1981.

Svendsen, Kester. "Milton and Medical Lore," *Bulletin of the History of Medicine* 13 (1943): 158–84.

———. *Milton and Science*. Cambridge, Mass.: Harvard University Press, 1956.

———. "Satan and Science." *Bucknell Review* 9 (1960): 130–42.

———. "Science and Structure in Milton's *Doctrine and Discipline of Divorce*." *PMLA* 67 (1952): 435–45.

Swaim, Kathleen M. *Before and After the Fall: Contrasting Modes in "Paradise Lost."* Amherst: University of Massachusetts Press, 1986.

Tate, W. E. *The Enclosure Movement*. New York, 1967.

Teskey, Gordon. "From Allegory to Dialectic: Imagining Error in Spenser and Milton." *PMLA* 101 (1986): 9–21.

Thirsk, Joan. "Enclosing and Engrossing." In *The Agrarian History of England and Wales, 1500–1640*. Ed. Joan Thirsk, 200–55. Cambridge: Cambridge University Press, 1967.

———. "Making a Fresh Start: Sixteenth-Century Agriculture and the Classical Inspiration." In *Culture and Cultivation in Early Modern England: Writing and the Land*. Ed. Michael Leslie and Timothy Raylor, 15–34. Leicester: Leicester University Press, 1992.

Townsend, Gavin. "Imagery in Lucretius." In *Lucretius*. Ed. D. R. Dudley. Studies in Latin Literature and Its Influence. London: Routledge and Kegan Paul, 1965.

Trinkaus, Charles. "The Astrological Cosmos and Rhetorical Culture of Giovanni Gioviano Pontano." *Renaissance Quarterly* 38, no. 3 (1985): 446–72.

Turnbull, G. H. *Hartlib, Dury and Comenius: Gleanings from Hartlib's Papers*. London: Hodder and Stoughton, 1947.

Turner, A. L. "Milton and the Arts of Design." In *A Milton Encyclopedia*. Ed. William B. Hunter, Jr., et al., vol. 1, 90–112. Lewisburg, Pa.: Bucknell University Press, 1978.

Verbeke, Gerard. "Ethics and Logic in Stoicism." In *Atoms, Pneuma, and Tranquility: Epicurean and Stoic Themes in European Thought*. Ed. Margaret Osler, 11–15. Cambridge: Cambridge University Press, 1991.

Webster, Charles. *The Great Instauration: Science, Medicine, and Reform, 1626–1660*. London: Gerald Duckworth and Co., 1975.

Weinberger, Jerry, ed. *Francis Bacon: New Atlantis and the Great Instauration*. Arlington Heights, Ill.: Harlan Davidson, 1989.

West, David A. *The Imagery and Poetry of Lucretius.* Edinburgh: Edinburgh University Press, 1969.

———. "Two Notes on Lucretius." *Classical Quarterly* 14 (1964): 98–102.

Westfall, Richard S. *The Construction of Modern Science: Mechanisms and Mechanics.* New York: John Wiley and Sons, Inc., 1971.

———. *Science and Religion in Seventeenth-Century England.* New Haven, Conn.: Yale University Press, 1958.

Whiting, George W. *Milton's Literary Milieu.* Chapel Hill, N.C.: University of North Carolina Press, 1939; rpt. New York: Russell and Russell, 1964.

Willey, Basil, ed. *Thomas Burnet. The Sacred Theory of the Earth.* London, 1684; rpt. Carbondale, Ill.: Southern Illinois University Press, 1965.

Wittkower, Rudolf. *Architectural Principles in the Age of Humanism.* 4th ed. New York: St. Martin's, 1988.

Wittreich, Joseph Anthony, Jr. *Visionary Poetics: Milton's Tradition and His Legacy.* San Marino, Calif.: Huntington Library, 1979.

Index

Abraham, 55
Abrams, M. H., 41
Adam and Eve: and desire, 128–29; and Eden, 55–56, 58, 147, 174; as human beings, 53, 132, 148–49; in *Paradise Lost*, 3, 29, 94–98, 126–30; and sin, 132, 137–38
Adams, Mary, 136
Ad Joannem Rousium (Milton), 153
Ad Patrem (Milton), 29–30
adultery, 115–16
Aeneid (Vergil), 19, 104, 147–50, 185n1
agriculture, 3, 10, 54–59, 62, 67–68, 171
Alberti, Leon Battista, 76
Alexander the Great, 105
Alexandrini, Georgius, 32, 60
Allen, D. C., 43–44, 96, 112, 177n2
Anatomy of Melancholy (Burton), 108–09
Anglican Church, 39
animism, 25–26, 136
Annales (Ennius), 104
Annotations on Mr. Milton's Paradise Lost (Hume), 48
anthropomorphism, 40–41, 50–51
Anxiety of Influence, The (Bloom), 20
Apollonius Rhodius, 18
Apologie de Raimond Sebond (Montaigne), 105
An Apology Against a Pamphlet (Milton), 14, 59, 182–83n8
Apuleius, 167
architecture: as art, 83; church, 78; Milton on, 74–76; and Pandaemonium, 79–82; in *Paradise Lost*, 74; in *Paradise Regained*, 77; principles of, 3, 10, 82–83; of Renaissance, 76–77, 82–84, 86, 173; Roman, 77, 173; of Vitruvius, x, 15, 82, 84, 165
Areopagitica (Milton), 40–41, 78, 167

Argonautica (Apollonius Rhodius), 104
Ariosto, Ludovico, 19
Aristotle, 156–57
Arnobius of Sicca, 132
Ars Poetica (Horace), ix
artifex omnium, 8
astrology: Dee on, 96–97; final stage of, 108; and human beings, 106, 111; Manilius on, 108, 127–29, 174–75; Milton on, x, 3, 96–97, 105–06, 111–13, 115; natural, 96, 105–06, 112; Phillips (Edwards) on, 112; in Renaissance, 99–97
Astronomica (Manilius), 98–101, 103–11, 114, 129, 164, 174–75
astronomy, 96, 102–03
atomism, 27, 32
Augustine of Hippo, 158–59
Augustus Caesar, 13, 76
authors: Greek, 10, 60; Latin, 1, 10–11, 13, 170; Roman, 15, 23–24, 28, 32, 60, 154, 159, 170

Babb, Lawrence, 111
Bacchus, 102
Bacon, Francis, 30–31, 39, 51–52, 108, 116–18
Baroni, Leonora, 33
Bate, Jonathan, 22
Beowulf, 75
Bible. *See also* New Testament, Old Testament, Scripture: on human action, 45–46, 132, 150–51; Milton on, 28–30, 57, 75, 178n2; and Wisdom of Solomon, 8
Blake, William, 86–87
Bloom, Harold, 20, 153
Boccaccio, Giovani, 23
botany, 35, 42–44
Boyle, Robert Sir, 27, 36
Bradshaw, David J., 159

Browne, Sir Thomas, 30, 37, 83
Bucer, Martin, 6
Budick, Sanford, 79
Burton, Robert, 108–09

Cable, Lana, 79
Cathedral design (Vitruvius), 88
Catholics, Catholicism, 34, 77–78, 80
Cato, Marcus Porcius, 3, 10, 16, 44, 60, 62–64, 155–56, 171; works by: *De Re Rustica*, 1, 32, 44, 59–60, 61, 67, 139–40, 171
Celsus, Cornelius, 1, 5, 18, 172
Choerilus of Samos, 104
Christ. *See* Jesus Christ
Christian Astrology (Lilly), 174
Christianity, 7, 25, 45, 107–08, 157–58, 163–69
Christopher, Georgia B., 37, 48–49
Church of Santa Maria della Consolazone, 93
Cicero, Marcus Tullius: theories of, 140–41, 156, 182n3; works by: *De natura deorum*, 140; *De officiis*, 5
Clement of Alexandria, 43–44
Columella, Lucus Junius: themes of, 1, 10, 28, 62–63, 139–41, 151, 171–72; works by: *De Re Rustica*, 1, 32, 44, 59–60, 61, 67, 139–40, 171
Comenius, Johann Amos, 3, 6–9, 12
Commonwealth. *See* England
commune bonum, 109
Conte, Gian Biago, 18–21
Copernicanism, 116–17
cosmology, 43, 45
Council of Trent, 116
Creation: and Earth, 26; and God, 94–95, 114; Milton on, 27, 36–37, 39, 42, 52–53, 55, 135–37, 177–78n2; in Scripture, 27, 55; views of, 40–43, 58
Cromwell, Oliver, 72–73, 78
Cunningham, J. V., 153

d'Alembert, Jean Le Rond, 52
Daniel, Clay, 111–12, 121
Darbishire, Helen, 82
Darnton, Robert, 51, 52
da Vinci, Leonardo, 73, 89, 92, 166
De aquis (Frontinus), 173
De Architecture (Vitruvius), 1, 76, 81–84, 88, 90–91, 92, 165, 173, 182n8
De augmenits scientiarum (Bacon), 108
De doctrina christiana (Augustine), 31, 36, 143, 158, 177n1
Dee, John, 81, 96, 112

Defence of the English People, A (Milton), 77
Defensio Secunda (Milton), 13
De medicina (Celsus), 5, 172
demulatio, 19–20
De natura deorum (Cicero), 140
De officiis (Cicero), 5
De rerum natura (Lucretius), 8–9, 98, 109–10, 136, 145, 174
De Re Rustica (Cato, Varro, Columella, Palladius), 1, 32, 44, 59–60, 61, 67, 139–40, 171
Didactica Magna (Comenius), 7
Diderot, Denis, 52
Diodati, Charles, 157
Doctrine and Discipline of Divorce, The (Milton), x, 3, 98, 111, 113–14, 116, 119, 127; medical imagery in, 114; philosophy in, 113; themes in, 98, 111, 127
Doctrine of Oeconomicks..., 10
Donne, John, 115
Dury, John, 3–7, 10–12
Dzelzainis, Martin, 5

Earth: and agriculture, 62; and Creation, 139; Milton on, 24–28, 102, 133–34, 139–41, 150–51, 185n1; nature of, 142–43; in *Paradise Lost*, 28, 133–39, 145–48, 150–51; Pliny on, 3, 24, 28, 143, 162–63; preexistence of, 25; Scripture on, 132; Seneca on, 141–43; Stoic theory of, 140
Eden, 55–58, 147–48, 174
education: philosophy of, 7; religious, 12; self, 14; universal, 7
Egypt, 158–59
Eikon Basilike, 70
Elements (Euclid), 81, 112
Elements of Architecture (Wotton), 81
Eliot, George, 56
Eliot, T. S., 21
Empson, William, 66, 133, 181n10
England, 5, 6, 56, 60, 70, 75, 80, 112, 156
Enlightenment, 13, 52
Ennius, Quintus, 104
Epictetus, 10
Epithalamion (Spenser), 127
Erasmus, 19, 21
etymology, 42, 44–45
Euclid, 81, 112
Europe, 13, 21, 75
Everard, William, 71

Fall (of man), 3, 40, 45, 89, 133, 141–43, 148–51, 174–75

Fallon, Robert T., 5, 185n4
Fallon Stephen, 32, 136, 186n6
Fish, Stanley, 100
Forman, Simon, 111
Foucault, Michel, 40
Fowler, Alastair, 31, 47, 65–66, 95, 141
Frontinus, Sextus Julius, 1, 4, 18, 173–74
Frye, Northrop, 68

Galileo Galilei, 31, 36, 177n2, 186n6
Gassendi, Pierre, 32
Geneva, Ann, 97
Geoffrey of Monmouth, 32
The Georgic Revolution (Low), 57
Georgics (Vergil), 99, 139, 171
Glisson Francis, 26
God: absolute authority of, 25; and Creation, 94–95, 114; and knowledge, 30–31, 37–40, 53; Manilius on, 110–11; Milton on, 34, 36–38, 46, 163, 168; plan of, 47; and science, 30; will of, 151
The Golden Ass (Apuleius), 167
"Great Instauration" (Bacon), 31
Greek: authors, 10, 60; instruction, 9, 13, 47, 153; language, 16; philosophy, 43
Greenblatt, Stephen, 119
Greene, Thomas, 20, 48, 145
Gust for Paradise, A (McColley), 42

Hale, John, 13
Hanford, James Holly, 4
Hartlib, Samuel, 3–4, 6–7, 12, 30, 35, 179n5
Harvey, William, 26
Haskin, Dayton, 29, 37, 40–41, 178–79n3
Heaven, 33–34, 45
Hell, 33–34
hermeneutic, 25, 108
Hesiod, 104
Hill, Christopher, 72, 97
Hippocrates, 172
History of Four-Footed Beasts and Serpents, The (Topsell), 51
History of the Kings of Britain (Geoffrey of Monmouth), 32
Hobbes, Thomas, 51, 98
Holland, Philemon, 24, 38
Homer, 21, 69
Homo ad Circulum (Vitruvius), 85
Homo ad Quadratum (Vitruvius), 85
Hoole, Charles, 22
Horace, ix, 13
horoscope, 111, 174
Hughes, Meritt, 25, 183n1
human beings: Adam and Eve as, 40, 132; and astrology, 106, 111; celestial nature of, 110; nature of, 16
humanism, 4, 6, 21
Hume, Patrick, 48
Hunter, William B., 123

Iliad (Homer), 69
imitatio and practice of, 19–20, 22
Israelites, 55, 158
Italy, 33, 93, 112

Janua linguarum (Comenius), 7
Jesus Christ, 33–34, 47, 60, 132, 157, 179n3
Johnson, Samuel, 15–16, 178n2
Jones, Inigo, 76
Jonson, Ben, 22
Jurisprudentia, 10

Kassell, Lauren, 111
Kepler, Johannes, 36, 113, 121, 123
Knoppers, Laura Lunger, 33, 102
knowledge: and God, 30, 37–40, 53; Johnson on, 16; natural, 2, 40–41; and nature, 38

L'Allegro (Milton), 56
language, 12, 16, 20, 96, 171
Lanham, Richard, 23
Lanyer, Aemilia, 22
Latin: authors, 10, 13, 170; language, 13, 16, 21, 171; literature, 2, 9, 23–24; poetry, 161; science, 12, 16
Lattimore, Richard, 69
Lewalski, Barbara, 58, 136, 180–81n6
Lewis, C. S., 150
Lieb, Michael, 79
Life of John Milton and History of His Time (Masson), 16–17
Life of Milton (Johnson), 15–16
Lilly, William, 97, 112, 174
Lockwood, Laura, 133
Low, Anthony, 57
Loewenstein, David, 79
Lucan, 33
Lucretius: studies of, 145–47, 151, 156, 169–70; themes of, 1, 3, 13–22, 26–28, 32, 98; works by: *De rerum natura*, 8–9, 109–10, 136, 145, 174
Lyacaeum, 6

Machiavelli, 34
Manilius, Marcus: on astrology, 108, 127–29, 174–75; on God, 110–11; Milton on, 19, 98–100, 129; Phillips (John) on, 112; on science,

13, 18; on solitude, 101; theories of, 100, 103–10, 153, 156, 164, 169, 183–84; works by: *Astronomica*, 98–101, 103–11, 114, 164, 174–75
Marjara, Harinder Singh, 30–31
marriage, 114–15
Marvell, Andrew, 22, 48, 98
Masson, David, 16–17
mathematics, 11, 83
McClung, William A., 84
McColley, Diane, 42, 58
medicine, 11, 113–14, 172
Merchant, Carolyn, 134
Meres, Francis, 22
Messeniaca (Rhianus), 104
Metamorphoses (Ovid), 161
metaphysics, 36
metempsychosis, 22
Milton, John: on adultery, 115; on architecture, 76; and astrology, x, 3, 96–97, 105–06, 111–13, 115; on Bible, 28–30, 57, 75, 178n2; biography of, 16–17; classical curriculum of, 2–6, 11–12, 15, 20, 23–24, 32, 89, 108, 153, 159, 170, 171–75; on contemporary issues, 3; on cosmology, 45; on Creation, 27, 36–37, 39, 42, 52–53, 55, 135–37, 177–78n; on creature, 37–41; on discourse, 176–77n3; on Earth, 24–28, 102, 133–34, 139–41, 150–51, 185n1; epistemology of, 32; on God, 34, 36–38, 46, 163, 168; Johnson on, 15–16; on language, 12; on Manilius, 19, 98–100, 129; on marriage, 114–15; Marvell on, 48; on medicine, 113; on Pandaemonium, 80–84, 89; Phillips (Edward) on, 1–2, 13–14, 59, 139; and Plowman imagery, 59; poetic achievements of, 3; on religious purpose, 12; on Satan, 31, 46, 89, 179n4; scholars on, 111; on science, 29–30, 42, 177–78n2; Shawcross on, 15; on sin, 43, 132; on solitude, 101–03; sonnets of, 1–8, 33; teachings of, 1–8; on theology, 43, 45; on Vitruvius, 73; works by: *Ad Joannem Rousium*, 152; *Ad Patrem*, 29–30; *An Apology for a Pamphlet*, 14, 59, 182–83n8; *Areopagitica*, 78, 167; *A Defence of the English People*, 77; *Defensio Secunda*, 13; *The Doctrine and Discipline of Divorce*, x, 3, 98, 111, 113–14, 116, 119, 127; *Of Education*, 2, 5–6, 8, 13, 35–36, 41, 51, 59, 76, 98, 139; Elegy 6, 157; *L'Allegro*, 56; *Paradise Lost*, 2–3, 19–20, 25, 28, 31, 33, 45, 48, 51–54, 59, 64–74, 76–77, 79–80, 94–98, 102–03, 106, 110–11, 132–40, 145–48, 151, 154, 159–66, 172–75; *Paradise Regained*, x, 3, 77, 79, 112–13, 154–56, 166; *Poems*, 5, 14; The *Readie and Easie Way*, 33, 74–75, 79, 156; The *Reason of Church Government*, 14, 101, 168–70; *Of Reformation*, 75, 108, 182n3; *Samson Agonistes*, 79
Milton, John Sr., 30
Milton Unbound (Rumrich), 164
Mitchell, W. J. T., 79
Montaigne, Michel de, 105
Montelion (John Phillips), 112
More, Henry, 36
Moses, 55, 116, 160
mythology, 19, 48, 51

Nativity, 156–57
Natural History (Pliny): on Earth, 24, 141, 162; on Fall, 38; on snakes, 50; studies in, 1, 10, 144–46
Natural Questions (Seneca), 141
natural science. *See* science
Natural Supernaturalism (Abrams), 41
nature: in Bible, 37; definition of, 31; divine, 38–39; in *Of Education*, 35, 51; and history, 38; and knowledge, 38; Lewis on, 150; in *Paradise Lost*, 15, 42, 51; and Romans, 15
Neuberg, Matt, 100, 175
New Testament. *See also* Bible, Old Testament, Scriptures: Corinthians, 115; and Matthew, 116, 132; and Paul, 115; and Peter, 43; Romans, 38
Norbrook, David, 33

OED. *See* Oxford English Dictionary
Of Education (Milton): and civic purpose, 2, 5–6; Edward Phillips on, 76, 98; on language, 17; Latin influence on, 139; on learning, 13; on nature, 35, 51; themes in, 5, 8, 36, 41–42, 52, 59
"Of Envy" (Bacon), 118
Of Reformation (Milton), 75, 108, 182n3
"Of Superstition" (Bacon), 116
Old Testament. *See also* Bible, New Testament, Scripture: Abraham in, 55; commandments in, 134; Deuteronomy, 115; Ecclesiates, 11–12, 63; Genesis, 19, 25–26, 39, 45, 57,

111, 114, 132; Moses in, 55, 116, 160; nature in, 37; Proverbs, 11–12; Psalms, 28–29, 132, 178–79n3
Orlando Furioso (Ariosto), 19
Ovid, 21–23, 33, 153, 161–62
Oxford English Dictionary (OED), 40, 67, 118, 134–35

paganism, 45, 60, 156–58
Palladius, Rutilius Taurus Aemilianus, 1, 3, 76, 171–72; works by: *De Re Rustica*, 1, 32, 44, 59–60, 61, 67, 139–40, 171
Pandaemonium: and architecture, 79–82; and Catholic Rome, 34; definition of, 78, 183n10; image of, 77–78, 80, 133, 166, 173; Milton on, 80–84, 89; and Mulciber, 3, 80; in *Paradise Lost*, 3, 76–77, 80; in *Readie and Easie Way, The*, 77
pansophy. See wisdom
Paradise Lost (Milton): Adam and Eve in, 3, 29, 94–98, 126–30; on agriculture, 3, 54–55, 58–59; on architecture, 74; Earth represented in, 28, 133–39, 145–48, 150–51; Fall in, 3, 19; Fowler on, 65–66, 95; heurustic imitation in, 20; Hume on, 48; Mammon in, 134, 137, 159–66, 173; Nativity in, 157; on nature, 15, 42, 51; Pandemonium in, 3, 76–77, 80; Plowman in, 56–57, 64–73, 181n10; poetry of, 31, 99, 130, 169; politics in, 33; proem to, 102–03, 160; on Satan, 2, 49–50, 97; scriptural authority in, 132; themes in, 3, 41, 45, 48, 77, 79, 110–11, 151, 154, 159–61, 172–75; theodicy in, 106; universe, 25
Paradise Regained (Milton): and astrology, x, 112–13; Roman influence in, 3, 77, 154–56; Satan in, 34, 77, 79, 166
Parker, William Riley, 78
Pascal, Blaise, 95
Pensée (Pascal), 95
Persica (Choerilus), 104
Petrarch, 19, 21, 23
Pharsalia (Lucan), 33
Phillips, Edward: and astrology, 112; on *Of Education*, 76, 98; on Latin curriculum, 10, 145, 172, 183n1
Phillips, John, 112; on Manilius, 112; on Milton, 1–2, 13–14, 59, 98, 139, 176n1; as scribe, 82
philosophy, 10, 32, 38, 40, 43, 47, 52, 132, 145
Pigman, G. W., 21
Plato, 6, 10, 153
Pliny: on Earth, 3, 24, 28, 143, 162–63; on Fall of man, 38; and Hobbes compared, 51; philosophy of, 16, 19, 156; on snakes, 50; studies of, 1, 144; works by: *Natural History*, 1, 50, 144–46, 162, 172
Plowman: Milton's images of, 3, 58–59; in *Paradise Lost*, 56–57, 64–73, 181n10
Plutarch, 10
Poems (Milton), 5, 14, 152
poetry, 12–14, 18–22, 29–31, 56, 59, 97, 159–61, 170–73
Pollio, Vitruvius. See Vitruvius
Polybius, 75, 182n3
Pontano Giovanni, 111
Poor Richard's Almanac, 64
Pope, Alexander, 100
Pope Urban VIII, 77
The Prelude (Wordsworth), 41
Protestants, 8, 77–78
Ptolemy, 108, 116, 183n1, 186n6
Puritans, 10, 25–26, 45–46, 92, 97
Puttenham, George, 22
Pythagoreus, 22–24

Radzinowicz, Mary Ann, 29, 58
Rajan, Balachandra, 13
The Readie and Easie Way (Milton): and architecture, 74; Pandaemonium in, 77; themes of, 33, 74–75, 79, 156
The Reason of Church Government (Milton), 14, 101, 168–70
Reformation, the, 6, 37
Reformation of Schooles, A (Comenius), 7, 9
The Reformed School (Dury), 12
Religio medici (Browne), 37, 83
Renaissance: architecture in, 76–77, 82–84, 173; art of, 32; astrology in, 96–97; and humanism, 4; intellectual achievements of, 21, 43, 60; masters, 5, 33, 73, 112; poetry of, 14, 19; secular in, 31; theorists of, 11, 22–23, 105–07
Renaker, David, 112–13, 123
Restoration, the, 33, 113, 156
Revard, Stella, 14, 154
rhetoric, 11, 18, 23, 111
Rhianus, 104
Rogers, John, 26
Roman: animist view of, 25–26;

architecture, 77; art, 34; authors, 15, 23–24, 28, 32, 60, 154, 159, 170; culture, 33; literature, 59, 154; republic, 75, 109, 182n2; state, 14; Stoics, 24–25, 139, 150, 186n6; texts, 1, 12–13, 108; wisdom, 10, 19
Roman Catholic Church, 78, 116
Romans, Book of, 38
Rome, 34, 78, 155, 171, 173
Romola (Eliot, G.), 56
Rosenmeyer, Thomas, 57
Rouse, John, 152
Rumrich, John, 164
Ruskin, John, 138

Sacred Wood, The (Eliot), 21
Samson Agonistes (Milton), 79
Sapientia, 8
Satan: hubris of, 15; Milton on, 31, 46, 89, 179n4; in *Paradise Lost*, 2, 49–50, 97; in *Paradise Regained*, 34, 77, 79, 166; and sin, 47
Schwartz, Regina, 55, 181n1
science: and astronomy, 96; and Galileo, 31; human, 58; and investigation, 38; Latin, 12, 16; Milton on, 29–30, 42, 177–788n2; natural, 3, 30, 48; and Romans, 15; and Scripture, 28–29, 36; study of, 17, 111, 129
Scripture. *See also* Bible, New Testament, Old Testament: on Creation, 27, 55; Earth described in, 28, 132; education of, 6, 47; on Fall of man, 45, 55
Seneca, Lucius, 28, 141–43
Serlio, Sebastiano, 76
Shakespeare, William: works by: sonnets, 22–23; *Venus and Adonis*, 22
Shawcross John T., 15
Sikes, E., 109
sin, 43, 47, 89, 132, 137–38, 172
Sirluck, Ernest, 116
Sixfold Commentary upon Genesis (Willett), 47
Smith, Nigel, 75
Smith, Rebecca W., 77, 83–84
solitude, 101–03
Spenser, Edmund, 127, 185n3
St. Peter's Basilica, 34, 77–78
Stevens, Paul, 79, 155
Stoicism, 24–25, 39, 107, 110, 139-40, 150–51, 169, 186n
Stratagemata (Frontinus), 1, 4, 173–74
Strier, Richard, 117
Summers, Joseph, 65
Svendsen, Kester, 113–14, 178n2, 186n6

Tate, W. E., 70
temptation, 46, 49–50
Theatre design (Vitruvius), 91
The Theatre of Insects (Mouffet), 52
Theogony (Hesiod), 104
theology, 36–38, 43, 47, 111
Thirsk, Joan, 60, 62
Thoreau, Henry David, 47
"To Cookham" (Lanyer), 22
"To Penshurst" (Jonson), 22
Topsell, Edward, 51
"Tradition and the Individual Talent" (Eliot), 21
Trinkaus, Charles, 111
The True Levellers' Standard Advanced (Winstanley), 71

"Universal Temple of Wisdom" (Comenius), 9
"Upon Appleton House" (Marvell), 22
The Usefulness of Experimental Philosophy, (Boyle), 27

"Valediction: Forbidding Mourning, A" (Donne), 115
Valerius Terminus (Bacon), 39
van Helmont, Jean Baptiste, 26
Varro, Marcus Terentius, 3, 10, 44, 58, 60, 155–56, 171; works by: *De Re Rustica*, 1, 32, 44, 59–60, 61, 67, 139–40, 171
Vasari, Giorgio, 76
Venus and Adonis (Shakespeare), 22
Vergil: themes of, 3, 28, 32, 108, 145, 159, 161; works by: *Aeneid*, 19, 104, 147–50, 185n1; *Georgics*, 99, 139, 171
Virgil. *See* Vergil
Vitruvius: architecture of, x, 15, 82, 84; art of, 85, 88, 90–91; Milton on, 73; principles of, 1, 3, 82–83; publication of, 76; works by: *De architectura*, 1, 76, 81–84, 88, 90–91, 92, 165, 173, 182n8; *Homo ad Circulum*, 85; *Homo ad Quadratum*, 85
Vitruvius figure (Vitruvius), 90

Webster, Charles, 42
Westfall, Richard, 30
Willett, Andrew, 47
Williams, R. D., 148
Winstanley, Gerrard, 71
wisdom, 7–11
Wittkower, Rudolf, 86, 92
Wordsworth, William, 41
Wotton, Sir Henry, 81

zoology, 35